Manchester Studies in Religion, Culture and Gender

Forever fluid

Manchester University Press

Manchester Studies in Religion, Culture and Gender

edited by Grace M. Jantzen

Religion and culture
Michel Foucault
selected and edited by Jeremy R. Carrette

Representations of the post/human
Monsters, aliens and others in popular culture
Elaine L. Graham

Becoming divine
Towards a feminist philosophy of religion
Grace M. Jantzen

Manchester Studies in Religion, Culture and Gender

Forever fluid

A reading of Luce Irigaray's
Elemental Passions

Hanneke Canters
and Grace M. Jantzen

Manchester University Press
Manchester and New York

distributed exclusively in the USA by Palgrave

Copyright © Hanneke Canters and Grace M. Jantzen 2005

The right of Hanneke Canters and Grace M. Jantzen to be identified as the authors of this work has been asserted by them in accordance with the Copyright, Designs and Patents Act 1988.

Published by Manchester University Press
Oxford Road, Manchester M13 9NR, UK
and Room 400, 175 Fifth Avenue, New York, NY 10010, USA
www.manchesteruniversitypress.co.uk

Distributed in the United States exclusively by
Palgrave Macmillan, 175 Fifth Avenue,
New York, NY 10010, USA

Distributed in Canada exclusively by
UBC Press, University of British Columbia, 2029 West Mall,
Vancouver, BC, Canada V6T 1Z2

British Library Cataloguing-in-Publication Data is available

Library of Congress Cataloging-in-Publication Data is available

ISBN 978 0 7190 6381 7 paperback

First published by Manchester University Press in hardback 2005

This paperback edition first published 2014

The publisher has no responsibility for the persistence or accuracy of URLs for any external or third-party internet websites referred to in this book, and does not guarantee that any content on such websites is, or will remain, accurate or appropriate.

Printed by Lightning Source

CONTENTS

Preface	*page* vii
Abbreviations	ix
Introduction	1

Part I Problems of rigidity

1 Rigid binaries and masculinist logic	8
2 More than one subject: Irigaray and psychoanalytic theory	33

Part II *Elemental Passions*

3 'Fragments from a woman's voyage': context and style of *Elemental Passions*	52
4 Interpretive synopsis of *Elemental Passions*	60
5 Images for a female subject	105

Part III Critical identities

6 Multiple subjects and fluid boundaries	124
7 Fluid logic	137
Bibliography	155
Index	163

PREFACE

'Let me go where I am not yet'. This is how Hanneke Canters translated Luce Irigaray's 'Laisse-moi aller où je ne suis pas encore', the words with which Hanneke intended to begin this book. Neither Hanneke nor anyone else could have foreseen the poignancy those words would have as this book goes to press. Hanneke began it at the start of a highly promising academic career. She had recently completed her PhD with a dissertation on the question of the female subject in Irigaray's Elemental Passions, and planned to take the investigation further in this book. Then she was found to have cancer. Work on the book continued between courses of chemotherapy, and gave Hanneke a strong sense of purpose; but eventually she could do no more. Hanneke died in September 2002.

It was Hanneke's great wish that her book should be completed and published. I had known Hanneke first when she was a visiting undergraduate at King's College, London; then as her supervisor for her MA in London and as external supervisor for her PhD in Sunderland. As editor of this series of Studies in Religion, Culture and Gender I was eager to consider her proposed book for publication, and delighted to work with her on it. Before she died I promised that I would do all I could to complete her book, which was then about half finished, and see it through the press. This volume is the result.

From very early in her academic career, Hanneke was sceptical of binary logic. Presented with Aristotle's Law of Excluded Middle with the example, 'either it is raining or it is not raining', Hanneke could be heard to mutter, 'But what about drizzle? What about drizzle?' With the raising of her feminist consciousness she came to see the ways in which binary oppositions have been used to define and oppress those who are deemed 'other' or 'opposite' to normative affluent white males: women, people of colour, gay and lesbian people, poor or disabled people. When Hanneke discovered the writings of Luce Irigaray, especially Elemental Passions, she used it to begin to work towards a more fluid logic, which she saw as a logic which would allow for the flourishing of the 'other', beginning with the female subject. She was, however, also critical of Irigaray's focus on sexual difference to the exclusion of other sorts of differences, and was concerned to extend her analysis to differences of race, sexual orientation, and ability.

Hanneke had begun to draw these strands together in her manuscript, but although she had given the issues much thought and written substantial drafts of several chapters, much remained to be done. Her manuscript was about half the length of this book. I have used her draft chapters as its basis, for the most part reproducing her work verbatim (though often treating the topics in a different order within each chapter for greater clarity), and adding much material, partly for clarification but also in large part to try to show the connection between the challenge to binary logic and the commentary on Elemental Passions. The Introduction and the first three chapters are substantially Hanneke's words, though reordered and considerably expanded. The large fourth chapter (the commentary on Elemental Passions) and the fifth chapter exploring its imagery follow Hanneke's plan and leave out none of her material, but also add much more, so that they are more than twice the length of her originals. The final section of the book was most problematic to complete. Hanneke had sketched a critique of Irigaray, which I have developed in chapter six. She also hoped to move the discussion forward by showing from the writings of Black American poets and song writers how that critique could be met. Here, however, her notes were not enough for me to go on, and, with regret, I have largely dropped this theme. What I have substituted is an analysis, in chapter seven, of what 'fluid logic' comes to, and how it might reconfigure our (gendered) approach to rationality. Hanneke was constantly thinking about these issues, and we had many

Preface

discussions on them, but the last section is substantially my work rather than hers, though I believe it to be congruent with the direction of her thought.

A central concern throughout has been to honour Hanneke's intentions and to allow her voice to be heard. This, however, presented a particular challenge. Her writing style is different from mine: she wrote more succinctly, sometimes abruptly, whereas I am more discursive. I have done my best to meld our work together for evenness of style and tried to retain her distinctive voice within the limits of consistency and overall readability. Inevitably, however, the additional material, especially from chapter four onwards, is more in my style than hers. All through the text I have used 'we' to refer to Hanneke's thoughts and/or mine, without breaking the flow to distinguish between us.

Hanneke's parents, Gerard Canters and Minke Hazewindus, were most helpful throughout. I am greatly indebted to them, not least for a meeting in Amsterdam at an early stage of my work on Hanneke's manuscript, in which we discussed the problems and possibilities of the book. Together we came to the view that it was more important to develop and clarify Hanneke's ideas for a wide readership than to preserve her draft chapters intact as a memorial of her exact words; and they gave me a free hand to do my best with the manuscript. I hope that they will find Hanneke's spirit shining through the final result.

I am most grateful, as was Hanneke, to Annemie Halsema, who has made valuable comments on the book as a whole and on draft chapters, has checked Hanneke's quotations, and has supplied the French text for the many quotations from *Elemental Passions*. She was also a most valuable presence at the Amsterdam meeting. This book could not have been completed without her.

Thanks also to Corneel Canters, Hanneke's brother, for technical assistance, especially with Hanneke's bibliography and other mysterious computer files; and to Barbara Underwood for her friendship and offers of help.

Alison Welsby and the staff at Manchester University Press have been sensitive and graciously helpful both to Hanneke and to me. Pamela Sue Anderson read the manuscript with great care for Manchester University Press and made perceptive comments: this book is much stronger as a result, and I thank her warmly for her thoughtfulness. I acknowledge with gratitude the interest and support of my colleagues and postgraduate students in the University of Manchester. My greatest personal thanks is to Tina Macrae, 'number one top support', for all her typing, encouragement and help, and above all for the light of her presence. Thank you.

ABBREVIATIONS

Cs	*Ce sexe qui n'est pas un* (1977)
EP	*Elemental Passions* (1992a)
FA	*The Forgetting of Air in Martin Heidegger* (1999)
ILo	*I Love to You* (1996a)
Jat	*J'aime à toi* (1992b)
Pe	*Passions élémentaires* (1982)
SG	*Sexes and Genealogies* (1993c)
SP	*Sexes et parentés* (1987b)
SpE	*Speculum of the Other Woman* (1985a)
SpF	*Speculum. De l'autre femme* (1974)
TS	*This Sex Which Is Not One* (1985b)

Introduction

A female subject?[1]

Laisse-moi aller où je ne suis pas encore. (Pe 30)
Let me go where I have not yet arrived. (EP 25)

These words, from Luce Irigaray's *Elemental Passions*, lie at the heart of this book. They characterize the journey towards female subjectivity undertaken by the woman within *Elemental Passions* as well as by those who engage with her in that adventure. 'Let me go where I have not yet arrived' captures the attitude of the feminist thinker who embarks on her project without prior knowledge of where it will lead her. It indicates the emerging woman subject in philosophy and psychoanalysis, and hints at the new avenues of thought which are opened up for women and men when the implications of female subjectivity are taken seriously. *Forever Fluid* presents an invitation to us as authors and to you our readers to move into uncharted territory without clear disciplinary demarcations, to discover what happens when female subjects are treated with the same consideration as male subjects have been.

The recognition of a female subject is relatively recent in Western philosophy. Through Western intellectual history the subject has been assumed to be normatively male. One of the first feminist writers to expose the grip of this assumption was Genevieve Lloyd in *The Man of Reason* (1984). Another groundbreaking article was Nancy Jay's 'Gender and Dichotomy' (1981). Both works are built upon by Moira Gatens in *Feminism and Philosophy* (1991) and a host of subsequent thinkers (Garry & Pearsall 1996; Battersby 1998; Code 1991; Harding 1991; Nye 1990). Through the efforts of these writers the dominance of the male subject in the history of Western philosophy and psychoanalysis has

---

[1] In this book we will speak of 'male' and 'female' subjects. There are of course significant differences in the terms masculine/male/man/men, and also in the terms feminine/female/woman/women. In *Forever Fluid*, however, we will use the terms 'male' and 'female' to indicate subjects of a different sex. For a discussion of these terms in relation to Irigaray, see Whitford 1991b. For more general problems on difficulties in translating Irigaray's French texts into English see Burke 1994b.

become clear. Where women are considered, they have seldom been taken as subjects. Rather, they have been seen as objects: an adornment for man, a partner in reproduction, at worst a snare and a seducer (Philo), at best a helpmate (Aquinas) or a guide (Rousseau). Women can help men experience oneness as a subject (Lacan) and can perhaps be of practical assistance as men ascend into the philosophical realm (Parmenides). Often women make no appearance at all (Descartes, Aristotle): many philosophical works read as though women's existence is of no relevance (Spinoza, Locke, Kant, Wittgenstein).

Once the conspicuous absence of the female subject from the philosophical canon is noted, however, the question cannot be avoided: how would things be different if women also had a place? Suppose women had a voice: what would they say? Luce Irigaray, contemporary French philosopher, psychoanalyst and linguist, has spent much effort in the search for a female subject and her significance. Irigaray's method in her early work, especially in *Speculum. De l'autre femme* (1974; SpE 1985a), consists of a very close and detailed reading of significant works of the Western canon. At least since Hegel, a central preoccupation of that canon has been the emergence of the subject in history: Irigaray shows how that subject is in fact male, not universal or genderless. Her approach can be characterized as the convergence of two strategies of reading – Derridean deconstruction and Lacanian psychoanalysis – always with the question of the woman subject to the fore (Grosz 1989; Weir 1996; Armour 1997). Using this method Irigaray is able not only to point out the dominance of the male subject, but also to explore the possibilities and implications of the emergence of the female subject, and to begin to indicate the vast consequences of that emergence for the canon itself.

Irigaray focuses almost exclusively on sexual difference, the difference between men and women. She argues that this difference has not been sufficiently recognized or acknowledged within Western thought. Woman, she holds, has been thought primarily in terms of man. Yet in order for both men and women to become subjects, it is necessary that both be granted their uniqueness. In order to emphasize this uniqueness Irigaray develops her concept of sexual difference, a concept which is developed, explained and revised in many places in her work. Crucial to her philosophy is the idea that the difference between men and women can be adequately thought only if terms are found that reflect each as a separate sexual subject. (For discussion of this see Halsema 1998: 190–216; Chanter 1995: 127–46; Whitford 1991b; Grosz 1989).

The consequences of the employment of sexual difference are far-reaching for the sexual subject of philosophy and psychoanalysis, as Irigaray shows in her writings from *Speculum* onwards. If the development of the subject is not conceived of in normatively male terms, as it has been from Plato to Freud, but if this subject is twofold from the beginning, then our philosophical frameworks also have to change. This results in a radical critique of Western philosophy. Concepts that have been associated with woman and the feminine and have therefore been excluded from philosophy are brought back within the domain: examples are passion, materiality and embodiment. The idea of a powerful rational agent who masters others and the world has to make way for mutuality and relational being; and the dichotomies of one and not-one, self and other, which construct subjectivity, are replaced by processes in which man and woman become subjects in relation to each other. It is already clear that this goes far deeper than simply adding some extra topics to the list of things philosophers think about. Rather, as we shall show in this book, it goes to the very heart of what it means to think at all. The binary logic characteristic of Western thought since Parmenides, with its rigid structures of 'either–or', is destabilized. Fluidity is as important as rigidity.

All this will become clearer as we proceed. But it immediately raises the question: how are such sexually different subjects to emerge? If they have been missing in Western thought and culture, what will enable their development? It is our suggestion that in her text *Elemental Passions* Irigaray works towards her goal of helping sexually different subjects find a voice. Her text also illustrates the consequences of this process for both subjects, as well as for the rigid structures of life and thought that have characterized male normativity. Although *Elemental Passions* has not received detailed study by English-language feminists until now, we believe that it is a highly significant text not only for understanding Irigaray but, more fundamentally, for rethinking the rigid categories of Western logic, as we shall try to show.

Other texts in Irigaray's corpus discuss the importance of sexually different subjects; some of them, especially *Marine Lover of Friedrich Nietzsche* (1991b) and *The Forgetting of Air* (1999), are written in ways that demonstrate the becoming of such subjects. In our interpretation, however, *Elemental Passions* is Irigaray's only book-length text which is entirely devoted to the enactment of two sexually different subjects emerging in relation to one another, showing their respective ways of thinking and their relations to the divine and to their surroundings. Although in various places in Irigaray's early work she had discussed the conditions for the becoming of a female subject, it is in *Elemental Passions* that she presents that emergence as happening within the text itself.

Consequently, *Elemental Passions* is not a straightforward text. The difficulties go beyond those which are often experienced by Anglo-American readers when they first encounter the quite different style of French philosophical writing. *Elemental Passions* is richly allusive, indeterminably poetry and philosophy, while also being performative. It is not written as a logical argument. Instead, the reader is invited to listen as a woman searches for her subjectivity in relation to a man; to listen, too, to his responses, and to ponder the implications. Both woman and man must change in order to become subjects in relation to each other. The reader bears witness to the process of change, with its pain and its rewards. As the woman in *Elemental Passions* develops more and more into a subject, the man sometimes reacts defensively, even violently. He does not adapt easily to the reconfiguration of the relationship from dominance to mutuality, and has trouble acknowledging the female voice that begins to sound. As we read the text, however, we find that the struggle for mutuality is worthwhile for both the woman and the man as their rigid difference is gradually replaced by a more fluid reciprocity. Moreover, in our reading this fluidity is key not only to the development of mutual subjects in the drama of the text, but also to a creative rethinking of the whole system of binary logic which has configured Western philosophy. Or so we will try to show.

Immensely significant as the development of sexually different subjects is, however, Irigaray's virtually exclusive emphasis on sexual difference is itself problematic. As many feminist writers have pointed out, the traditionally male philosophical subject has other significant characteristics besides his sex. Over the centuries he has implicitly been white, heterosexual, middle class, affluent, able-bodied, and young to middle-aged. The unacknowledged assumption in much of Irigaray's writing, including *Elemental Passions*, is that all these implicit characteristics are shared by the man and the woman of its drama; the only significant difference between them being sexual difference. But why make this assumption? What forms of racism, homophobia, and prejudices of class, age and ability are left unchallenged or even covertly reinscribed if these alterities are passed over in silence? In chapter six of this book, after exploring the richness of *Elemental Passions*, we will revisit the question of multiple subjects, multiple differences, to show how the insights Irigaray has developed can be taken further than she herself has gone.

Fluidity: a term with many meanings

In this book, fluidity is a pivotal term. It denotes several important issues, different from one another and yet flowing into each other. Firstly, it refers to a logic generated by the emergence of (sexually) different subjects. The traditional construction of subjectivity in terms of one and not-one, A and not-A, demonstrates a way of thinking structured according to rigid binaries or dichotomies. But in the emergence of mutual but different subjects as performed in *Elemental Passions*, these binaries are displaced by a more fluid logic. The rigid binary according to which the other is defined as the opposite of the one, what the one is not, is replaced by a mutuality of respect and reciprocity. The implications of this understanding of fluidity (as well as how it must be qualified) will be one of the central themes of this book, in relation to both philosophical logic and psychoanalysis.

A second meaning of fluidity refers to the female subject herself. As Irigaray performs the emergence of the female subject in *Elemental Passions*, she shows how this subject passes out of the boundaries in which she has been positioned by philosophy and psychoanalysis alike. In order to explore difference and newness both she and the male subject have to renounce re-enactment of traditional roles and change the parameters within which subjects can develop. Thus Irigaray's female and male subjects are continually becoming, forever fluid. They are never finished; they are always developing further. Moreover, the fluidity of the subjects ensure that they cannot be made into rigid objects to be pinned down and controlled.

The language with which Irigaray writes of the development of these subjects is also fluid. This brings us to our third meaning of fluidity. The language of *Elemental Passions* is poetic, full of (unanswered) questions, playful and elusive. Like the female subject who emerges within it, Irigaray's language escapes possession. It eludes the reader time and again. In order to think and write of a female subject without making it something fixed, Irigaray makes liberal use of imagery. As Rosi Braidotti has remarked, 'one has to learn to read the images that mark Irigaray's texts and maximize their power of inspiration' (1991: 249). Some of the images we encounter in *Elemental Passions* are a song, a cloud, a flower and lips. Not only do these images display fluidity in themselves, they also flow over into one another, and are of central importance for the emergence of fluid subjects.

Lastly, we would like to urge that fluidity can also be used to go beyond Irigaray and to conceive of multiple subjects with all sorts of differences, who take up ever-changing positions in relation to each other. Fluidity is helpful in understanding what might go on among female subjects who find themselves in different positions of power, for instance, or among male or female subjects when sexual difference is only one of the differences to be negotiated, or between subjects of the same sex who nevertheless have much work to do to empower one another in mutuality. In other words, we will propose that Irigaray's insights and her development of a language of fluidity in which female subjects can emerge can be extended to the creative performance of other sorts of difference.

The structure of the book

This book is divided into three parts, each of which has several chapters. Part I discusses the grip of rigid binary thinking on Western culture and begins to show something of Irigaray's challenge to it, especially in her earlier work. In Chapter 1 we consider the centrality of binary logic for Western philosophical thinking exemplified by Parmenides, and show how Irigaray appeals to Empedocles to destabilize the hegemony of the binary system and to introduce the idea of a fluid logic. In Chapter 2 we consider the same binary system with its implicitly male subject in its psychoanalytic manifestation. Irigaray has been heavily influenced by Jacques Lacan, the French psychoanalyst at whose *Ecole freudienne de Paris* (the Freudian School of Paris) Irigaray worked until the publication in 1974 of her *Speculum*. Lacan dismissed her after this publication. We investigate

Introduction

Lacan's investment in the subject as male, and Irigaray's insistence on the emergence of the female subject.

Part II, the heart of the book, is an analysis of *Elemental Passions*. First we situate *Elemental Passions* in relation to Irigaray's other writings, and give an overview of its strategies and themes. Then in Chapter 4 we offer a chapter-by-chapter commentary with special reference to the emergence of the female subject and the importance of fluidity as central to the mutuality of sexually different subjects. After we have commented on the chapters, we return in Chapter 5 to selected parts of them for a more detailed study of some of the key images which Irigaray uses; and we show how these images of fluidity offer creative ways of thinking otherwise than in oppositional binaries, whether in relation to philosophical logic or to psychoanalytic subject formation.

In Part III we begin by considering criticisms of Irigaray's work, and suggest ways in which it could be taken forward. We recognize in particular the inadequacy of thinking exclusively in terms of sexual difference, and argue for the recognition of multiple alterities. We suggest, however, that Irigaray's thinking on fluidity and the performance of subjectivity can be appropriated for the celebration of many kinds of difference, and that her images enable us to think the conditions of the development of multiple subjects in relation to one another, to nature, to society and to the divine. In the final chapter we revisit one last time the rigid binary systems of philosophy and psychoanalysis and show how these fields of thought could be enriched by intellectual and subjective formation that is forever fluid.

PART I

Problems of rigidity

CHAPTER 1

Rigid binaries and masculinistic logic

In Irigaray's philosophy of sexual difference love is of ultimate significance for the development and mutual relationship of two subjects. But what sort of love is this? How should it be understood? In *Elemental Passions* Irigaray draws a distinction between two kinds of love:

> Love can be the becoming which appropriates the other for itself by consuming it, introjecting it into itself, to the point where the other disappears. Or love can be the motor of becoming, allowing both the one and the other to grow. For such a love, each must keep their body autonomous ... Two lives should embrace and fertilize each other without either being a fixed goal for the other. (EP 27)

> L'amour est le devenir qui s'approprie l'autre en le consommant, en l'introjectant en soi-même, jusqu'a sa disparition. Ou l'amour est le motuer du devenir qui laisse l'un et l'autre à leur croissance. Pour un tel amour il faut que chacun garde son corps autonome ... Que deux vies s'embrassent et se fécondent l'une l'autre, sans fin arrêtée en l'un ou en l'autre. (Pe 27–8)

Irigaray argues that love between two sexually different people is fruitful when each recognizes the other as distinct and autonomous. It is destructive when one erases the other, whether by trying to merge or by domination. Neither should be a fixed goal for the other, they should embrace *sans fin arrêtée*.

Paradoxically love which seeks to consume or erase the other is love which is operating according to rigid boundaries of self and other and cannot tolerate difference. On the other hand, love which cherishes autonomy and difference in self and other has no need for rigidity and control. A recognition of the other as genuinely different allows for mutuality and thus the break-down of rigid boundaries. It renders dichotomies unnecessary. It operates with a fluid logic.

Philosophy has operated with a rigid binary system of logic ever since its inception in ancient Greece. Indeed, binary logic is arguably its starting point and framework. But what would happen if love, along with logic, were allowed to be the springboard of our thought? Love, after all, is at least as important as rationality in making us human; or, better, to be human is to be capable of loving thought and thoughtful love. Suppose we were to take this seriously in our ideas

Rigid binaries and masculinistic logic

of epistemology: indeed, how can we not? Part of the implication of Irigaray's insistence on the importance of mutual love is that when love of sexually different subjects is given the consideration it deserves a new philosophy emerges, a philosophy in which fluidity is significant. In this chapter we will show something of the grip of rigidity on Western philosophy since its inception and point out its consequences with regard to subjectivity and power. We will also see how Irigaray reaches back to alternative sources of philosophy as she looks for the conditions for the emergence of the female subject. In Part II we will see how fluidity is significant for that emerging subject, and how it calls forth new philosophical categories.

Binary beginnings

The Pythagorean table of opposites, which was developed in the sixth century BCE, is an early articulation of a binary system. As reproduced by Aristotle (*Met.* 1.5.986a) the ten contrasts of this table are as follows:

limit	unlimited
odd	even
one	many
right	left
male	female
rest	motion
straight	curved
light	dark
good	bad
square	oblong (Aristotle 1941: 698)

The precise significance of these pairs of contrasts for the Pythagoreans themselves can only be conjectured. Pythagorean teachings were multiple and developing, and their original thought cannot now be recovered (Cornford 1922, 1923; Barnes 1982). It seems clear, however, that the terms of each column were conceptually linked with one another, and that those of the left-hand column were considered superior to those of the right-hand column. Thus for example limit, one, rest, light, good and male were linked together and seen as superior to their counterparts of unlimited, many, motion, dark, bad and female. It follows that all the terms, including pairs with terms that to us seem gender neutral such as odd–even, had specifically gendered values for the Pythagoreans. F. M. Cornford, in his study of the Pythagorean table, shows the importance of this gendered linkage:

Thus the Dyad, as the first even number, stands for the female receptive field, the void womb of unordered space, the evil principle of the Unlimited. The Triad is its opposite, the good principle of Limit, the male whose union with the Unlimited produces the limited. (1923: 2)

Cornford illustrates both the gendered nature of the pairs of contrasts and the values which were attached accordingly. In particular, the male is valued positively, the female negatively.

The pairs of opposites in the Pythagorean table serve to reinforce each other. Together they form a structure in which maleness is associated with a clear, determinate mode of thought while femalenesss is linked to vagueness and the indeterminate. Pamela Anderson points out that reason is constructed as male and as that which 'limits, unifies, enlightens, orders, rests, straightens' (1997: 9). Reason has thus been defined in opposition to the female: chaotic, multiple, moving, darkness (Jantzen 1998b: 266–70). This construction can be discerned in the assumptions of subsequent thinkers even when they differed in other respects from Pythagoras.

Parmenides' ascent to logic

One such account is found in the fifth-century BCE thinker, Parmenides. Parmenides holds that ultimate reality must be One, and criticizes the Pythagorean school because it 'derives a manifold world from an original unity' (Cornford 1922: 137). Parmenides' alternative is an account which recognizes only one unchanging Being; the 'many' of ordinary experience is only appearance or illusion.

Everyone agrees that Parmenides had an enormous influence on the development of logic. However, there is disagreement on how this influence should be evaluated. Jonathan Barnes, like many experts on Presocratic philosophy, is happy to describe Parmenides in glowing terms as 'a giant figure'; what is more, he introduced into Presocratic thought a number of issues belonging to the very heart of philosophy (1982: 155). Others, writing from a feminist perspective, have pointed out that Parmenides was the first to make a rigid division between the realm of sensory experience and the realm of thought, a division that has plagued Western philosophy ever since, to the disadvantage of women (Cavarero 1995: 37).

Parmenides wrote his philosophy in the form of a narrative poem in hexameters, the same style as Homer had used. Unlike Homer, however, the story that Parmenides narrates is not a story of a battle or a sea voyage but the story of a journey towards the discovery of truth. Only fragments of the poem are preserved. This, together with the facts that Parmenides' language is at times obscure and that readers of today are not always aware of his background assumptions, gives rise to multiple and sometimes conflicting interpretations (for the translation and interpretations of the poem, see Coxon 1986: 44–50;

Barnes 1982: 155–99; Nye 1990: 9–23; Hussey 1997: 130–73).

In its main outline, however, the poem is clear enough. It opens with a prologue written in the first-person narrative. Parmenides is driven through the sky by sun maidens in a horse-drawn chariot: 'On this I was carried, for on this the sagacious mares were carrying me, straining at the chariot and guided by maidens along the way' (Coxon 1986: 44). The maidens bring Parmenides to the gate which marks the paths of day and night and is guarded by Dike, which can be translated 'Justice'. Coxon comments on the specific words Parmenides uses here. He shows that the phrase 'journeys of night and day' echoes Homer. The gate signifies the boundary between the 'perpetual light of the divine world and the relative darkness of the human world'. In Parmenides, however, the further step is made that light is associated with knowledge and reason, darkness with not-knowing. When we recall Pythagoras' table of opposites, the gendered associations of these metaphors are apparent. It is no accident, therefore, that Irigaray also chooses to employ imagery of light and darkness, but with very different consequences as we shall see.

The maidens persuade Dike to let Parmenides through the gates, and they lead the chariot to the goddess of truth. With Parmenides' arrival at the goddess of truth, the poem proper begins. The remainder of the poem is taken up with the goddess initiating Parmenides into logic. She addresses Parmenides as follows: 'Come then, I will tell you (and you must spread the story when you have heard it) what are the only roads of inquiry for thinking of' (Coxon 1986: 52–3). The goddess teaches Parmenides that there exist two kinds of knowledge with two corresponding paths: the way of truth for those initiated into logic and the way of opinion which the masses follow. The way of opinion is described as a way

On which mortals with no understanding stray two-headed, for perplexity in their own breasts directs their minds astray and they are borne on deaf and blind alike in bewilderment, people without judgement, by whom this has been accepted as both being and not being, the same and not the same, and for all of whom their journey turns backwards again. (Coxon 1986: 54–5)

Muddled mortals who have not proceeded far enough on the road which eventually leads to logic wander around 'two-headed'. That is, they believe that they can apply 'is' and 'is not' to one and the same thing which means that their thinking goes in two directions at the same time. The logical truth, so the goddess discloses, is that reality is One, an unchanging whole. But this teaching is attainable only to those (few) who have learned logical reasoning and are not deceived by their senses. 'Only one story of the way is still left: that a thing is. On this way there are very many signs: that Being is ungenerated and imperishable, entire, unique, unmoved and perfect' (60–1). The goddess is insistent. Either something is eternal and unchanging or it is not and never will be. One can ask of the world or of anything in it,

Problems of rigidity

How and whence grown? I shall not let you say or conceive, 'from Not-being', for it cannot be said or conceived that anything is not; and then what necessity in fact could have urged it to begin and spring up later or before from Nothing? Thus it must be either entirely or not at all. (64–5)

This clear-cut distinction between 'is' and 'is not' also applies to the two paths of knowledge. The path of logic is the path that is real. The other path seems to provide knowledge but in fact leads nowhere. The path that leads to truth is described by Parmenides as the 'path of persuasion' (52). Page duBois suggests that, from the context of the time, this could be interpreted to mean that truth is revealed under duress, just as a slave was 'persuaded' to tell the truth by being tortured: 'like the slave who yields the truth to the torturer, the "what-is" is bound in domination, and delivers up its truth under necessity' (1991: 101).

In summary, the four main aspects of Parmenides' thought are, first, that there are two paths purporting to lead to knowledge, a true one and a false one. Second, the true way is the way of logic. Third, this logic stipulates that there is a rigid distinction between what is and what is not – either something exists or it doesn't; either something has a quality or it does not: Aristotle was to call this the Law of the Excluded Middle. Fourth, when Parmenides applies this logic to ordinary experiences of change it leads him to the conclusion that these experiences are illusory: something either 'is' or 'is-not', and what is cannot change.

A feminist critique of Parmenides

Feminists have taken issue with all four of these aspects of Parmenides' thought. They show that the imagery itself is a clue. The people who assist Parmenides in his journey – the two sun maidens, Dike, and the goddess – are all female. Even the horses are mares! Parmenides is the only male figure to appear. From a feminist perspective it is ironic that females assist Parmenides in his quest for knowledge and yet are excluded from it themselves: having given him their aid, they are then dropped from consideration.

Classical scholars commenting on Parmenides' writings have regularly followed Parmenides in erasing the importance of the female figures, focusing mainly on the content of Parmenides' poem and either ignoring the form or dismissing it as obstructive. For example, Jonathan Barnes remarks that it is 'hard to excuse Parmenides' choice of verse as a medium for his philosophy' (1982: 155) and says flatly that the interpretation of the allegorical prologue 'is for the most part of little philosophical importance' (156); though in the preface to the second revised edition of his book Barnes recognizes that he has 'ignored the literary form' of Parmenides' writing. Although he does not regard this lack as too significant, he asserts that if he were to write the book again he would 'take a less nonchalant attitude to questions of style and form' (xvi).

Rigid binaries and masculinistic logic

Similarly, Edward Hussey's main concern is with Parmenides' logic. He includes a small section on Parmenides' narrative form and his use of images, but complains about Parmenides' choice of poetry as his literary form: 'the constraints imposed, by the metre and vocabulary of epic verse, on the exposition of matter for which they were never designed, are bad enough' (1997: 131). But in response to Hussey, we ask: who decides what is the appropriate material for poetry, and by what criteria? What assumptions are built into a contention that philosophy and poetry should be kept separate, not allowed to flow into one another?

In contrast to Barnes and Hussey, Moira Gatens has argued that philosophers should take responsibility for the representations which they employ, and should scrutinize the particular images of their philosophy and their implicit assumptions and passions (1996: xii). Andrea Nye (1990) and Adriana Cavarero (1995) do just that. Both of them regard the metaphors in Parmenides' poem as significant for his logic, and argue that his imagery cannot be ignored. Nye points out the centrality of desire in Parmenides' poem: it is desire which motivates his journey and he is passionate in his encounter with logic. Nye argues that in the poem this desire for logic is a displaced sexual desire. Sexual desire for another person – which can be marred by uncertainty, ambivalence, confusion and fear – is replaced by desire for logic, which can receive absolute satisfaction. The images of the prologue support this interpretation. Dike's heavy iron gates swing wide and reveal an opening through which Parmenides' chariot is driven, 'mimicking the physical consummation of desire'. In Parmenides' encounter with the goddess, physical satisfaction is replaced by the satisfaction of an absolute logic (Nye 1990: 9–22). Adriana Cavarero probes the fact that Parmenides is supported in his search for truth and initiated into logic exclusively by women: 'it is astounding that female figures inaugurate the route toward abstract thought, where philosophy celebrates its patriarchal glory' (1995: 38). It is almost as if the female figures who assist Parmenides 'serve merely as sacrificial food for the journey toward the realm of philosophy that will exclude them' (39).

It might be objected to this that the figure with the most power in the poem is female: it is the goddess, not Parmenides, who is represented as supreme, and it is she who initiates him into logic. She receives and welcomes Parmenides and teaches him her knowledge. In response to this objection we would point out that it is important to remember that this is a poem written by Parmenides to convey his philosophy; it is not a historical account of a meeting with an actual goddess/woman. All the words the goddess speaks in the poem are Parmenides' words, put into her mouth for his own purposes. By making the goddess say exactly what he wants her to say, Parmenides can simultaneously make her serve his wishes and yet make it seem as though it is she, not he, who is responsible for the teaching of the poem. Although the poem is full of female figures, they are all given supportive roles. The real hero of the narrative is the male philosopher. The

Problems of rigidity

women are there to serve, initiate, and then step back into the wings, leaving the stage for the male protagonist. It is a classic example of the refusal of a female subject in philosophy; significantly it is in this context, where the male protagonist is the only real subject, that a rigid logic is the result. Although Irigaray does not explicitly discuss Parmenides, his strategy is a classic example of what many of her writings expose: erasure of the woman upon whom nevertheless his whole structure depends.[1]

Birth and truth

As Cavarero interprets his poem, Parmenides' journey upward through the sky to the goddess emphasizes the vast distance he wishes to place between ordinary knowledge and logic, between the realms of sensory experience and pure truth. She interprets his journey as the philosopher's ascent to his new, perfect home. Parmenides leaves the world of muddled mortals behind: 'in effect the philosopher abandons the world of his own birth in order to establish his abode in pure thought' (1995: 38). Nye also uses the metaphor of birth: she says that 'removed from the uncertain pleasures of the flesh, Parmenides is reborn' (1990: 19). Man gives birth to himself, in a second birth, assisted by a woman: this birth is seen as more perfect, more pure, than biological birth from a woman.

There are evident parallels here to other stories in which men give birth. There is the story of the birthing of Eve by God the Father from Adam's rib in the Hebrew narrative of the creation: the male God and the man together produce the woman and, through her, all of humankind. In Greek mythology the goddess Athena is born from Zeus's head. In Plato's *Symposium*, Diotima's speech (put into her mouth by a male philosopher in much the same way as Parmenides ventriloquizes the goddess) advocates love between men which results in the birth of philosophical insight. Plato's teaching is that this love, which begets through the soul, replaces the lesser love between man and woman which procreates through the body and results in the creation of another human being. The Christian rite of baptism, similarly, can be interpreted as masculine birthing: the priest (traditionally male) rebirths a child with a small amount of water 'in the name of the Father, the Son and the Holy Spirit'. Evangelical Christians celebrate their rebirth by calling themselves 'born again'. Genevieve Lloyd presents a modern secular variant when she points out that the rationale for mothers sending their sons to the front in times of war is, perversely, to assist them in rebirthing themselves: 'in giving up their sons, women are supposed to allow them to become real men and immortal selves. Surrendering sons to significant deaths becomes a higher

---

[1] The tactics of this exposure have much in common with Derridean strategies which excavate the crucial repressed or denied assumption of arguments: Irigaray as usual shows its sexual dimensions. The jury is out on the question of which of them had the greater influence on the other.

mode of giving birth' (Lloyd 1986: 76). In each of these cases, the right of reproduction is appropriated by males, while women are denied their subject position: at best they are ancillary or in a supportive role.

Yet as Cavarero points out, none of these 'rebirthings' would be possible unless there had been an initial birth from a mother. The philosopher, the Christian and the soldier seem to forget that they could not have chosen their new birth, or their new philosophical home, or their manliness, had they not first been born into the world. Luce Irigaray makes much of this forgotten debt to the woman: repeatedly she argues that men want to forget to whom it is that they owe their existence (FA; SG21; etc.). Part of her intention in her analysis of the mother–son relationship is to draw attention to the fact that woman brought man into the world before he could decide to rebirth himself. Irigaray contends that man's independence is an illusion. Moreover, the idea of man's second birth denies to woman her generative power. It relegates her to the role of assistant, and erroneously posits the male as the sole creator, whether of philosophy, as in Plato's *Symposium*, or of eternal life, as in Christian rites, or even of language, as we shall see in Lacan in the next chapter. This male creator does not need woman, except perhaps as his assistant.

Now, actual birth is messy. There is a great deal of fluid: indeed lubrication is essential if the birth is to be possible at all. The masculinist appropriations of birth are much neater and cleaner: there is no blood or shit or mucous. At most there is a trickle of clean water, as in Christian baptism. Moreover we can see how that which is born, in these masculinist birthings, is solid, rigid: the absolute logic of Parmenides; the hard manliness of the soldier; the unswerving conviction of the born-again Christian. Although the detail of the argument will emerge in later chapters, we can already begin to notice how the lack of a subject position for women is related to the emergence of rigid binaries, and catch a hint of how subversive attention to fluidity will be to this masculinist pattern. When Parmenides has reached the realm of truth, materiality and fluidity are placed outside of the philosophical domain. Irigaray's work endeavours to bring this rejected aspect, which has been associated primarily with women, back into philosophy; she works to restore the woman subject and the fluidity and bodiliness which the woman subject represents.

A or not-A

Although in some respects Parmenides can be read as challenging Pythagoras, his philosophy reinforces the notion of binary oppositions. Parmenides is taught by the goddess that what is, is, and what is not, is not. This concept of being excludes notions of change and becoming. Parmenides writes 'And how could what becomes have being, how come into being, seeing that, if it came to be, it is not, nor is it, if at some time it is going to be. Thus becoming has been extinguished and is unheard of' (Coxon 1986: 66–7). The world of appearances is deceptive, for, contrary to what our senses tell us, change does not exist. This means that the mind must take precedence over the senses. The world as we experience it has no being. It belongs to 'what is not', or nothingness. The only thing that exists is revealed by pure logic: the eternal, unchanging One.

According to Parmenides' logic, becoming would be the emergence into existence of something that had not existed previously. Given a binary logical structure where something is either A or not-A, the only way to conceive of becoming is to describe it as the opposite of being, as nothingness. Deriving from Parmenides and the development of his ideas in Greek thought, the idea of negation and nothingness had a pervasive influence on modern continental thought from Hegel through Kojève to Sartre and Merleau-Ponty. Throughout this trajectory it is possible to trace how the negation of becoming or change, and the depiction of the world as nothingness, leads to the silent exclusion of women from philosophy. It is after all women who are involved in the domain of change: giving birth, rearing children, taking care of the material conditions of life, dealing with death. Women's work has traditionally been concerned with changes in the household as well: cooking and preparing food, mending and washing clothes, cleaning the home, and taking care of dependants. It is striking how many of these activities crucially involve fluids. Moreover, as Andrea Nye has said, 'the world of women involves not only heterosexuality and birth but also death. Not only must man bear the indignity of birth, he must also look forward to bodily decay and eventual destruction' (1990: 15). These are fearsome and fluid occurrences: it would be much less frightening if one could escape them into a realm of pure and rigid thought.

We can now begin to recognize the relationship between Parmenides' logic and Pythagoras' oppositions, and how they reinforce one another in the exclusion of the woman subject. In Parmenides' logic subjectivity is constructed through rules of identity and sameness. Something either is or is-not. Changes are illusory. Now, if we consider the dualisms mind/senses, immortality/mortality, unchanging logic/processes of change, being/becoming, we can see that the first term is frequently associated with men, the second with women. The male subject is thus constructed as the norm. This leaves woman described as the not-man, and erases her as a subject in her own right. Two sexually different beings are reduced to one, the same and the not-same, the man and the not-man. Moreover, a subject who constructs himself by the attempted erasure of what-he-is-not will carry with him a fear of the other. The difference between 'the one' and 'the other' is therefore made into a fearful gulf; and the (repressed) fear of difference can result in violence directed towards the 'other'.

Once again it is through Hegel that this logic has its largest impact upon modern continental thought. In Hegel's *Phenomenology* (1977), the distinction and then the conjunction between the same and the not-same, the one and the other, is the motor that drives developing consciousness in its journey to Absolute Spirit. If there is a single vignette in Hegel's writing that has had a greater impact on subsequent thought than all others, it is his story of the master and the slave; and it would not be putting the case too strongly to say that all of *Elemental Passions* should be read under its sign.

Hegel begins by insisting that 'self-consciousness exists ... only in being acknowledged' (1977: 111); the self needs the not-self, the other, even to recognize itself. Much as it needs the other, however, the other is also a threat to the self, its negation, its *not-self*: moreover this is as true for the second as for the first. 'Thus the relation of the two self-conscious individuals is such that they prove themselves and each other through a life-and-death struggle' (111–12). Yet if one or the other were actually to be killed in this 'trial-by-death' it would defeat the purpose of the struggle. What both of them wanted was recognition: the dead recognize no one. The victor in the struggle therefore does not kill his opponent but makes him his slave. By being forced to serve the master's desires, the slave is forced to recognize the master and give him the affirmation and acknowledgement of his selfhood that he craved. Stanley Rosen summarizes Hegel's account as follows:

So long as he [the other] is independent, I am alienated from myself; I cannot be certain of my own truth or value. Since my independence turns upon my ability to negate or assimilate whatever I desire, I must risk my life in a struggle with the other for mastery of desire. My goal, however, is not to kill him but to reassert my independence within the medium of self-consciousness by forcing him to recognize me as independent. I struggle not to kill but to prove my manhood, to show that I am independent enough to be prepared to die. (Rosen 2000: 158)

By reducing the other to a subordinate position whose chief function is to serve the master and reflect his self-consciousness back to him, the master has gained his object, though of course he will have to be ever vigilant, and exert continuous control lest the slave escape his domination.

Hegel's account was taken up in various registers in twentieth-century France. Alexandrè Kojève, in his enormously influential lectures on Hegel in Paris in the 1930s, emphasized the violence involved in the demand for recognition, and transposed the Hegelian theme into an explanation of history and warfare (Kojève 1969; cf. Drury 1994). Simone de Beauvoir, in *The Second Sex*, explicitly took the Hegelian account of master and slave as a model of the struggle between the sexes (Beauvoir 1954; cf. Chanter 1995: 55–68). And Jacques Lacan developed his psychoanalytic theory in terms of the driving force of desire for recognition (1977, 1982a), a theory that can be expanded beyond the individual to Western culture in what Teresa Brennan explores as 'the ego's era' (1993: 26–78).

The atmosphere in which Irigaray wrote *Elemental Passions* was heavy with the long shadows of Hegel's account of the struggle for mastery, and there are allusions to it in almost every chapter of her book, as we shall see. Ever and again she shows how 'you-man' tries to dominate the woman and receive recognition from her. He uses violence, confinement, appropriation of her language, and many other tactics to assert his mastery over her, since she is his other, not-self, not-A to his A, and is thus an object of both threat and desire.

But Irigaray emphasizes a further element of the Hegelian account. In Hegel's rendition, enslavement is not the final outcome. The master becomes aware that recognition from someone who is compelled to give it is of little value: for affirmation to be satisfying it must be freely given by an equal. The slave, for his part, by his work for the master develops for himself a self-respect which takes him above his position as a slave. In the Hegelian *Bildungsroman* the eventual result is that the two win through to mutuality, their binary opposition overcome. Can the same mutuality be achieved in relation to sexual difference? This is the central question of *Elemental Passions*.

Feminist critiques of binaries

It is the awareness of the use of power and efforts to mastery which accompany the construction of dichotomies that lie at the heart of feminist critiques of binary logic. It is not the case that feminist philosophers reject binaries in all contexts: there are situations in which binaries are manifestly useful (see Gatens 1991: 92). However, binaries are often cast as dualisms in which domination and subordination are implicit, and constructed as oppositional and exclusive: this has typically been the case in relation to masculine and feminine gender identities (Plumwood 1993: 31). Moira Gatens, for example, shows how dichotomous thought 'can covertly promote social and political values by presenting a conceptual division as if it were a factual or natural division' (1991: 92). Thus, oppressive power relations can be reflected and reinforced by apparently neutral philosophical distinctions.

A ground-breaking investigation of such power-filled distinctions was undertaken by Nancy Jay. Jay's 'Gender and Dichotomy' (1981) is a study into the use of logical dichotomy in Emile Durkheim's concept of religion. Jay argues that Durkheim's use of the profane/sacred binary is not empirically grounded but is instead an a-priori conceptual framework imposed on the empirical data. The profane/sacred binary is linked (as in Pythagoras' system) with other dichotomies, such as female/male. Jay ultimately argues that explanations of societies which use formal dichotomous logic are resistant to change and serve to support the position of those with power.

Be that as it may, it is significant that Jay argues that the construction of gender differences as a classic binary has important consequences. To understand these consequences it is necessary to understand Aristotle's formulation of three basic rules of logic, already evident but not articulated in Pythagoras and Parmenides. Aristotle's laws are, first, the Principle of Identity (if anything is A, it is A);

second, the Principle of Non-Contradiction (nothing can be both A and not-A); and third, the Law of the Excluded Middle (everything must be either A or not-A). Jay points out that according to these laws, firstly, 'continuities between terms is a logical impossibility for distinctions phrased as contradictories, as A and not-A': there is a rigid and impermeable division between them; secondly, 'in A/Not-A dichotomies only one term has positive reality'; and thirdly, 'the structure of A/Not-A is such that a third term is impossible: everything and anything must be either A or Not-A' (1981: 44).

Moira Gatens takes up and explains Jay's position. Drawing on Jay, Gatens argues that the way a dichotomy operates is that one term, the one that is valued positively, determines the other one. Instead of the distinction being formulated as between something (A) and something else (B), it is set up as a distinction between something (A) and its opposite (not-A). This means that whatever is not A becomes defined solely by the fact that it is not the same as A, rather than for itself or in its own terms. We can now see more clearly how it is that the process of constructing differences as opposites of which one term is taken as the norm has meant that woman has been defined primarily as not-man (not-A). Qualities which were not deemed suitable for men – such as irrationality, weakness, and dependence – were attributed to women, whether or not actual women showed these qualities (Jantzen 1997b: 389–90). Moira Gatens makes a similar point: 'From ancient Greece to our own time women have been defined not so much in terms of any positive qualities that they possess but rather in terms of the male qualities that they lack' (1991: 94). In the course of this book, it will become clear that Irigaray challenges these definitions of women as lacking certain qualities or as deficiency in her development as a female subject; and that this challenge is related to a rejection of rigid binaries in favour of fluidity as a category of logic which has received far too little attention.

In Irigaray's writings it is the gender binary which is seen as paramount. She concentrates on the characteristics historically attributed to women and sets out to disrupt the binary opposition 'Man and not-Man' through a fluid language which defies dichotomies. For Irigaray, the dichotomy 'Man and not-Man' is the ultimate binary opposition which grounds Western thought. If this dichotomy can be dismantled, it would signal the unravelling of other dichotomies. Through the course of this book we will be exploring this claim and its implications.

However, we would wish to signal at the outset that, in our view, sexual difference is not the only or even necessarily the most important binary. Rather, which binary is most significant is context-dependent. It is only within specific historical and cultural circumstances that it can be decided which difference(s) in power, expressed as dichotomies, need to be addressed as primary. For example, in the opening pages of the autobiography *I Know Why the Caged Bird Sings*, the Afro-American writer Maya Angelou writes, recalling her girlhood:

Problems of rigidity

I was going to look like one of the sweet little white girls who were everybody's dream of what was right with the world ... Wouldn't they be surprised when one day I woke out of my black ugly dream, and my real hair, which was long and blond, would take the place of the kinky mass that Momma wouldn't let me straighten? My light-blue eyes were going to hypnotize them. (1969: 1–2)

Breena Clarke writes of a similar sentiment in *River, Cross My Heart* (1999). Central to this novel, set in Georgetown, Washington DC in the 1920s, are the segregated locations for swimming. The white children swim in a pool; coloured children in a dirty canal. The main character, Johnnie Mae, is outraged by this injustice. In contrast to the girl in *I Know Why the Caged Bird Sings*, Johnnie Mae does not seek the solution in crossing over to the other side of the dichotomy and becoming white. Instead, she contrives to get access to the pool as she is: a black girl and a good swimmer.

The point is that, different as these accounts are, in both of them sexual difference, though it plays a role, is not central. Of over-riding importance is the difference between black and white. Not the opposition man–woman but a different binary is the focus of injustice and struggle: the books illustrate our contention that it is the context which determines which dichotomy is primary at a particular moment. We will argue that Irigaray does not pay sufficient attention to binaries other than sexual difference, even though her strategies of fluidity can be used in relation to other differences as well.[2]

Moreover, it is important to recognize that, as Val Plumwood (1993: 42–3) and Patricia Hill Collins (1991: 67) argue, dichotomies form interlocking structures of thought which serve to uphold oppression. In their view, it would not be enough to select only the gender binary, man–woman, and analyse this in order to change all the power relations which Western philosophy reflects. Just as in Pythagoras' table, each term was linked with all the others in its column, so also throughout Western culture gender binaries have been linked with other forms of binary. A clear example is the way in which race is defined in our society: in our society 'white' is the norm (A) and 'black' includes everything that is 'non-white' (not-A); moreover 'white' as the norm is linked with maleness while blackness is often feminized.

The distinction between white and black is not an innocent one, or merely empirically descriptive. The categories are intricately linked with power. Whiteness indicates a privilege: the whiter one is, the more privileged. As Richard Dyer has described it in his book *White*, 'given the overwhelming advantage of being white, in terms of power, privilege, and material well-being, who counts as white and who doesn't is worth fighting over' (1998: 52). Dyer argues that the

---

[2] This inattention has also been true of Anglo-American feminists. White feminists during the 1970s thought they spoke for all women when they addressed issues of gender. As black women showed them, they ignored their own whiteness and failed to see that race was another area of power struggle (see Hall 1995; Collins 1991).

privilege of whiteness is reflected in, for example, aesthetics and beauty ideals. He points out that 'much of the history of Western make-up is a history of whitening the face' (48); however the trend for tanning, he contends, does not reflect a desire on the part of white people to become black. Paradoxically, a suntan emphasizes the person's 'racial' whiteness (49–50). Similarly, Debbie Weekes in 'Shades of Blackness' discusses the impact of race for black women's self-conceptions of beauty, and argues that these women take the degrees of skin colour and hair texture as measures for blackness (1997: 319).

In situations where the effect of race on people's lives is taken to the extreme, such as during the apartheid regime in South Africa, rigid racial categories take on an even more sinister meaning. Under apartheid, specific rules determined whether one belonged to the category 'white' or 'black'. Within this system, people were forced into colour categories which substantially determined where they lived, where they worked, how much they were paid, on which bench they could sit and which toilet they could go to, 'white' or 'black'.

It could be objected that in the case of apartheid there was a third category, the category of 'coloured/kleurling'. This defined someone who was neither 'black' nor 'white' but something in between. As it was set out for practical usage, 'the term "Coloured" in South Africa is in general confined to persons of mixed race ...The exact legal definition of a Coloured person is an extremely complex point, but for all practical purposes it may be taken as anyone who is not African, Indian or European' (Brookes 1968: 22). The existence of the category, however, did not upset the binary structure of white–black any more than does a sun-tan. If anything it reinforced this structure, since only if a person were a specific combination of black and white could they be classified as 'coloured'. Difference was forced into a binary opposition, in which one term became the norm against which the other term was defined; and the whole was bound up with the use of power.

These examples show that it is important to ask what kinds of dichotomies imply values, and what their link is to power and domination. Plumwood argues that any dichotomy can be arbitrarily imposed on people (1993: 47). The rationale for the imposition, she holds, need not lie in the terms of the opposition itself, let alone in the empirical data, but in the values that are attached to these terms. One can think of numerous instances in the course of history where apparently neutral empirical distinctions have been employed to oppress people. The example of apartheid is obvious. Another example is hair and eye colour in twentieth-century middle Europe. During the Nazi regime blond hair and blue eyes were seen as characteristic of the Aryan race. Richard Dyer points out that the basis for upholding the Aryan race was a quest for the origins of white people, a white genealogy. Central to the Aryan myth was the issue of purity: not surprisingly, the white race was seen as the purest race (Dyer 1998: 20–2). In the light of such examples, we can see that it is always crucial to ask: in whose interests are particular dichotomies singled out and enforced? Or, as Jay puts it, 'one can ask in *whose* interest it is to preserve social dichotomies, *who* experiences change as disorder' (1981: 53).

Another example, from the work of Page duBois in her book *Torture and Truth* (1991), shows how the legitimation of using force depends on keeping particular dichotomies in place. DuBois addresses the connection between power and truth in her analysis of the role of torture within the legal system of ancient Greece. She shows that the dichotomies operative in the social order were held intact by those in power. This also influenced the prevalent idea of truth. The aim of duBois' analysis is to recognize that 'the very idea of truth we receive from the Greeks ... is inextricably linked with the practice of torture' (7). Although the difference in treatment of witnesses within the legal system of ancient Greece seems to stem from the solid distinction in status, slave or free, duBois shows that a slave could become free in a number of ways, for example by buying himself or herself out with saved money or through a will. Conversely, a free person could become enslaved by being taken prisoner in a war. DuBois argues that the enforcement of the dichotomy between free person and slave, illustrated in the use of torture in ancient Greece, functioned to set a rigid boundary between slave and free person.

> The discourse on the use of torture in ancient Athenian law forms part of an attempt to manage the opposition between slave and free, and it betrays both need and anxiety: need to have a clear boundary between servile and free, anxiety about the impossibility of maintaining this difference. (1991: 41)

Although in reality the boundary between the slave and the free person was fluid, this fluidity had to be denied. Aristotle held that it was the nature of a free person to speak the truth, and the nature of a slave to lie unless tortured. Thus it was in the interest of those in power to maintain the boundary between freed and enslaved people, since this distinction justified the use of torture for those who were not free, who were 'other'. The opposition between self and other therefore resulted in a concept of the other as an object from which truth could be extracted through force: 'the logic of our philosophical tradition ... leads almost inevitably to conceiving the body of the other as the site from which truth can be produced, and to using violence if necessary to extract that truth' (duBois 1991: 6).

A similar example can be found in the attitude to nature of the early modern philosopher Francis Bacon, which further illustrates the claim that the attitude towards knowledge in the Western philosophical tradition leads to the construction of the object of knowledge as the 'other' and to the use of violence in order to persuade the 'other' to fulfil the bidding of the one who 'knows'. Bacon presents his argument about philosophy and nature in his book *The Refutation of Philosophies*. In his discussion of Plato, Aristotle and the Scholastics, he argues that to obtain knowledge about nature one should seduce nature to give up her secrets. This is necessary, he asserts, because

> I had not supposed ... that we were on such familiar terms with nature that, in response to a casual and perfunctory salutation, she would condescend to unveil for us her mysteries and bestow on us her blessings. (1964: 129)

Bacon argues that 'men' should trust their observations about nature and endeavour to learn how she operates. Although in one sense Bacon treats nature as a machine, with rules of performance which can be discovered, in another sense he treats nature as a woman who can usually be persuaded to part with vital knowledge. If she resists, force can be used to penetrate her secrets.

Bacon used sexual metaphors to describe man's quest for scientific knowledge, which he saw as the rightful domination of nature: his hope was to 'establish a chaste and lawful marriage between Mind and Nature' (131). According to Bacon, man should seduce nature so that she submits to him, like a woman submits to a man in marriage. Usually this would be voluntary; but it should not be forgotten that in Bacon's time (and long after) it was considered legitimate for a man to demand sexual 'rights' even if the woman did not consent. Feminist philosophers have pointed out the extent to which constructing nature as 'other' and female has legitimated the domination of nature and the resulting exploitation of the earth (Lloyd 1984: 10–18; Merchant 1983). Luce Irigaray, in her return to Empedocles' elemental philosophy discussed at the end of this chapter, begins a rethinking of the traditional opposition between culture and nature, male and female, by replacing an exclusively binary logic with one in which fluidity is also an important category, as we shall see.

But what about drizzle? Feminist alternatives to binary logic

Those who insist on the importance of the Laws of Logic would argue that without binary oppositions no sense could be made of the world. Now, it should not be thought that those who look for a more fluid logic suppose that there is no place for binaries: there are many sorts of discussion in which binaries are necessary. But although there are many situations in which binary logic is appropriate, there are also many others in which it seems unhelpfully rigid. Take the simple example of rain: one can easily think of a situation in which it is neither raining nor completely dry, as for example when there is a slight drizzle. The simple distinction 'Rain or not-Rain' is not sufficient. A third term is needed, something that indicates a situation of both A and not-A, or something between A and not-A, to describe this situation accurately. Yet as we have seen in relation to the category of 'coloured' in the apartheid regime, a simple introduction of a third term is not enough to destabilize the binary. Something more radical is needed.

Problems of rigidity

Irigaray is not the only feminist to look for ways to destablize the hegemony of binary logic. Anglo-American feminists also have been searching for alternatives. Val Plumwood (1993) addresses the dualisms male–female and culture–nature specifically, though not exclusively, in her construction of a feminist ecology. Margrit Shildrick (1997) works towards a feminist ethics of difference which questions and disrupts binary oppositions. Janice Moulton (1992a) argues that the use of dichotomies is reflected in the method of philosophy itself, which she terms 'adversarial': in her view, this method does not yield the best results, and she presents an alternative model which explicitly relates ideas to the contexts in which they are developed. Her method challenges the idea that knowledge is neutral and unconnected to the context out of which it arises, and advocates cooperation instead of competition in the search for knowledge (see also Jantzen 1998b: 70–1). Lorraine Code (1991) and Sandra Harding (1991) have applied Moulton's insights to epistemology and science respectively, and taken them forward.

One of the most telling paradigms for the destabilization of binary logic is that of pregnancy, a specifically female experience. The notion of a pregnant woman disturbs the neat distinction between self and other. A woman who is pregnant is neither one nor two, but simultaneously both one and two. The foetus she carries is indeterminably neither other nor self, or both other and self. If one thinks of reproduction as central to human experience, then it does not make sense for a woman who is carrying a child to distinguish sharply between herself and an other. The differentiation is gradual: even the event of birth, which marks the physical separation between mother and infant, does not sever identification; without continued bonding with a mother or mother-figure the infant could not survive. Caroline Whitbeck (1992), taking pregnancy and birth as her paradigm, outlines a feminist ontology in which the self–other relation is taken as central, and atomistic individualism is an aberration. She argues that such atomism denies our very humanity, and that it lies at the heart of binary structures which operate within philosophy. In Whitbeck's view, a healthy self–other relationship 'generates a multifactorial interactive model of most, if not all, aspects of reality' (1992: 63). Christine Battersby, using the same model, argues in her construction of a feminist metaphysics for a subject who develops in interaction with other subjects: the 'other', for Battersby, is encountered 'within, as well as without' (1998: 8).

Although there is little to indicate that Luce Irigaray had read these Anglo-American feminists, she uses similar ideas – especially those of pregnancy, the individuation of the infant, and the development of the female subject – to challenge rigid binary logic and to show the significance of fluidity. Irigaray's early essay 'When our Lips Speak Together' can be read as an attempt to think about the logic of self–other experience in relation to pregnancy, though it can also be taken as applying to any close relationship:

Rigid binaries and masculinistic logic

> We are luminous. Neither one nor two. I've never known how to count. Up to two. In their calculations, we make two. Really? Two? Doesn't that make you laugh? An odd sort of two. And yet not one. Especially not one. Let's leave *one* to them: their oneness, with its prerogatives, its domination (1985b: 207)

Irigaray uses the role of the mother as a starting point to unmask the pretence of a (male) subject that he is absolutely independent.

Again, as we shall see, in *Elemental Passions* Irigaray shows the significance of the fact that a foetus in the womb is part of the mother's body. The mother supplies it with the oxygen, blood and warmth it needs to grow. Thus, the mother's own body is for the foetus its food and shelter. At the same time, the foetus develops into a separate entity. This messy, fluid process of growth and becoming cannot be accounted for with binary logic, which recognizes only the Law of A or not-A. In Irigaray's logic, the notion of becoming plays a crucial role. As she says, evocatively,

> What is the rigour of your thought? The superb confidence of someone moving inside a fleshly fabric borrowed from the other. The limitless appeal of someone entrusting his survival to the destiny of mortal women ... A sovereign power, miming and undermining the whole of the resources from which it draws. (EP 82)

> La rigueur de ta pensée? Superbe aisance de qui se meut dans un tissue de chair emprunté à l'autre. Séduction sans fin de qui confie sa survie au destin de mortelles ... Puissance souveraine, mimant et minant le tout de ce qu'elle y prend comme ressources. (Pe 101)

In contrast to this recognition of the significance of birth as a paradigm for philosophical thinking, philosophers have usually concentrated on death as a central philosophical category. Adriana Cavarero, in her questioning of Parmenides' obsession with pure thought at the expense of change and becoming in the world, asks what it is about not-being that drives Parmenides to categorize the whole world and all of ordinary experience as illusion? She argues that it is death. What is implicated in the notions of becoming and change is death, non-existence. In death is revealed what change and becoming are ultimately taken to mean: namely ceasing to exist. Cavarero claims that 'the patriarchal tradition has always thrived on the category of death' (1995: 7): it has shaped Western thinking from Plato's rendition of the death of Socrates to Heidegger's philosophy of 'Being towards death' (for further analysis, see also Battersby 1998; Jantzen 1998a: 108–21).

One example of this is Georges Bataille, a French playwright and philosopher who pondered the connections between subjectivity, violence and death in a way that influenced Irigaray. For Bataille, all three come together in eroticism and reproduction. The aim of the act of making love is, according to Bataille, 'a total blending of two beings'. Yet Bataille suggests that in the act of heterosexual intercourse, one of the partners, the woman, dissolves. For the male partner, discontinuity with his lover is what he therefore experiences. As Bataille puts it in a quotation which links male subjectivity, eroticism and power:

Problems of rigidity

> Possession of the beloved object does not imply death, but the idea of death is linked with the urge to possess. If the lover cannot possess the beloved he will sometimes think of killing her; often he would rather kill than lose her. Or else he may wish to die himself. (1962: 20)

It is clear that, in Bataille's thinking, the two beings who are united in intercourse are not in positions of equality. The power and longing to possess lie with the man. Bataille's remarks show the tenor of his thought: 'Each being is distinct from all others ... He is born alone. He dies alone. Between one being and another, there is a gulf, a discontinuity' (12).

From a feminist point of view, such an exclusive focus on discontinuity and death in relation to subjectivity and love is perverse and life-threatening. The following quotation from the novelist Breena Clarke illustrates a different perspective: 'Folks always say, "You come into this world alone, and you must leave it alone." They ought to know better. Because it isn't so. It's not that way at all. The child comes to life very much attached and stays attached and is mired all its life in a soup of relations' (1999: 77).

In *Elemental Passions* Irigaray accepts Bataille's ideas of discontinuity as an accurate description of masculinist structures. However, she works to develop an alternative route to communication and continuity between subjects. Rather than think towards the domination and possession by one (male) subject of the 'other' (woman), Irigaray starts from what she sees as inherent difference between sexual subjects. In the terms of this discussion, she sees man and woman as A and B, not as A and not-A. Recognition of the difference between them leads to love and respect between subjects which enable both to become in their own distinctive ways, enable them to be neither one nor two, both one and two. Thus the development of the female subject is directly linked to the idea of a fluid logic, destabilizing the hegemony of rigid binaries with their hierarchies of domination.

Becoming JewGreek

It is already apparent that there are significant parallels between Irigaray's thought and the work of Anglo-American feminists on binaries, especially in telling examples such as that of pregnancy. These parallels, however, do not on the whole indicate mutual influence: they have been developed independently. As we shall show in Chapter 6, there has unfortunately been little interchange between Anglo-American feminists and Irigaray until relatively recently.

There is, however, another influence much nearer to home for Irigaray which so far as we are aware has not been investigated for its impact on her writing, and that is the effect of Rabbinic patterns of thought upon Freud and Derrida and through them upon Irigaray. This suggestion may at first seem far-fetched: Irigaray is not Jewish and never engaged in sustained discussion of Jewish issues or even of the Hebrew Bible. But Freud and Derrida, both of whom obviously had enormous influence on Irigaray, can be shown to have adopted Rabbinic patterns of thought which are quite different from the Greek patterns based on binary logic that have structured the West.

Susan Handelman, in her important book *The Slayers of Moses* (1982), explores the impact of Rabbinic methods of interpretation upon modern Jewish thinkers, and shows how different its style is from Greek or subsequent Christian thought. As she presents it, Greek thought from Parmenides onwards is focused on Being. Words are names, not substances; language, including metaphor, is an attempt to get at Being beyond words. The Principle of Bivalence, as Handelman names the binary system of A or not-A, is fundamental to this use of language, 'the firmest of all principles' as Aristotle said (*Metaphysics*: 1.3.1005b). It is the only way in which truth and falsehood can be constituted; and it is only through truth that we can attain Being. In Christian thinking this emphasis on true belief as the only way to knowledge of God (and thus the possibility of the presence of the divine) was taken up in patristic thinkers including Augustine and restated with emphasis in Protestantism. The requirement of binary logic as the *sine qua non* of true belief continues in Western philosophy and science under a thin veneer of secularism.

In Jewish thinking, Handelman argues, quite different assumptions prevailed. Christians looked to Christ as Truth, word made flesh, and took the pattern of his suffering. 'For the Rabbis, however, the primary reality was linguistic; true being was a God who *speaks* and creates *texts*, and *imitatis deus* was not silent suffering, but speaking and interpreting' (Handelman 1982: 4). The text itself is living: it is not a letter which kills while the spirit gives life as Pauline christendom would have it. This living text is open to endless interpretation, like a well that never runs dry. In the Midrash and the Talmud are collected commentaries and debates on the written Torah: they (and subsequent interpretations) are the 'Oral Torah'.

> For the Rabbis, the oral Torah is precisely what lies between the lines, so to speak: the explanations, the filling in of the lacunae, the elucidations of the enigmas, and the probing into what was not explicitly written: It is the text within the text. The written Torah is something like a notebook in which every jotting condenses a whole train of thought. (40)

Handelman describes the boundaries between the written and the oral Torah as 'fluid'. There is not a rigid demarcation between scripture and interpretation as there is in Christian thought, with the former authoritative over the latter. Neither is it necessary that the interpretations should all be consistent with one another. What is important is not a rigid or static system of truth in which binary logic holds sway, but rather endless living engagement with the living text.

It is immediately obvious that although both Freud and Derrida each in his own way took some distance from orthodox Jewish piety, the style of Rabbinic interpretation was congenial to them. In the case of Freud, the psychoanalytic method depended upon both the patient and the analyst freely associating upon the 'text' of the patient's life. There is no rigid 'right' or 'wrong' association; nor do contradictions matter; the issue is not one of establishing truth but of enabling the patient to engage with their past so that they can move forward in freedom. We could say that for Freud, and for psychoanalytic theory and practice after him, the becoming of a subject is bound up with this pattern of interpretation. Imposing binary logic on psychoanalytic process would stifle it.

Similarly Derrida has famously written against the idea of a fixed and rigid truth and the full presence of Being which such truth is meant to betoken. Like the Rabbis, Derrida emphasizes writing and the text, whose meaning lies in difference and is ever and again deferred. Derrida, immensely influenced here by Levinas, claims that the Greek *logos* with its ontology of Being and its binary logic is 'ontological or transcendental oppression', a totalitarian thought regime from which we can be liberated only by the 'parricide of the Greek father Parmenides' (Derrida 1978: 82, 89).

Absence, otherness, the 'trace', all of Derrida's primary terms, comprise a vocabulary that seeks to evade the either/or trap of being-or-nonbeing of Greek philosophy. Derrida's reality is not being but absence; not the one, but the other; not unity but plurality, dissemination, writing and difference. (Handelman 1982: 172)

The patterns of thought which characterize Derrida's playfulness, deferrals, and the endless possibilities of interpretation with their emphasis on difference are patterns which echo those of the Rabbis.

Both Freud and Derrida are crucial influences on Irigaray. Although Irigaray shows no awareness that their style is Rabbinic, she, like them, is suspicious of Greek ontology and its binary logic, and emphasizes otherness, difference, fluidity. *Elemental Passions* with its poetic allusions and associations can be read, at one level, like a transcript of sessions with a psychoanalyst; at another like Derridean deconstruction of the 'one' and the 'other'. With Irigaray, however, these strategies of interpretation are applied in the first instance to sexual difference: in her view it is the binary between man and not-man which founds all the other binaries of Western thinking, and it is this which must be deconstructed and replaced with mutual, fluid interaction. As we proceed, we will keep finding parallels between Irigaray's thinking and that of Freud and Derrida, with Irigaray always moving towards the register of sexual difference.

Empedocles

Since binary logic got its grip on Western thinking through ancient philosophy, Irigaray too turns to an early figure, Empedocles, to set her argument in motion. His logic of interactive forces, which initiate and conduct processes of change, allows for a notion of becoming which Irigaray finds helpful.

To understand Irigaray's use of Empedocles, it is helpful to place it in the context of her wider project. As far back as her essay 'Divine Women' (*SG* 57),

Irigaray signalled her intention to write a tetralogy based on the four elements, linked, in her mind, with the passions, and each of them connected to the work of an influential male thinker.

> I had thought of doing a study of our relations to the elements: water, earth, fire, air. I was anxious to go back to those natural matters that constitute the origin of our bodies, of our life, of our environment, the flesh of our passions. (SG 57/SP 69)

The first book, on water, was *Marine Lover of Friedrich Nietzsche* (1980/1991b). The second was *Elemental Passions* (1982/1992a), with earth as its central element though with awareness of all the elements and the forces between them. The third was *The Forgetting of Air in Martin Heidegger* (1983/1999), taking air or breath as its theme. The fourth, on fire, has not been written as such, though Philippa Berry, among others, argues that the centrality of fire in *Speculum* (1974/1985a) could warrant the interpretation that '*Speculum* is the missing "fire book"' (Berry 1994: 231). Whether or not this is the case, there can be little doubt of Irigaray's longstanding interest in the elements, taking them, often, as metaphors that can be used to elucidate sexual difference. The philosopher to whom *Elemental Passions* points is Empedocles.

Empedocles lived in Sicily in the fifth century BCE. Only fragments of two of his main works have survived. One was a detailed work of natural science, called *On Nature*. The other, *Purifications*, was about human conduct and fate. The style of Empedocles is poetic: he wrote in hexameters, in the style of Homer's *Odyssey*. In this respect he was also like Parmenides, with whose ideas he engaged. The metaphysics of Empedocles is in part developed as an answer to Parmenides' idea that there exists only one thing, Being, and that all the changes one perceives are illusory. Empedocles, by contrast, argued that there are four elements – water, air, fire and earth – which he called the four roots, and that these are the constituents of the cosmos and all things in it, including human beings. Everything is made up of specific combinations of these elements. The changes that we witness are in fact processes of accumulation and dispersion of the elements. Earlier Presocratic philosophers had also written about the elements: Thales, Anaximander and Heraclitus each took one of the four as the primal element – water, air, and fire respectively – and Anaximander argued that the four elements changed into each other. But none of their surviving works shows their thought as clearly as we find in Empedocles' writings (Wright 1981, 1997; Barnes 1982, 1987; Kirk & Raven 1969).

According to Empedocles, the processes of change are caused by two forces which attract and disperse the elements, Love and Strife respectively. Empedocles puts it as follows:

> And in wrath [strife] all [fire, air, water and earth] are distinct in form and separate, and they come together in love and are desired by each other.

From these all things that were, that are, and will be in the future have sprung: trees and men and women and beasts and birds and water-nourished fish (Wright 1981: 218–19)

The powers of Love and Strife cause an unending cosmic cycle. The recurrent phrase is 'as time circles round' (Wright 1981: 210). Love binds all matter together. This results in a universe in which the elements are evenly mixed. Next comes a period of increasing Strife during which the elements are separated. At the point of total Strife the universe collapses and subsequently a new universe is formed in which Love increases and the elements mingle again. Then a period of total Love occurs during which everything is again concentrated until Strife begins to gather and everything gradually falls apart, till total destruction results, upon which another new world is created and Love increases (Kirk 1969: 326–32; Barnes 1982: 310).

In her introduction to the fragments of Empedocles, M. R. Wright argues that Empedocles chose the two forces of Love and Strife 'from the observed fact that these have had the greatest influence on the behaviour of men, causing them to approach each other and act together in friendship or shun and destroy each other in enmity' (1981: 31–2). Not only in human behaviour but also in the cosmos itself, changes are caused by Love and Strife. The four roots and the two forces are, in Wright's words, 'ungenerated, unchanging and indestructible' (1997: 183). While the elements are material and can be witnessed, the two forces are immaterial and should be observed in contemplation. Love, for example, which is present within the 'limbs of mortals', causes humans to think 'thoughts of love' and perform 'deeds of union': Love is also called 'Joy' and 'Aphrodite', the goddess of sexual love (Barnes 1987: 166; Larrington 1992: 68–9). Empedocles describes the processes of change:

I will tell a two-fold story. At one time they grew to be one alone from being many,

and at another they grew apart again to be many from being one –

fire and water and earth and the endless height of air,

and cursed Strife apart from them, balanced in every way,

and Love among them, equal in length and breadth.

Her you must regard with your mind: do not sit staring with your eyes.

She is thought to be innate also in the limbs of mortals, by whom they think thoughts of love and perform deeds of union,

calling her Joy by name and Aphrodite. (in Barnes 1987: 166)

Although Love and Strife are represented as two forces working against one another, however, they should not be thought of as simple opposites. They are not binaries, A and not-A. Rather, they are two 'motors of becoming' which cause things to mingle and separate, flowing in and out of one another.

For Irigaray, therefore, Empedocles is a starting point for a different way of thinking from that represented by Pythagoras and Parmenides and taken forward in the binary logic of Western philosophy. This is so in three respects. First, Irigaray draws from Empedocles an emphasis on the elements themselves, the material base of our existence. As she says in her essay 'Divine Women',

> We still pass our daily lives in a universe that is composed and is known to be made up of four elements: air, water, fire and earth. We are made up of these elements and we live in them. They determine more or less freely our attractions, our affects, our passions, our limits, our aspirations. (SG 57)

It is this materiality that establishes us bodily in the universe. In contrast to much Western philosophy, which emphasizes conceptual rationality, Irigaray's return to Empedocles results, as Margaret Whitford says, in 'the material of passional life' with a vocabulary that is 'more immediate and direct in its language than the abstractions of conceptualisation, yet without the immobilizing tendencies of the concept' (Whitford 1991b: 61).

Second, with the return to the elements, the materiality of our existence, Empedocles emphasizes the passions, and again Irigaray follows him. Love and Strife, the operative forces between the elements, are also understood as the most basic of passions determining human behaviour. As she says,

> The passions are a matter of fire and ice, of light and darkness, of water and drowning, of earth and finding or losing one's footing, and of breathing in the deepest and most secret aspects of life. Our passions are transformed or transform us into phenomena that can be watery or heavenly, solar or volcanic, blazing with light or lost in shadow. (SG 58)

For Irigaray, moreover, the passions of Love and Strife are of particular importance in the development of sexually different subjects. Elizabeth Grosz explains Irigaray's method as follows:

> Empedocles' representation of the four elements ... provides a startling yet apposite metaphor of the meeting of different substances, a perilous meeting which, through Love, can bring productivity and unexpected creation, and through Strife can break down apparent unities and stable forms of co-existence. It is thus a rich metaphor for contemplating the possibilities of autonomy and interaction between the two sexes. (Grosz 1989: 169)

It is striking that in this return to the Presocratics and their emphasis on the passions, and her connection of the elemental passions to the development of sexually different subjects, Irigaray is continuing a pattern found in psychoanalytic writing. Returning to the passions is in accordance with both Freud and Lacan. Freud traced his own primal forces of 'Eros' and 'Thanatos' back to Empedocles' notions of Love and Strife; Lacan refers to Heraclitus' notion of Strife rather than Empedocles' (Lacan 1977: 21; Bowie 1991: 28). In *Elemental Passions* Irigaray too explores, in her poetic and allusive way, the interaction between Love and Strife, with Love as the motive which enables both woman and man to become subjects. Love as an Irigarayan 'motor of becoming' is the force that helps men and women bridge the gap between them, a gap held in place by fear of the other and the craving for power which manifests itself in Strife.

These two ways in which Irigaray draws upon Empedocles, namely the emphasis on the material elements and the recognition of the centrality of the passions, each also show an aspect in which Irigaray clearly differs from Empedocles. The first is her figuration of the elements as female, and the second is her introduction of the concept of sexual difference. For Irigaray, the return to materiality involves a return both to the elements and to woman. Both, she argues throughout her writings, have been 'forgotten' or erased and both should be retrieved and incorporated within philosophy. Only then will the development of a female subject within philosophy be possible. Furthermore, the analysis of life and death as the coming together and dispersing of the elements is not enough for Irigaray. It is only when sexual difference is introduced that the analysis becomes fruitful for her purposes.

The third way in which Irigaray draws on Empedocles, connected with the other two, is her idea of fluidity, which corresponds to the mingling of the elements by the power of the passions in Empedocles' philosophy. For Irigaray as for Empedocles, reality is in constant flux, driven on by the elemental passions. Not only are the rigid binaries of Parmenidean logic therefore inadequate to understand the flow of reality; they are also actually a technology of control, operating in the service of Strife to limit the development of the woman subject. As we have seen in an earlier part of this chapter, a philosophy that insists on an exclusive use of binary logic is not value-free. For the development of subjectivity such logic has been detrimental to those with little access to formal power. Irigaray's adoption of a fluid logic in her development of sexually different subjects thus poses a creative challenge to the rigid binaries of traditional Western philosophy and to its implicit power structures.

It also poses a challenge to the constructs of masculinist psychoanalytic theory: we shall turn to this in the next chapter.

CHAPTER 2

More than one subject:
Irigaray and psychoanalytic theory

As original as Irigaray's work is, it is nonetheless situated firmly in the French philosophy of the twentieth century. Some of the dominant themes of that philosophy were drawn from Hegel, either in agreement or disagreement with him (Descombes 1980: 12): themes such as the nature of the subject, identity and difference, and the role of desire (Butler 1999; Gutting 2001). As we will see in the course of this book, Irigaray takes up these themes, but in every case is alert to the effect of gender in relation to them. Rather than ponder the nature of the subject, for example, as though it were a universal subject (and therefore implicitly male), Irigaray discusses sexually different subjects; rather than consider desire in itself, Irigaray works with sexually different desire.

This emphasis on desire and sexual difference obviously intersects with the psychoanalytic theories of Freud and Lacan, theories which had enormous impact on French philosophers of the time. Irigaray, in common with most other psychoanalytic theorists, believes, first, that understanding human sexuality is crucial for understanding culture; and second, that it is through images, dreams, and associations of ideas that sexuality can best be understood. In the middle section of this book we will explore some of the images she chooses in *Elemental Passions* to explore the development of women subjects. In this chapter we wish to discuss Irigaray's uneasy relationship with the psychoanalytic theory of Freud and Lacan, an uneasiness which mirrors her relationship with the trajectory of Western philosophy, which she both appropriates and tries to destabilize.

We saw in the previous chapter how the idea of rigid binary logic has been central to Western philosophical thinking since Pythagoras. We also saw that it is not innocent: binary thinking has regularly been used by the group that constructs itself as normative to oppress the group which is constructed as its other. Irigaray uses the psychoanalytic emphasis on sexual development to assert that sexual difference is the most basic of all differences. What she seems to imply is that if, as in Western culture, sexual difference is constructed in terms of a binary, whereby man is the norm and woman is the not-norm/not-man, then all the other binaries of Pythagoras' table follow. Putting it the other way around, if the binary of sexual difference could be disrupted and reconstructed in a way that allowed for the becoming of women in their own right (and not simply as not-man), then all binary thinking would have to undergo change, with major consequences, not just epistemological but also moral and political. In Irigaray's terms, fluidity would be as important a metaphor for logic as is rigidity.

In the final section of this book we will critically evaluate this claim, asking among other things whether the category of sexual difference can actually bear all the weight which Irigaray puts upon it: is it, for example, more basic than differences of race, culture, and ability? To whom is it more basic? We will also ask whether Irigaray, in her insistence on the man/woman dichotomy, in some respects falls into precisely the sort of rigid binary that she seems to be rejecting. In this chapter, however, we want to explore the ways in which the psychoanalytic theories of Freud and Lacan which rest upon and reinforce binary logic are used and criticized by Irigaray in her development of the idea of the woman subject and thus of sexual difference. The remaining chapters will focus on images in *Elemental Passions* and beyond. It is in reaction to the theories of Freud and Lacan that Irigaray develops her ideas on subjectivity and language. In order to be able to interpret *Elemental Passions* and conduct the search for female subjectivity further, we therefore need to understand these ideas first.

Freud's theory of the development of sexuality

In 'Female Sexuality', first published in 1931, Freud argues that boys and girls develop along the same lines until their third year. Not content with this account, Freud returned to the issue of female sexuality two years later. In his 'Lecture 33 on Femininity' he explains that it is with the Oedipus complex that the ways of the boy and the girl diverge. It becomes clear, Freud maintains, that the development of a little girl into a normal woman is 'more difficult and more complicated' than the development of a little boy into a normal man (Freud 1986c: 416).

To describe this stage of early childhood, Freud used the ancient Greek myth of Oedipus who, without knowing it, killed his father and married his mother (Freud 1986b: 32). The Oedipus complex as Freud develops it illustrates the implicit Western ideal of heterosexual monogamy. The son has to let go of his desire for his mother because she belongs to the father. The assumption, of course, is that a woman will have a sexual relationship with one man only, the father of her son. The Oedipus complex introduces the father as a paternal figure with authority who forbids his children to be in love with their mother. Up till this point, mother and child exist in what the child perceives as a dependent union, a dyad where the two terms are mutually dependent. Then the father comes along and pronounces the mother as *his* love object. The child cannot marry the mother because she is the father's wife. For the boy this means that he has to project his feelings onto other women. He realizes that if he pursues his love for his mother, his father will punish him in the same way as he has punished the girl: it is obvious to the little boy that the father has taken the girl's penis away. Freud calls the boy's fear of punishment the fear of castration.

It is clear that in the development of the Oedipal drama Freud (and later Lacan) regards the child as male. Only later does he work out what the drama may mean as applied to female children: it is of course a classic case of A and not-A, the male as norm and the female as not-male, the other. Although in Freud's work with dreams and with the unconscious he tends to allow the free flow of associations which we saw in the previous chapter characterized Rabbinic patterns of thought, when it comes to sexual difference he operates with a rigid binary. The boy is the paradigm; the girl deviates from it and becomes the not-boy. As Freud understands the situation, for the girl it is the father's interference which means that she has to substitute love for her mother with love for her father. This means that, unlike the boy, she has to change not only the object of her love but also has to learn to love someone of a different sex from the original object. To make things even more complicated, she has to come to terms with the fact that she does not have a penis.

Freud argues that a break with the mother is needed for the Law of the Father to operate. For the little boy this is a gain, because he can enter into the father's world and make it his own; but for the little girl it is a loss: she is forever barred from entry. In Freud's analysis three paths of development of sexuality are open to the little girl who is faced with this loss. The first is a revulsion from sexuality altogether. The little girl is so disappointed that she does not have a penis that she completely abandons clitoral masturbation, which she had previously practised (1986c:426); the young woman becomes passive in other areas of life as well. The second possibility is an eternal longing for the penis to the extent that the girl, and the woman when she grows up, acts masculine and takes a 'homosexual choice of object'. The third path is the one that leads to the 'final normal female attitude' or 'definitive femininity'. The girl realizes that her clitoris is not a mini-penis after all. Her active clitoral sexuality makes way for a passive vaginal sexuality. This in turn calls for an active male sexual partner. Thus, the girl first directs herself to her father and later takes her husband as object. In this third instance the woman's longing for a penis is replaced by a longing for a baby: 'her happiness is great if later on this wish for a baby finds fulfilment in reality, and quite especially so if the baby is a little boy who brings the longed-for penis with him' (1986c: 426). Indeed, Freud states that 'a mother is only brought unlimited satisfaction by her relation to a son' (431): she 'regards him with feelings that are derived from her own sexual life: she strokes him, kisses him, rocks him, and quite clearly treats him as a substitute for a complete sexual object' (1986d: 358).

Problems of rigidity

Irigaray and Freud

It is obvious that Freud's theory fits neatly into Western patriarchal family structure, which it both reflects and reinforces. Although Irigaray accepts Freud's contention that analysis of their psychosexual development is crucial if we are to understand adult human beings, her main point of critique is that Freud conducts his study through a male lens. For example, she argues that one should be suspicious of Freud's statements firstly that one should 'become' a woman and secondly that this process is more difficult and more complex than becoming a man. According to Irigaray, Freud's tacit assumptions are revealed here. For example, Freud begins his essay 'Female Sexuality' as follows:

> During the phase of the normal Oedipus complex we find the child tenderly attached to the parent of the opposite sex, while its relation to the parent of its own sex is predominantly hostile. In the case of the little boy there is no difficulty in explaining this ... With the small girl it is different. (Freud 1961: 225)

The rest of his essay is devoted to explaining how the little girl is different from the little boy: the reader is made to identify with the little boy and to see the little girl as strange. Elsewhere, Freud stipulates that it is a universal assumption among children that everyone has a male sex organ: 'the assumption that all human beings have the same (male) form of genital is the first of many remarkable and momentous sexual theories of children' (Freud 1986d: 334). Irigaray points out that Freud's whole 'economy of representation' is 'an organized system whose meaning is regulated by paradigms and units of value that are in turn determined by male subjects' (SP 22; cf. 82–3). This economy, Irigaray explains, gives rise to a desire for the same. And already, alarm bells should start ringing. What does 'the same' mean? Who will be taken as norm and who will be made into 'the same', and how? Will force be used? Our suspicions should be thoroughly aroused, since in the previous chapter we saw that throughout the history of Western philosophy man has thought of 'the other' as 'not the same as himself': female, black, not-Western, without formal education, slave. Not-A.

For Freud, the desire for the same is mirrored in woman's desire for the penis. Freud's assumption is that a woman will want to be the same as a man. The only possible reaction he can think of, when a woman realizes that she is not a man, is severe disappointment. This, he argues, gives rise to jealousy in the form of penis-envy. But Irigaray points out that his whole theory is based on the masculinist assumption of the supreme value of the penis: what would happen to Freud's theory if women make different assumptions, and perhaps have different wishes and desires? (Sp 51). What if woman is B rather than not-A? Irigaray argues that the desire for the self-identical is reflected in the methods and aim of psychoanalysis, and that the self-identical is modelled upon the male. It therefore excludes female desires other than those which fit into (patriarchal) theory (Sp 32–4 ff.).

Irigaray strengthens her point by showing how man's desire for sameness is brought out in Freud's account of female desire. The motive for Freud's claim that a woman can only be satisfied by a male child concerns man, Irigaray argues, not woman. In the son, the father sees himself reflected. He has reproduced an image of himself through his wife who is now also mother: 'What a triumphant revenge for the anxieties of an Oedipus who *sees himself coming out (again)* from a womb he has himself fertilized' (Sp 78).

Irigaray criticizes Freud for making woman's reproductive capacity the most central aspect in his account of female sexuality (Sp 28). She comments ironically on Freud's account of intercourse: 'Woman is nothing but the receptacle that passively receives his *product*, even if sometimes, by the display of her passively aimed instincts, she has pleaded, facilitated, even demanded that it be placed within her' (Sp 18). Moreover, Irigaray is critical of Freud's claim that the little girl must detach herself from the mother and take the father as love object in order to develop into a normal woman. Does this not, Irigaray asks, have as a result that the girl has to reject representations of her own sex and eventually comes to devalue her own sex? In 'men's signifying economy' she is nothing but a lack, a hole, a gap (Sp 40, 76). In addition, and in a way that will have considerable bearing on the text of *Elemental Passions*, Irigaray criticizes the emphasis placed on the visual in Freud. Because the little boy (or is it Freud?) cannot see female genitalia he supposes that the girl does not have them. However, questions which Irigaray raises are: whose gaze is this? Why is this gaze deemed so valuable? What is left out or ignored if the gaze is valorized, and how does this reflect and reinforce patriarchal values? All these questions will return in Chapter 4.

Summing up, Irigaray criticizes Freud on the following points. She argues that Freud looks at the little girl's development and at women's sexuality through a male lens of the self-same. This means, for example, that Freud believes the fact that woman has no penis *must* mean that she is eternally longing for one: perhaps as he imagines a castrated man would do? Women's (sexual) desires are only discussed in terms of her relation to the goals fit for women in a patriarchal society. The roles available to women in such a society are those of daughter, wife, mother, or, when something has gone wrong in their development, lesbian or hysterical: Lacan will add 'mistress' to these roles.

The girl's love object must be the father. Irigarary asks, however, what this must mean for the image that the little girl has of her mother and of herself as a woman? According to Freud, a girl cannot take her mother as a role model for her development as a female subject; it is her father who is the subject, not her mother. A woman who desires to be a subject in her own right and to exist in a relation of equality to a man, amounts to a woman who wants to be a man, Freud argues. A 'proper' woman should accept her natural role as mother, as bearer of sons.[1] In

---

[1] A wonderful example of this kind of psychoanalytic thinking can be found in the Dutch film Nynke. This film follows the first part of the life of Nynke van Hichtum, a famous Dutch writer who lived at the turn of the century between the nineteenth and twentieth centuries. Being

Freud's thinking, man is the norm, woman is the other: A and not-A. It is, according to Irigaray, a central instantiation of the binary logic which underlies the Western philosophical and cultural tradition, rendering it oppressive and impoverished.

Lacan's theory of child development

Lacan develops Freud's theories on subjectivity and language further. Although Lacan presents himself as an interpreter of Freud, in the view of most commentators he in fact develops a new theory of subjectivity (Bowie 1991; Flax 1991: 91): in the words of Carolyn Burke, Lacan is both a 'faithful disciple' and a 'new Master' (Burke 1994a: 40). One main difference between Freud and Lacan is their view of language. For Freud a subject's unconscious can be articulated in language by someone else, a psychoanalyst for example. For Lacan, however, a subject is constituted through and within language (see Ward 1996: 30–2). This means that whilst Freud believed that a psychoanalyst could arrive at a subject by unravelling her unconscious, Lacan holds that the task of a psychoanalyst is to unravel the meanings of the unconscious by understanding how it functions as a system or structure, analogous to language.

Like Freud, Lacan distinguishes various phases in the development of subjectivity. To begin with, a child experiences its mother and itself as inseparable, as one entity. Slowly, it begins to recognize itself as a separate being. Eventually, a separation between mother and child is enforced by a third party, the father, who represents patriarchal power. This separation occurs simultaneously with the child's entry into language. These stages correspond to specific drives – respectively needs, demands and desires – and to specific ways in which the child relates to the world and to itself.

As a newborn baby, the child is dependent upon the mother for its survival. Its relationship to the mother is characterized by needs, such as the need for shelter, food and love. The baby experiences itself and the mother as a continuum. It does not distinguish between itself and the mother's body or itself and other objects. Therefore, it does not have a clear sense of identity but can be characterized as a bundle of impressions and experiences.

At approximately six months the child gains the ability to recognize itself in the mirror when it sees its own reflection; it enters the mirror stage. In Lacan's famous article 'The Mirror Stage as Formative of the Function of the I as Revealed in Psychoanalytic Experience' (1977: 1–7) he explains this stage as follows.

---

regulated to the role of housewife and mother actually makes Nynke ill. She is admitted to a psychiatric ward at the academic hospital in Groningen. After much research, the psychiatrist who treats Nynke pronounces her to be an incurable hysteric. He explains to his students that the problem with Nynke is that she aspires to a career, like her husband. Such a woman, he argues, is doomed to hysteria (Verhoef 2001).

Irigaray and psychoanalytic theory

Contrary to a monkey which grows tired of its reflection as soon as it realizes that it is only a reflection and not another animal, the human child is fascinated with its own image. The mirror presents a child with a contradictory experience: on the one hand, it has little control over its bodily functions, is still dependent on another human being and experiences itself as fragmented; yet on the other hand it sees itself reflected in the mirror as a whole person. This discovery of (potential) wholeness gives rise to joy on part of the child. It is the beginning of the subject's experience of itself as an 'I'. The child begins to fantasize unconsciously about itself as a whole, as one. This experience generates what Lacan calls the Imaginary.

However, the child's reflection which both is and is not itself, also gives rise to anger and frustration. There is a rupture between the child's experience and its perception. As Elizabeth Grosz explains,

> The child identifies with an image that is manifestly different from itself, though it also clearly resembles it in some respects ... The subject, in other words, recognizes itself at the moment it loses itself in/as the other. This other is the foundation and support of its identity, as well as what destabilizes or annihilates it. The subject's 'identity' is based on a (false) recognition of an other as the same. (Grosz 1990: 41)

This frustrating experience of inhabiting a fragmented body which looks like a whole resurfaces later in life in dreams of disjointed limbs and in symptoms of hysteria. Images which accompany these experiences are castration, mutilation, dismemberment, dislocation, devouring and bursting open of the body: Lacan takes the fifteenth-century painting of hell by Hieronymous Bosch as an illustration of experiences of this kind (Lacan 1977: 4–5).

The realization that its reflection is different from itself also leads the child to understand that the mother is a being separate from itself. The painful recognition of the mother's separate existence creates a gap, a lack for the child. It wants a return of the closeness, the oneness it experienced in the earlier stage. The child wants to be continually affirmed in its existence, and wants the mother to be present at all times. Now the physical needs it had turn into demands for the mother's presence, demands for her love and attention. However, whereas the needs could be fulfilled, the child's demands can in the nature of the case never be met to its satisfaction; it will never get the mother's full love and affirmation. The mother is other, with needs and wishes besides the child and which the child cannot fulfil: she is (m)other. As Lacan puts it:

> demand annuls the particularity of everything that can be granted by transmuting it into a proof of love, and the very satisfactions that it obtains for need are reduced to the level of being no more than the crushing demand for love. (1977: 286)

The child consoles itself with its own image in the mirror. Later, it will have language as a substitute. However, it is clear that the child will never be completely consoled. The gap, the longing for a re-union with the (m)other will remain, and will influence all subsequent relationships.

Through the turbulence of the Mirror Stage, the child has learnt that its mother is separate from itself; nevertheless it still experiences itself and its mother as a dyad. Grosz describes it as follows: 'The dual imaginary mother/child relation is bound up with a narcissistic structure of mutual identifications. Each defines the identity of the other in a closed circuit' (1990: 67). The child is dependent on the mother for its existence and the mother can smother, 'murder', it with her care. But according to Lacan, in order for subjectivity to develop, it is necessary that there should be genuine differentiation between one and another such that there can be exchange between them. This means that the child cannot develop into a subject so long as it exists in this dyad of mutual identification without real differentiation.

Lacan therefore argues that for the child to develop into a subject who can exist in its own right, and not simply in terms of the mother/child dyad, the introduction of a third term, the father, is necessary. A third figure, the father, enters the mother–child relationship in the Lacanian version of Freud's Oedipal drama. The father-figure who forbids the child to be in love with his mother and forces him to be separate from her represents patriarchal power. He represents the law, religion and language which is the currency of exchange. The symbol for patriarchal power is the phallus. The punishment for not obeying the Law of the Father is castration: the phallus of the male child is taken away. Although Lacan insists that the phallus is not the same as the penis but symbolizes male power, it is nevertheless the case that for Lacan only those with a penis can have access to the phallus: 'It is in *the name of the father* that we must recognize the support of the symbolic function which, from the dawn of history, has identified his person with the law' (Lacan 1977: 67).

The above shows how Lacan applies Freud's concepts of the Oedipus complex, fear of castration and penis envy. In Lacan's account, the father figure initiates the little boy into the symbolic and grants him the phallus on condition that he obey the father. Should the little boy fail to do this, then the father will take the phallus away. Drucilla Cornell remarks in this context that the price the little boy pays for this is that he will always live in fear that the phallus will be taken away from him. She argues that this produces a subordination to an imaginary father which manifests itself in hierarchies between men. Another consequence of man's fear and anxiety is, according to Cornell, that man constructs a fantasy of superiority over women (Cornell 1995: 89; see also Brennan 1993).

Be that as it may, according to Lacan the male child must give up the desire for his mother and will thus obtain the phallus, the symbol of power, as a result. Since the price of this power is repression of his desire for the mother, the unconscious comes into existence, an unconscious from which repressed desire always returns. Nevertheless, at a conscious level, as an 'I', a subject, a possessor of the phallus, the male child functions within the symbolic, language and culture. Teresa Brennan describes the function of the Lacanian symbolic very clearly:

The symbolic places human beings in relation to others, and gives them a sense of their place in the world, and the ability to speak and be understood by others. It does this by enabling them to distinguish themselves from others, and through establishing a relation to language. (1989: 2)

The child's earlier demands have turned into desire. Just as the demand for the (m)other was insatiable, so also is the desire for the (m)other insatiable. Graham Ward explains it as follows: 'the desire can never be satisfied because it is the very demand for the other which constitutes and keeps the other as other' (1996: 31). Contrary to the earlier demand, however, this desire cannot be articulated. It is repressed and resides in the unconscious. The only way a subject's desire for the (m)other can even temporarily be satisfied is through being desired himself, since in fact his desire for the (m)other is a desire for recognition of his own subjectivity. Therefore when a subject is desired his existence is affirmed. And in this lies the whole story of male efforts to dominate, to make the (m)other recognize him and thus feel himself whole and affirmed.

For the female child the Lacanian psychosexual development story is significantly different. With the interference of the father-figure, it becomes clear what the girl is: not a boy. She is defined by a lack. As with Freud, the girl is not defined separately but in contrast to the boy: she is not-A to the boy who is A. She does not have the phallus, the symbol of power and value. She cannot identify with the father but only with the object of his love, her mother. The only way the girl can obtain the phallus is through male lovers when she grows up, and through the male children she will produce in relationship with them, just as Freud had said.

Nevertheless the girl, too, has to give up being in love with her mother, even though she must simultaneously identify with her in terms of her sexuality: the girl, like the mother, must be feminine. This means that in relation to the Law/Name of the Father, the girl is an object, passive. It also means that she does not have a subject position in her own right, but only as constituted by the Law of the Father. Moreover, since language is one aspect of this Law, with the phallus as the ultimate signifier, it means that the girl has no language of her own. She can only speak (and think) in a male tongue, as prescribed for her by the father. It is true that the boy also enters into language and culture and obtains the phallus through submission to paternal power, which is the Law of the Father. In doing so, however, the boy becomes a subject in his turn, a wielder of language and of the Law. For the girl, no such subject position is possible. Within the male symbolic, women are not recognized as potential subjects who can think and speak in their own right. According to Lacan, women are defined by a lack.[2]

---

[2] One way of understanding Lacan's emphasis on lack is to see it in relation to the theme of negation and nothingness that formed so central a part of French reflections on Hegel, especially as interpreted by Kojève (1969) and reconceived by Sartre (1969). See also Drury 1994: 17–39; Descombes 1980: 32–6.

It is tempting to ask why a girl would assent to giving up her love for her mother, when all she gets from this is removal of all possibility of a subject position. Why would she want to submit to the Law of the Father? These questions, however, are misguided. It is not a matter of wanting or assenting. This is precisely what patriarchy means: both the girl and the boy are forced to recognize the phallus, but for the girl it offers no power. She finds herself in a subordinated position. Perhaps the only asset is that she will grow up to be a 'normal' woman and fit into the roles which a patriarchal society has carved out for her: the binary 'other' of the man.

It thus becomes ever clearer both how Freudian–Lacanian psychoanalytic theory reflects and reinforces binary logic, and also how that logic is in fact a tool of patriarchy. For women to be subjects, to speak in our own tongue, to be able to develop in mutual relationship with men (rather than merely as (m)other to men) it is necessary to destabilize that logic and with it that aspect of psychoanalytic theory. Putting it the other way around, if we can find a way for women to emerge as subjects in our own right, then that very process will undermine the rigidity of binary logic and psychoanalytic theory. The project of the development of women subjects as well as male subjects for mutual relationship is all of a piece with the development of a logic of fluidity as a necessary counterpart and corrective to rigid binary thinking.

Language and the phallus

To see all this more fully, it is helpful to look a little further into the connections which Freud and Lacan make between language, subjectivity and the phallus, since Irigaray's view of female subjectivity and language is developed in reaction to these theories. Freud used the Fort!Da! game to explain how a child copes with his mother's absence. This game was played by a little boy, Freud's grandson Ernst, who was in a room by himself. The little boy had a 'wooden reel with a piece of string tied round it'. He threw the reel away, holding onto the thread while exclaiming 'ooo' and then pulled it back, saying 'aaa'. Freud interpreted these sounds as respectively 'Fort' (gone) and 'Da' (there). The little boy repeated this game endlessly. In Freud's interpretation this game was a symbolization of the mother's departure and return. He says that Ernst was a good little boy who never cried when his mother left him. Freud posits that the boy mastered his mother's absences through this game in which he controlled her departure and return (Freud 1986a: 224–5).

Lacan accepts the significance of Freud's Fort!Da! game. He interprets it, however, in linguistic terms, as the first articulation in language (ooo/aaa; fort/da) of the child's desire. According to Lacan, a linguistic relation is substituted for the actual relation to the mother: the desired object, the (m)other, is substituted by the reel which is in turn substituted by language, the sounds ooo and aaa. Lacan says:

the child begins to become engaged in the system of the concrete discourse of the environment, by reproducing more or less approximately in his *Fort!* and in his *Da!* the vocables that he receives from it. *Fort! Da!* It is precisely in his solitude that the desire of the little child has already become the desire of another, of an *alter ego* who dominates him and whose object of desire is henceforth his own affliction. (Lacan 1977: 104)

Lacan posits that the mother is substituted by language in which the child becomes a subject. We have seen that in Lacan's account of the mirror stage, the split in the subject-to-be occurs. The child experiences its first loss of the (m)other and will forever try to get back to its union with her. The child also experiences the split between its experience of itself as a fragmented body and the way it is perceived by others as a whole. From that moment onwards, it searches for affirmation of itself through reflection by the (m)other. For Lacan the Fort!Da! game marks the transition from the mirror stage into the symbolic through the articulation of sounds. It illustrates how the (boy)child masters the mother's absence by himself and finds language as a solace.

For his argument on language, Lacan draws on Saussure. Saussure argues that language consists of signs. A sign is a combination of what is signified and a signifier. The relation between signifier and signified is arbitrary. Language should be understood as a system of signifiers and signified which only have meaning in relation to each other. Saussure explains: 'In a sign, what matters more than any idea or sound associated with it is what other signs surround it' (Saussure 1995: 118). For example, 'green' can only be understood in relation to 'blue' and 'yellow', not in and of itself; 'child' and 'adult' take their meanings from one another, and so on. One cannot understand the meaning of a sign in isolation. Although there is no reason to think that Saussure was influenced by Rabbinic patterns of thinking, it is easy to see how his work would be congruent with it: just as interpretations of the Torah are not to be taken in isolation but flow into and out of one another, so also the meanings of signs are fluid and derive their significance from the other signs with which they are surrounded.

Lacan adopts much of Saussure's theory of language, especially his insistence that signs draw their meaning from their relationship with one another rather than by pointing to some essence. However, contrary to Saussure, Lacan argues that there is *one* signifier which is not thus relative; rather, by its nature it guarantees the meaning of all the other signifiers. It is fixed, rigid. Stiff? For Lacan, this signifier is the phallus:

The phallus is the privileged signifier of that mark in which the role of the logos is joined with the advent of desire. It can be said that this signifier is chosen because it is the most tangible element in the real of sexual copulation, and also the most symbolic in the literal (typographical) sense of the term, since it is equivalent there to the (logical) copula. (Lacan 1977: 287)

For Lacan the phallus is 'the signifier of the desire of the Other' (290). Put simplistically, one could say that for man this desire is a desire for affirmation, for woman this means a desire to cover up her lack. Even though in one sense the phallus is the guarantor of meaning, however, in another sense it also is relative, since the phallus only has meaning, power and value for a man if it is confirmed by an other, just as Kojève had interpreted Hegel's vignette of the master and the slave. For this reason man seeks recognition from female lovers. Lacan asserts that a man does not love women because of who they are individually but because he needs them to affirm himself. Both a virgin and a prostitute can serve as an example of 'another' woman, and thus can confirm man's phallus, according to Lacan:

If, in effect, the man finds satisfaction for his demand for love in the relation with the woman, in as much as the signifier of the phallus constitutes her as giving in love what she does not have – conversely, his own desire for the phallus will make its signifier emerge in its persistent divergence towards 'another' woman who may signify this phallus in various ways, either as a virgin or as a prostitute. (290)

In sexual intercourse, man does not primarily seek an encounter with a sexually different being. Instead, intercourse provides a way to arrive at himself.

For Lacan, therefore, woman's role is to enable man to experience oneness, self-recognition. Woman dissolves within this process: she has no subject position of her own, but is defined as a lack, in order that she may be receptive to the man who needs her. We are only a short step from the line of reasoning we saw in Chapter 1 in relation to Bataille with regard to subjectivity and eroticism. For Bataille (following Kojève) a male subject desires total submission from his female sexual partner in order to experience oneness (see Drury 1994: Chapter 8).

In Lacanian terms, a man sees a reflection of himself in the woman he loves. A woman's desire is for a man so that she can cover up her lack of the phallus: 'it is for that which she is not that she wishes to be desired and loved' (Lacan 1977: 290). In this way the phallus as a symbol is constitutive of heterosexuality; but also of culture and of language. It is therefore obvious that language and culture will be patriarchal.

The entry into language can moreover be seen as another example of man's second birth: the biological birth out of the mother resulted in the child of flesh and blood, the entry into language through the Law of the Father gives rise to the subject. The maternal blood ties are replaced by the name of the father which from now on marks the child. In this process the mother's contribution to the development of the subject is 'forgotten'. There are obvious echoes here of Parmenides' ascent to heaven and of Plato's birth of the philosopher. Both of these Greek philosophers believed that a 'second birth' was necessary for man to become a philosopher. In the analyses of Parmenides' poem by Nye and by Cavarero we saw that women are bystanders in man's process of becoming a thinking subject. Women may assist men; they cannot, however, take part in the thinking process as subjects. Here we see that Lacan presents a similar argument with regard to language and the phallus. Through phallic language man can become a subject, but in order to succeed he needs woman's help. This woman can be man's mother and/or sexual partner. For women, however, the route to subjectivity through phallic language is closed: all she can ever be is a receptacle and a mirror for men.

Irigaray's critique of the Fort!Da! game

In the next section of the book we will show how Irigaray in *Elemental Passions* presents an alternative to the Freudian–Lacanian view of women, showing how women can be subjects, have language, and thus disrupt the masculinist economy of sameness and rigidity. *Elemental Passions* is, however, not the only place where Irigaray challenges Freud and Lacan; and it is useful for clearer understanding of what she is doing in *Elemental Passions* to consider her earlier interaction with psychoanalytic theory, particularly in relation to the Fort!Da! game. Freud, as we have seen, interprets the game his little grandson played as a way in which the male child masters his mother's absence, whereas Lacan interprets it in linguistic terms. In his view, the little boy substitutes his mother with language. In this section, we will present Irigaray's critique of both Freud's and Lacan's interpretations of the Fort!Da! game and show how she starts her development of a female language from their accounts.

Freud and Lacan developed their theories from the perspective of male subjects and subsequently added that the girl's development is different from that of the boy, and that therefore women had to be theorized as different from men. This results in the kind of reasoning we have seen in the previous chapter, namely in conceptualizations of A (man) and not-A (woman). Irigaray in contrast argues that the development of a female child is different in the sense that it cannot be explained solely in terms of the development of a little boy, and that if we begin with the boy as the model for both sexes we will get the whole project started on a misguided trajectory. This is crucial. Throughout her work, Irigaray argues that women are irreducible to men, and need to be defined in different terms, so that man and woman can be described as two sexually different subjects, as A and B instead of A and not-A.

In relation to the Fort!Da! game, Irigaray asks what a girl's reaction to the absence of her mother would have been. She lists three possibilities. Firstly, the girl can feel lost to the extent that she is unable to live without her mother. Anorexia, Irigaray argues, is an expression of this inability:

She (the girl) is overcome by distress if she is deprived of her mother, she is lost, she cannot survive, and does not want to, she neither speaks, nor eats, is anorexic in every way. (SG 97)

Secondly, the child can play with her doll. In playing, the girl transfers maternal affects to a quasi-subject. This could be said to pave the way for intersubjectivity. The third possibility takes this one step further. It can be interpreted as a forerunner of language in Irigaray. The child dances. By dancing she constructs a space for herself:

a vital subjective space, space which is open to the cosmic maternal world, to the gods, to the other who may be present. This dance is also a way of creating for herself her own territory in relation to the mother. (97–8)

Irigaray maintains that if the girl-child speaks it is in a playful way 'without giving special importance to syllabic or phonemic oppositions'. The language the child speaks 'corresponds to a rhythm and also to a melody' (98). The aspects of Irigaray's description of the language of the female child are non-oppositional, playful, rhythmic and melodic. The Fort!Da! movement, the out-in movement, is 'too linear and too analogous with the movement of the penis or of masturbation' (99). The boy needs an external object for his gratification, symbolized by the reel. The girl does not need an object at all, what is important for her is that her lips touch:

In order to touch himself, man needs an instrument: his hand, a woman's body, language ... And this self-caressing requires at least a minimum of activity. As for woman, she touches herself in and of herself without any need for mediation, and before there is any way to distinguish activity from passivity. (TS 24)

Instead of the Fort!Da! binary, girls make circular movements, through dancing or skipping for example. A girl creates a space for herself in the shape of a circle. This means, Irigaray argues, that a girl's relation to space is different from a boy's. Instead of the rigid dichotomy 'Fort/Da', 'gone/here', there is the fluid border which marks the changing inside and outside of the girl's space.

Contrary to the boy, the girl does not enter language through an object. The boy enters language by identifying with the phallus and thus making the (m)other into an object. The girl however, Irigaray argues, wants to speak with the (m)other. Although a boy speaks in absence of the mother, a girl speaks in relation to her mother, in her presence. The little girl does not have a need for the phallus but rather has a need to become, to create herself. In a direct contradiction of Lacan, Irigaray argues that 'the need for the phallus which is imputed to them [women] is an *a posteriori* justification of the obligation placed on them to be mothers and legal wives' (99).

According to Irigaray, the possibility for becoming is however impeded by the mother's reaction. In *I Love to You*, Irigaray argues that the little girl initially addresses the (m)other as a subject. The mother however, because she has herself been socialized within the male economy, encourages a subject–object relation. In other words, the way in which the boy enters language is sanctioned; the way in which the girl tries to do so is blocked. Here we see how a phallic mother leaves her daughter no option but to accept her role within patriarchy, as she herself has done. Irigaray puts it like this:

> The little girl shows her mother a loving intention, an ethical one, as it were. She sets up a just and communicative micro-society between her mother and herself ... Unfortunately, the mother does not show the same intersubjective respect for her daughter ...The mother commands, the daughter is to listen and obey. The elder seems to repeat to her daughter what has been forced upon her as a woman. A dominant male culture has intervened between mother and daughter and broken off a loving and symbolic exchange ... And yet young girls still dream of accomplishing intersubjective communication. (ILo 130)

If we follow Irigaray's line of argument, it becomes clear that she intends to find a way to reinstate the little girl's desire for intersubjectivity in love. The dominant male culture has replaced this female reciprocity with dichotomies of subject and object, lover and loved. What Irigaray attempts in *Elemental Passions* is to develop two subjects, man and woman, in love, starting from a lost female perspective. Woman initiates this reciprocity in her quest for female subjectivity. Irigaray's strategy in *Elemental Passions* highlights some of the crucial points of her theory and addresses some of the objections her critics raise, which we will consider further later in the book.

It is clear that Irigaray believes that woman should return to a lost, hidden girlhood with a forgotten way of communication. Her hidden yet budding subjectivity needs to be uncovered so that she may become a subject in her own right. Philosophically, this return to a lost personal beginning corresponds to a return to the forgotten origins of (Western) philosophy. According to Irigaray these philosophical roots can still be discerned in the surviving fragments of Empedocles' theory of the elements. This way of thinking also explains Irigaray's method of uncovering hidden meanings within texts coupled with a simultaneous process of working towards a new way of thinking and of relating to each other and the universe, in short towards a new way of living.

There are, however, some obvious objections that can be raised. For example, if we all live within patriarchy and use phallic language then how can we break out of this? How is it that one person, Irigaray, can see beyond the rim of the phallic horizon? What vantage point is she speaking from? These questions also point to the inescapable limits of Irigaray's theory: if Irigaray can critique phallic language and subjectivity then others can probably do so too. And they may perceive a different kind of 'new reality'. How should we then choose between different utopias? We will return to these critical questions in Chapter 6, after we have considered in more detail Irigarary's work in *Elemental Passions*.

Irigaray and Lacan

It is a matter of consensus among commentators on Irigaray that the relation between Irigaray and Lacan is complex and uneasy (Burke 1994a: 39; Weed 1994: 91). This complexity arises out of the fact that at times it is difficult to distinguish between places where Irigaray cites or paraphrases Lacan, appropriating his insights as her own, and other places where she criticizes him in her own voice. Jane Gallop, for example, in commenting on Irigaray's early work, argues that Irigaray, 'the daughter', has been seduced out of her resistance to psychoanalysis by the 'father', Lacan, while at the same time the father has been seduced out of his illusion of self-control. This, Gallop contends, calls into question how far Irigaray is radical in her analysis of both Freud and Lacan. Is Irigaray posing her own questions, or is she asking of Freud and Lacan what they want her to ask and is she in fact picking up the cues from their texts (Gallop 1982: 56–79)?

In broad outline, Irigaray adopts a Lacanian psychoanalytic perspective, often interjecting her own writing into that of Lacan. However, she is also deeply critical of it. Thus Berg suggests that Lacan is in fact Irigaray's main addressee, at least in *Speculum* and *This Sex Which Is Not One*. 'All of Irigaray's [early] work is in some sense to be understood as a dialogue with Lacan, although his name is spectacularly missing from her books' (Berg 1982: 16). Irigaray's main criticism of Lacanian psychoanalysis is, as we have already seen, that it takes man as its subject. She argues that it does not provide a general, universal theory of child development, but one of *male* development, taking the male as the norm, A, and the female as the other, not-A. This critique, therefore, links concerns about binary logic with the question of sexually different subjects.

One of Irigaray's most detailed, sophisticated analyses of Lacan, occurs in her essay 'Così Fan Tutti' (TS 86–105). In this article Irigaray responds to Lacan's seminars *Encore*, especially to 'God and the Jouissance of the Woman' (Lacan 1982b). 'Così Fan Tutti' is a wordplay: it refers, of course, to Mozart's opera, but whereas his title was 'Così Fan Tutte' meaning 'All women are/act like that', Irigaray replaces the final 'e' of 'Tutte' with an 'i', 'Tutti', to mean 'All men are/act like that. In Irigaray's essay it is not the women, nor even the male protagonist Don Alfonso, but Lacan, or, as Weed playfully writes, 'Don Jacques', who is exposed (Weed 1994: 88; cf. Gallop 1982: 154n.).

The implication of Lacan's theory of language and subjectivity is that women cannot speak about their desire. In Lacan's seminar *Encore* this is exactly what he says:

There is a *jouissance* proper to her, to this 'her' which does not exist and which signifies nothing. There is a *jouissance* proper to her and of which she herself may know nothing, except that she experiences it – that much she does know. She knows it of course when it happens. It does not happen to all of them. (1982b: 145)

Driven to apparent exasperation Lacan exclaims:

What gives some likelihood to what I am arguing, that is, that the woman knows nothing of her *jouissance*, is that ever since we've been begging them – last time I mentioned women analysts – on our knees to try and tell us about it, well, not a word! (146)

In this seminar Lacan first states that women do not know anything about their experience of their *jouissance*, their (sexual) pleasure. He then argues for this with two points. Firstly he refers to female analysts, his colleagues, who remain silent when he asks them to tell him about female *jouissance*. Secondly he points to those he calls mystics who 'sense that there must be a *jouissance* which goes beyond' (147). The main example he gives of a mystic who experiences this pleasure is Saint Theresa. Lacan argues that:

> you only have to go and look at Bernini's statue in Rome to understand immediately that she's coming, there is no doubt about it. And what is her *jouissance*, her coming from? It is clear that the essential testimony of the mystics is that they are experiencing it but know nothing about it. (147)

Irigaray remarks in response to Lacan's exclamations are scathing. She points out that 'the question whether, in his logic, they can say anything at all, whether they [women] can be heard, is not even raised' (TS 90). If the rest of Lacan's theory is accepted, then it follows that women cannot speak about themselves. It also follows that sexual desire which is articulated has to be male desire, for women only experience a lack. Therefore, Irigaray suggests that on his own terms Lacan should not be surprised to encounter silence on the issue of women's pleasure.

Furthermore, Irigaray asks why Lacan needs to go and look at the statue by Bernini in the first place. She asks sardonically: 'In Rome? So far away? At a statue? Of a saint? Sculpted by a man? Whose pleasure are we talking about?' (91). She remarks that it would have made more sense for Lacan to consult Saint Theresa's writings on her experiences of pleasure. However, she asks pointedly, would Lacan, as a man, have been able to understand them?

> how can one 'read' them when one is a 'man'? The production of ejaculations of all sorts, often prematurely emitted, makes him miss, in the desire for identification with the lady, what her own pleasure might be all about. (91)

Irigaray's mention of ejaculation above is an obvious reference to man's role in heterosexual intercourse and at the same time refers to (Jacques) Lacan, who has remarked that his teachings are like the 'mystical ejaculations' of St Teresa (Lacan Ò982b: 147). Irigaray responds that Lacan, like most men, is so preoccupied with his own (sexual) performance that he fails to listen to women.

In sum, Irigaray's answer to Lacan's questions about female sexuality is that Lacan looks in the wrong places and hears with ears that fail him. In his theory there is no place either for women's sexual pleasure or for female speaking subjects. Within a patriarchal structure and within phallic language women cannot be heard. So why should Lacan be surprised not to find women who speak of their sexuality when he starts looking? Irigaray concludes that

> Mastery clearly acknowledges itself, except that no one notices it. Enjoying a woman, psychoanalyzing a woman, amounts then, for a man, to reappropriating for himself the unconscious that he has lent her. (94)

Problems of rigidity

But why should man be allowed to do this? Why should Lacan's theory go unchallenged? Might it not be the case that a woman subject could emerge after all? What would be the conditions of her possibility? In *Elemental Passions* Irigaray experiments with language, with the fluidity of images and poetic allusion, to see how sexually different subjects could develop, in mutual relationship with one another. In doing so, she challenges not only the masculinist assumptions of psychoanalytic theory, but also the binary logic upon which it rests. It is to *Elemental Passions* that we now turn.

PART II

Elemental Passions

CHAPTER 3

'Fragments from a woman's voyage': context and style of *Elemental Passions*

Elemental Passions makes few concessions to the reader. Both in style and content it is elusive, open to various interpretations. Unlike most texts of traditional Western philosophy and psychoanalysis which argue a thesis or develop a point of view, Elemental Passions invites the reader inside, makes suggestions to enable the reader to set off on her own journey rather than follow predetermined steps laid out by somebody else. The original text of Elemental Passions plunges directly into allusive poetry and images, leaving the reader to find her own bearings. However, in a Preface written for the Japanese edition in 1988, Irigaray offers some clues:

> Elemental Passions offers some fragments from a woman's voyage as she goes in quest of her identity in love. It is no longer a man in quest of his Grail, his God, his path, his identity through the vicissitudes of his life's journey, it is a woman. Between nature and culture, between night and day, between sun and stars, between vegetable and mineral, amongst men, amongst women, amongst gods, she seeks her humanity and her transcendency. Such a journey is not without its trials (EP 4)

The interpretation we offer here tries to elucidate that journey, in particular in relation to the way in which the development of the woman subject is interconnected with issues of logic. We wish to emphasize, however, that ours is only one possible interpretation. It is not intended as *the* definitive interpretation: indeed we would doubt that the idea of a definitive interpretation could properly be applied to this text, just as Rabbinic strategies rejected the idea of a single interpretation or truth of Torah. Instead, it opens the way to multiple readings, multiple journeys. This is the one we have travelled: we hope it opens paths for others.

Context

In an interview for the feminist journal *Hypatia* in 1995, Irigaray distinguished three phases in her work (Hirsh and Olson 1995). The first is a critical analysis of philosophy and psychoanalytic theory, showing their erasure of women, and by provocative close reading and acute questioning, 'jamming the theoretical

Context and style of *Elemental Passions*

machinery' of these supposedly gender-neutral texts of the Western canon. The most scholarly text of this phase is *Speculum. De l'autre femme*, her doctoral thesis, which was published in 1974 and translated into English in 1985 as *Speculum of the Other Woman*. The way the title is written immediately illustrates the problems of translation with regard to Irigaray. In her own view, the English title misrepresents the French by omitting the full stop. She remarks that 'it should have been put, *Speculum on the Other Woman* or *On the Other: Woman*. That would have been best' (Hirsh and Olsen 1995: 99). This, Irigaray says, is just one example of the many misunderstandings of her work in the English-speaking world (Hirsh and Olsen 1995: 98–100; see also ILo 59–62). In France the response was immediate. The publication of *Speculum* in 1974, followed by the essays collected in *This Sex Which Is Not One* in 1977, was perceived correctly as a direct challenge to the masculinist psychoanalytic establishment. Jacques Lacan responded by dismissing Irigaray from her teaching position in his *Ecole freudienne de Paris*.

The second phase of Irigaray's work, dating from approximately 1980 to 1987, continues the critique, but also moves forward in creative exploration into the conditions for a female subject. Key theoretical works of this period include *L'Ethique de la différence sexuelle* (1984) and the important book of essays published in 1987 as *Sexes et parentés*. It was also during this time that she worked hard on the tetralogy of the four elements, beginning in 1980 with *Amante marine, de Friedrich Nietzsche* and continuing with *Passions élémentaires* in 1982 and *L'Oubli de l'air chez Martin Heidegger* in 1983. In these books Irigaray experiments with a poetic style, in which she weaves together words from the philosophers with whom she engages in these texts, allusions to other thinkers of the Western tradition, and an intricate web of images and concepts of her own creation. At the same time, however, from about 1985 onward she also writes essays more directly concerned with bringing about changes in society. This is reflected both in an interest in political ideas and groups as well as in a more accessible style of writing (Whitford 1991a: 10–13).

In her third phase, from 1987 to the present, Irigaray continues to combine the creatively poetic mode with political and social intervention in the investigation of how two sexually different subjects can exist. Among other writings are *Je, tu, nous. Pour une culture de la différence* (1990) and *J'aime à toi. Esquisse d'une félicité dans l'histoire* (1992). More recently, Irigaray has turned to the East for further writing on air, breath and spirit.

Beyond the corpus of her own work, *Elemental Passions* must also be situated in relation to the whole trajectory of Western philosophy and psychoanalysis, and in particular to the major continental thinkers of the twentieth century: Heidegger, Sartre, de Beauvoir, Levinas, Foucault, Merleau-Ponty, Derrida and Deleuze. Important as it would be to locate her work in conversation with these thinkers, however, we have chosen not to undertake this in any detail here, since it would be a large project in itself.[1] Rather, we have devoted our attention to the text of Elemental Passions itself, though with the recognition that our commentary would benefit from further detailed work on the penumbra of thinkers whose air Irigaray breathes.

The reason for this intensive focus on Elemental Passions is that it has hitherto received very little attention. This is the first detailed study of the text in any European language, though it has received brief mention in several places. For instance Annemie Halsema (1998: 15n.4) refers in passing to Elemental Passions as an example of a text by Irigaray which balances between philosophy and literature. In addition, a number of authors use isolated passages of Elemental Passions either in support of their arguments or as epigraphs, but without contextualizing them or discussing them further (Shurmer-Smith & Hannam 1994: 116–17; Boothroyd 1996: 11; Vasseleu 1998: 118; Kozel 1996: 114). It is our suggestion that detailed study of Elemental Passions is thus long overdue. It is a text crucial for understanding Irigaray's second phase, and is an enactment of the becoming of sexually different subjects. As such, it is a performative text, not merely a descriptive one; and although this makes any interpretation necessarily unstable and incomplete, it also enables creative engagement.

Style and language

The performative nature of the text is reinforced by elusive, poetic language which renders any interpretation even more tentative. The style of Elemental Passions reflects the fluidity and the motion of its female subject. In this respect it is similar to the style of 'When Our Lips Speak Together', about which Burke has written:

> To mime the relations of 'self-affection', Irigaray tries out a language of immediacy, which hovers between the written and the spoken and stresses the sense of touch in the here and now. A language of flux, it refuses rigid definitions and avoids images or metaphors that stabilize meaning in too permanent a manner. (Burke 1980: 68)

The open-ended and poetic style of Elemental Passions allows for a fluid free association of ideas and images that does not permit any rigid binaries to establish themselves. The reader is unsettled through the text's continual questioning. Moreover, Irigaray presents touch (rather than, say, the gaze) as crucial for the female subject.[2] This also is borne out by her style: one could argue that the text touches itself like two lips speaking together as recurrent themes are revisited. Themes such as identity and difference in man's appropriation of woman, the philosophical categories of time and space, death and birth, and the formation of subjects through the love between man and woman occur repeatedly throughout

---

[1] Some aspects of it have been undertaken by, among others, Braidotti 1986, 1994b,c; Grosz 1994a; Kozel 1996; Chanter 1995; Vasseleu 1998.

[2] There are obvious affinities here with the thought of Maurice Merleau-Ponty (1962, 1964), though as usual he does not consider sexual difference.

Context and style of *Elemental Passions*

Elemental Passions. They are revisited only partly in order to move events between man and woman or the argument about subjectivity forward; their more important function is to create awareness and understanding in the reader. Although we will suggest below a loose narrative structure of *Elemental Passions*, we believe that its aim is not to present a linear argument but to open the reader up to a different mode of thinking. There is therefore no substitute for an immersion in the text itself. We offer a commentary; but we wish to repeat that the commentary will only serve its purpose if it leads the reader *into* the text. On no account should it be read *instead* of the text.

In her style as much as in her content, Irigaray's writing has features of Lacan's. Lacan's seminars and papers are notoriously difficult to understand. He frequently crosses the borders between psychoanalysis, philosophy and poetry, and refers to art and literature to illustrate his theories. He speaks in riddles, allusions and metaphors. Malcolm Bowie argues in his exposition of Lacan that the aim of this style is to entice the reader to enter the theory the way Lacan intends them to. Part of that entry is to be in a manner that questions the theories themselves, and their purposes. Bowie describes Lacan's approach as follows:

One of Lacan's recurrent purposes as a writer is to amplify theories to the point where they become deranged, to supercharge them with meaning in such a way that they no longer have uses or applications ...

Lacan's writing seeks to tease and seduce. It is full of feints, subterfuges, evasions and mimicries. (Bowie 1991: 35, 200)

Irigaray's style of philosophy shows similarities. In her early books, especially *Speculum*, her close reading of theorists such as Freud, Plato and Descartes asks such detailed questions of their intentions and the consequences of their writings, especially for women, that the theoretical machinery of the original text is jammed. The theory is destabilized, not so much by counterargument as by showing what it really comes to when gender is taken into account. Particularly in her second phase, Irigaray also wants to seduce both the philosopher she engages with (Nietzsche in *Marine Lover*, Heidegger in *Forgetting of Air*) and her reader (Burke 1987). The reader cannot simply 'consume' her books but is made to participate in them by engaging with the allusions and free associations.

To readers in the English-speaking world, Irigaray's texts have at times seemed unnecessarily complex and incredibly elusive, especially in the multiple layers of their allusions to writers in the philosophical and literary canon of the West. Partly because of this she has been criticized, perhaps not unjustly, for being elitist. Irigaray is not unlike Lacan in sometimes betraying an apparently arrogant attitude towards their audience. Compare, for example, Lacan's condescending comments in his notorious 'God and the *Jouissance* of the Woman':

You may have noticed – and naturally I am speaking to the few seeming men that I can see here and there, luckily for the most I don't know them, which prevents my prejudging as

Elemental Passions

> regards the rest – that occasionally it can happen that there is something which shakes the women up [*secouer*], or helps them out [*secourir*]. If you look up the etymology of these two words in Bloch and Von Wartburg's *Dictionary*, which I delight in and which, I am sure, none of you even have in your libraries, you will see the relationship between them ... (Lacan 1982b: 145)

He is at best patronising, at worst openly contemptuous of his audience. Irigaray can also be dismissive of the honest and intelligent efforts of her translators.

> Why do they make this mistake? Because they fail to listen and lack the imagination that corresponds to what I mean. (Hirsch & Olsen 1995: 98)

Both sometimes display an arrogant attitude, though Irigaray's impatience is notably milder than Lacan's persistent habit of insulting and belittling his audience (Gallop 1982: 37). Moreover, one should bear in mind that both psychoanalysis and continental philosophy are renowned for their opaque style (Macey 1988: 8). Within the French context, many writers including Derrida, Hélène Cixous and Julia Kristeva combine literature, philosophy, psychoanalysis and poetry. In comparison with them, Irigaray's style is in fact not exceptionally strange or complex (see Duchen 1988; Halsema 1998).

A further crucial respect in which Irigaray's style should be situated in relation to Lacan is with regard to their ideas of gender and imagery. Lacan provides no other image for woman than lack, hole, gap. Irigaray, in direct challenge, holds that woman needs to look for images that will reflect herself. She needs images which will make it possible for her to be different from man and not definable merely in his terms. They will enable her to become a subject. Elizabeth Berg, discussing Irigaray's early work, argues that Irigaray's images are necessarily empty. Irigaray, she says, views woman as a blank canvas upon which man projects his image: within a phallocentric system of representation woman serves as mirror to man. Although Irigaray develops images for women, she does not want to continue woman's function of mirror for man nor remain the blank space upon which man can project images. In order to hold open the blank spaces in masculine representations, Berg argues that Irigaray develops images that are 'empty': they capture the disruptive tension which is present in masculinist representations. Thus Irigaray maintains the potential for subverting masculinist discourse (Berg 1982).

By the term 'empty' Berg does not mean to say that Irigaray's images have no meaning and thus could be used to denote anything from liberating to oppressive views of women. Rather, 'woman is described in terms of analogies which themselves resist definition, and are therefore less subject to phallocentric reappropriation' (17). This means that they can serve as temporary meanings for woman's subjectivity but guard against a theory or structure in which woman would, once again, be the object. Berg's view of Irigaray's images is in accordance with Whitford's interpretation of Irigaray's use of language. Just as men have a 'house of language', a language as a dwelling place as Heidegger argued, so women too need coverings (Whitford 1991b: 43–5; see also Chanter 1995:

146–51). However, women's language should not constrict them, imprison them, or constrain their movement through a fixed definition. Braidotti (1994a) has proposed the idea of women's language as nomadic tents. To use our own favoured metaphor, we are suggesting that at least in relation to *Marine Lover* and *Elemental Passions* fluidity is a highly appropriate way of thinking about Irigaray's imagery and her overall use of language.

One of the consequences of the fluidity of Irigaray's language is that it is extremely difficult to translate. The words cannot be pinned down: the writing is poetic, elusive and associative; and the associations which are often immediately apparent in French are clumsy or lost altogether in translation. Commentary is therefore simultaneously heavy handed and inadequate: much is left out even while other parts are laboured. As a rule we have chosen to refer to the English translation; but to make specific points we refer also to the original French. In the commentary of the next chapter and in the discussion of images in Chapter 5 we have cited both the English and the French text for the reader's convenience.

Structure and narrative

One of the first things with which the reader of *Elemental Passions* is confronted is an 'I' and a 'you'. Who are they? To identify them, it is helpful to remember that this is not the first time an 'I' and a 'you' have appeared in Irigaray's writings. In the essays from her first phase, 'When Our Lips Move Together' and 'And One Doesn't Stir Without the Other' in *This Sex Which Is Not One*, an 'I' and a 'you' figure. In these cases both pronouns refer to women: to women as lovers, as mother and daughter, or even as different dimensions of one woman. Commentators disagree slightly about how the pronouns function in these essays. H. V. Wenzel interprets the 'you' of 'And One Doesn't Stir' specifically as the 'I's mother. She therefore reads this essay as a monologue with fixed subject and object positions (Wenzel 1981: 58). Carolyn Burke reads the pronouns in a less fixed way; and especially in 'When Our Lips' argues that the use of personal pronouns draws the reader into 'an exploration of plurality' (Burke 1980: 67–8).

In the case of *Marine Lover* the case is somewhat clearer. It is easy to read the 'I' and the 'you' respectively as Irigaray and Nietzsche, and *Marine Lover* as the difficult love relationship between them. More generally, it could be supposed that the books of the tetralogy on the elements constitute amorous dialogues between an 'I' who is Irigaray or woman gaining access to a subject position and to philosophy, and a 'you', the philosopher that specific text engages with, or the dominant male with whom the woman is interacting. In all these texts, the use of the pronouns 'I' and 'you' serves to unsettle subject and object positions. It allows for fluidity and reciprocity between the two. If it is not always clear to whom the pronouns refer, we suggest that the ambiguity is deliberate. Through an unsettling of subject and object positions, these texts disrupt binary logic.

Elemental Passions

Who, then, are the specific 'I' and 'you' of *Elemental Passions*? It seems clear that the 'I' of *Elemental Passions* is female: I-woman. In the Introduction which was added in 1988, Irigaray writes that the book is about a woman who goes in search of her identity, a search which has many difficulties.

But these do not discourage her from her quest, as she attempts again and again to discover how I-woman can enter into a joyous nuptial union with you-man. She finds that this cannot occur unless *you* relates to *he* and *He*, and *I* relates to *she* and *She*. (EP 4)

Both 'I' and 'you' therefore are connected not only with individuals but with the divine horizon, *He* and *She*, the 'spirit of divinity circulating between' women and men (2).

This does not, however, mean that identities are entirely fixed or stable. Especially about the identity of 'you', Irigaray is sometimes ambiguous. Usually she uses the familiar form, *tu*, for you-man, and in most cases it reads as an intimate address to a father, son, lover and/or philosopher. Sometimes, however, *tu* could refer to you-woman: mother, daughter, lover or even two aspects of one woman who strives to become a subject. 'You' in the plural (*vous*) could refer to you-men, you-women, or you-men-and-women; *vous* can also of course be used as formal address for either you-man or you-woman. The meaning of 'you' changes repeatedly in *Elemental Passions*. Our interpretation of it will be based on the context and on grammatical clues. Unless these give clear indications to the contrary, we will usually interpret 'I' as 'I-woman' and 'you' (*tu*) as 'you-man' in the development of Irigaray's theme of the becoming of sexually different subjects in intimate mutual relationship.

This theme, we suggest, gives rise to a loose narrative structure for the book. *Elemental Passions* is a short book. It consists of fifteen chapters which are each between two and ten pages long in English translation. Some of the chapters read as a sort of narrative, in which there is a story-like text in which the events and characters develop. It is narrated by a female voice, I-woman. The term 'non-narrative' is used to indicate those chapters which are not like a story between an 'I' and a 'you', though once again no rigid distinctions can be sustained and the divisions between narrative and non-narrative are at best loose and tentative. As we present them, the non-narrative chapters are meditations on images that arise as the story unfolds.

In the narrative, written from a female perspective, we witness the developing relation between a man and a woman in which both struggle to become subjects. This narrative, which could be characterized as a love story, is interrupted with non-narrative meditations which increase in number as the book proceeds. It is as if man needs to learn to listen differently before he can hear woman speak. The narrative as well as the meditations prepare both him and the reader for new receptivity. In our reading of *Elemental Passions*, the narrative chapters are 2, 3, 4, 5, 8, 9, 13 and 14. Themes such as embodiment, man's imposition of his notions of time and space on to woman, mastery and sexual love are introduced at the beginning and subsequently revised and reiterated. This repetitive style aims to undo both linear, goal-oriented thinking and binary logic and serves to open up the space for subjects to develop. It also shows that becoming subjects, male and female in mutual relation, is an ongoing process.

For convenience, we present below our suggested overview of Elemental Passions, before proceeding to chapter-by-chapter commentary. For the most part, the commentary will confine itself to exposition of the text, reserving critique to Part III.

Schematic overview

I   Prologue: the stage is set for the story to unfold.
II   Narrative: man searches for his origin. Silence as weapon and strategy.
III   Narrative: woman leads man to womb. Man imposes his binary framework of time and space onto woman. She is halted in her becoming a subject.
IV   Narrative: man regards woman either as his unique reflection or as ground of his being.
V   Narrative: Breakthrough I: differences are at last acknowledged. The challenge for man and woman is to develop their relationship and retain their sexually different subjectivities.
VI   Interlude I: image of flower.
VII   Meditation I: the light of reason.
VIII   Narrative: Backlash I: man tries to reimpose his framework of time and space. Differences are denied and the debt to the maternal is not acknowledged by man.
IX   Narrative: Breakthrough II: I-woman and you-man enjoy their differences.
X   Interlude II: lips and boundaries.
XI   Meditation II: space, time, infinity and movement.
XII   Narrative: Vision of future: sexual difference leads to refiguring of procreation.
XIII   Narrative: Backlash II: man finds it impossible to accept sexual difference; woman and man have to be separate if woman is to become a female subject.
XIV   Narrative: man cannot bear to be alone but cannot acknowledge sexual difference either.
XV   Epilogue.

CHAPTER 4

Interpretive synopsis of *Elemental Passions*

One: prologue

The first chapter can be regarded as a Prologue. Irigaray begins with short, staccato sentences.

White. Immense spaces. White, a rush of breath. Be swift, marry this breath. Remain in it. Make haste. Let it not abandon me. Let me not turn from it. Be swept up: my song. (EP 7)

De grands espaces. Blancs. Un grand souffle, blanc. Rapide, épouser ce souffle. Y rester. Dans la hâte. Qu'il ne m'abandonne pas. Que je ne le laisse pas. Y être entraînée : mon chant. (Pe 7)

The short sentences of this first paragraph attract the attention of the reader and convey a sense of urgency. Twice in this small paragraph words which depict speed, 'rapide' (quick) and 'dans la hâte' (hurry, make haste) occur. What is the hurry? Who should make haste, and why? What is urgent, and what will happen if a quick response is not made?

It is I-woman who is speaking these words, both for herself and to you-man; and the object of her hurry is a song, woman's song, an expression of her love for 'you'.

You give me a blank white mouth. My white mouth, open, like an angel in a cathedral. You have stopped my tongue. What remains is song. I can say nothing but sing.

A song, for you. But that 'for you' is not a dative. Nor that song, a gift. Not received from you, not produced by me, nor for you, that song: my love with you. Intermingled. Escapes from me. A cloud. (EP 7)

Tu me donnes une bouche blanche. Ouverte, ma bouche blanche, comme les anges dans les cathédrales. Tu m'as coupé la langue. Me reste le chant. Je ne peux rien dire que chanter.

Chanter pour toi. Mais ce pour toi n'est pas un datif. Ni ce chant, un don. Pas reçu de toi, pas produit par moi, ni pour toi, ce chant : mon amour avec toi. Mêlées. S'échappe de moi. Nuée. (Pe 7)

From the first paragraph we are left with the question: why must I-woman hurry with her song? The second and third paragraphs raise another question, which helps to answer the first: how and why do 'you give me a white mouth'? Why white? Mouths are usually pink or red. A white mouth is a dead mouth, a statue, perhaps, 'like an angel in a cathedral'. It looks as though it could speak, but it cannot. The man, she says, has made her mouth 'white', like a plaster angel, and thus has stopped her speech: the 'I' cannot use her tongue or her language anymore. But if she is quick, if she hurries, before her metamorphosis into a statue is complete perhaps she can still sing. Perhaps her music, her song telling her love for him, will stop him from turning her into a statue, and thus will save them both. He, after all, also wants love, and a statue, even a statue of an angel, cannot give him love. Though he can control it completely, it can never fulfil his desires. Only a real live woman – a woman who is free to be herself and to speak and sing in her own voice – can do that.

Woman's love is a love which cannot be appropriated, cannot be owned. 'My love with you' is characterized as a song which is not, the text says, 'a gift': it is not part of an economy of exchange like a marriage dowry. In previous chapters we have shown how the appropriation of women by men is interconnected with binary logic. If the subject – of philosophy or of culture – is exclusively male, then, as Lévi-Strauss has shown (1949), women can be owned by men and can serve as gifts between them. From the very beginning of *Elemental Passions*, Irigaray signals that woman's song, woman's love, is not the sort of gift which allows man to claim her as his possession.

By giving her love to you-man in her song, I-woman's breath mingles with the air and forms a cloud (nuée). It is not an exchange-gift; but it invites the man to respond with his own song, his own love, not by making her into a statue but by letting their song, their love, intermingle like a cloud. Woman's song is an invitation to a different logic, a logic not characterized by rigid binaries and which does not thrive on ownership and appropriation, but mingles like breath in a cloud. This mingling is 'spilling out without a break' (diffusion sans arrêt) (EP 7/ Pe 8). The words 'sans arrêt', literally 'without stopping', are significant. They occur frequently in *Elemental Passions* in descriptions of a female subject and indicate the movement towards fluidity.

The air is full of I-woman. You-man however does not recognize this nor does he hear the song she sings.

You do not hear. So many words divide us. Divide us from the song. How could that white effusion reach you? That intense candour still cannot be heard. (EP 7)

Mais tu ne l'entends pas. Tant de mots nous séparent. Séparent du chant. Comment t'atteindrait cette effusion blanche? La force de la candeur reste inaudible. (Pe 7)

Man has stopped his ears, filled his ears with his own words, his own language, and can neither sing nor hear the woman's song. Throughout her writings Irigaray argues that in our present phallic language there is no place for either song or silence, no respect for breath (See ILo 121–8; FA). This implies a lack of respect for life, a preoccupation with death. In the womb, Irigaray reminds us,

Elemental Passions

we are provided with oxygen through our mother's blood; and once outside the womb, oxygen, breath, is essential for life. Yet our language does not seem to respect breath, forgets air. Indeed it seems to want to replace it.

Speech, instead of bearing breath, takes its place, replaces it, which invariably stifles and preoccupies the place for silence. (ILo 122)

La parole, au lieu de porter le souffle, en tient lieu, s'y substitue, ce qui essouffle et préoccupe toujours le lieu du silence. (Jat 188)

For Irigaray, the lack of respect for breath in our language is thus related to a denial of the mother. It reflects a lack of respect for life, for oneself and the other, the unacknowledged debt to the mother as the one who gives life. Our bodily and physical existence is connected with our logic and our language, and reflected in our metaphysics.

The urgency of Irigaray's beginning, therefore, is the urgency of I-woman's invitation to you-man to listen to her voice, respond to the song, mingle his breath with hers in the cloud.

Call yourself. Give, yourself, names.

Recall yourself once more: I insist, into the air. (EP 7–8)

Appelle toi. Donne, toi, des noms. Rappelle toi encore : j'insiste dans l'air. (Pe 8)

If you-man will respond to this invitation, will mingle with I-woman in harmonious song, there is hope. Until he hears her song and joins in her breath, the fruitful relationship between man and woman as two sexually different subjects remains only a promise, an invitation. It is this promise with which the closing paragraph of chapter one leaves us.

Seeing, hearing, speaking, breathing, living, all these wait to be made fecund by an innocent potency. (EP 8)

Le voir, l'entendre, le parler, le respirer, le vivre attendent la fécondation d'une puissance innocente. (Pe 8)

Human actions performed by the senses and the body, such as seeing, hearing, and even breathing, need fertilization (*fécondation*). We interpret this to mean that these everyday biological functions are performed but are not fruitful in the Irigarayan sense: it is not until two subjects, male and female, are allowed to come into being that our actions and our language become procreative and fertile. This is the first use of the crucial idea of 'innocent force' or 'potency' (*puissance innocente*) in Elemental Passions. Although Empedocles is not explicitly mentioned, the chapter indicates the pattern of the tension between Love and Strife. Which of these two elemental passions will gain the ascendency?

In sum, the opening chapter of Elemental Passions introduces the key concepts and themes we are about to witness: the images of a song, a cloud, love, fecundity and potency (*puissance*); women's struggle for a female language and female subjectivity and man's tendency to cut off her speech, the tension between Love and Strife. The main events that will shape the succeeding narrative are suggested: you-man tries to appropriate I-woman by forcing her to speak like he does; he does not succeed, nor does he understand I-woman because she is different from him; I-woman offers him her love which is a love that allows for (sexual) difference; and we are left with a promise of the possibility of new relations between the sexes. It is as if the stage is set, the story-line presented, and now the performance of the text is ready to commence. For this reason we consider the first chapter to be a prologue.

Two: narrative

In chapters two to five the narrative begins to unfold. The second chapter starts as follows:

Was it your tongue [*ta langue*] in my mouth which forced me into speech? Was it that blade between my lips which drew forth floods of words to speak to you? And, as you wanted words other than those already uttered, words never yet imagined, unique in your tongue [*ta langue*], to name you and you alone, you kept on prying me open, further and further open. Honing and sharpening your instrument ... piercing further into my silence. Further into my flesh, were you not thus discovering the path of your being? ... And I was speaking but you did not hear. I was speaking from further than your furthest bounds. Beyond the place you were penetrating to reveal the secret of resistance to your tongue [*ta langue*]. (EP 9)

Ta langue, dans ma bouche, m'a-t-elle obligée à parler? Cette lame entre mes lèvres, est-ce elle qui tirait de moi des flots de paroles pour te dire? Et, comme tu voulais des mots autres que ceux déjà prononcés, des mots encore inouïs pour te nommer toi et toi seul, unique en ta langue, tu m'ouvrais de plus en plus loin. Tu effilais et amenuisais ton outil ... pour frayer plus avant mon silence. Plus avant dans ma chair, m'aillais-tu découvrir le chemin de ton être? ... Et je parlais, mais tu n'entendais pas. Je parlais de plus loin que ton plus lointain. Au-delà d'où tu pénétrais pour dévoiler le secret de ce qui résistait à ta langue. (*Pe* 9)

In the French original, the first two sentences begin with nouns: 'ta langue' (your tongue) and 'cette lame' (that blade) respectively. The grammar of these questions, starting with a noun instead of a weak verb 'was it' (as in the English translation), emphasizes the importance of the words 'tongue' and 'blade', and indicates from the outset the insistent violence of the exchange. The French word for 'tongue', *langue*, means both language, as in 'mother tongue', and 'tongue' as the bodily organ. Your tongue/language, that blade, that sharp instrument are all inserted by 'you' into 'my' mouth, my lips, my silence and my flesh. What does this mean?

Our interpretation begins from the premise that 'I' is I-woman and 'you' is you-man, as in the previous chapter: this is supported by the masculine form 'toi seul' in the phrase 'to name you and you alone'. Woman's lips are being spread apart against her will; they are wrenched open and she is forced to speak. What is inserted is a tongue/language, an instrument. From Irigaray's other writings we are aware of her discussion of lips as twofold, the mouth and the labia (TS 28–33). The significance of the image of two pairs of lips for Irigaray will be discussed in the next chapter; suffice it to say here that for Irigaray women's double lips, always touching, symbolize the fact that woman's subjectivity cannot be reduced to 'one', whether this is one sex organ, one definition, one place or one language. In this it contrasts with phallic or male language which imposes clear oppositional boundaries.

If this is correct, then the passage – like much else in *Elemental Passions* – admits of a three-fold interpretation which can be thought of as concentric circles. At the centre is the literal sexual violation of the woman. In the light of Irigaray's general argument about the violation of female lips by male sexual intervention (sometimes under a medical pretext), 'that blade between my lips' can be read as a penis or a speculum. This violation has connotations of rape, loss of virginity, and masculine appropriation of reproduction.

The second level of interpretation continues Irigaray's engagement of Lacanian theories of language and its roots in psycho-sexual development: it is his tongue/language which the man forces into the woman's mouth, causing her to lose her own speech and subjectivity and instead reflect his. What is required of woman is that she speak of you-man, 'to name you and you alone' in continuous reaffirmation. Man's aim is to get woman to speak of him in 'words never yet imagined'. This is a variant of the need of man, in Lacan's terms, to be reflected by (multiple) women. Woman is asked to speak to man in ever new words in order to establish his subjectivity over and over again. He wants her to be 'virgin material' (*matière vierge*) for him (EP 10/ Pe 10), having no history, no subjectivity of her own, so that she is an unqualified support for his project of mastery, 'for the building of your world to come' (EP 10). And yet the woman is aware that if man's desire is premised upon a lack, moreover a lack which she was expected to fill by her affirmation of him, then that 'world to come' could never be attained: 'how could it ever be reached if, in that quest, once again you wanted yourself as you already are?' (EP 10).

At that level of interpretation we can see that Irigaray makes allusions also to the history of philosophy and its binary logic. She alludes to Empedocles' ideas of the recurrence of Love and Strife. She also points towards Heidegger and his theme of man's desire to build for himself a home to dwell in, using 'what has been held in reserve': but Irigaray sees that what has fundamentally been held in reserve is the woman. Thus I-woman says, 'You cling to me as to your ancient home'; but by doing so in a rigid way that precludes becoming, such clinging only opens up 'that gap-death'. Interwoven with the allusions to Heidegger there are echoes of Sartre's *Being and Nothingness*, especially his assertions about sex as mastery and repetition without fulfilment, and, again, Lévi-Strauss's theories of gift and exchange.

How many times, without end, will you return to make use of that gift within me? Leaving, ceaselessly leaving, so that you can come back and create, in the spacing of that ever more repeated to-and-fro, a nothingness which you seek to master by dint of repetition. (EP 11)

Combien de fois, sans fin, reviendras-tu disposer en moi de ce don? Partant, et ne cessant de partir, pour pouvoir faire retour et créer, en l'espacement de ce va-et-vient toujours plus rebattu, un néant que tu t'efforces de maîtriser à force de répétitions (Pe 12).

And yet that 'incrustation of your nothingness' (*incrustation de ton néant*) can only make things worse.

This brings us to the third level of interpretation, that of the narrative of *Elemental Passions*. As we read this text, we take this chapter as indicating the relationship between I-woman and you-man in Western culture, a relationship characterized by masculine violence: sexual, linguistic and philosophical. This is the place from which I-woman must start in her efforts to remedy the situation. In response to you-man's attempts to force her to speak, she points out that 'I was speaking but you did not hear'. As we saw in the Prologue, woman speaks, but man does not hear her, does not want to listen to what she says. The aim of woman's speech is not to provide a static reflection of man; it is rather an attempt to encourage him to think and listen differently and to open himself up to her voice.

I was speaking, not so that you would stay where you already were, but so that you would move beyond. (EP 10)

Je parlais, non pour que tu demeures où tu étais déjà, mais pour que tu arrives outre. (Pe 10)

Man does not hear. Irigaray suggests that by first probing inside woman and then getting as far away from woman as possible on his all-male philosophical or technological quests, man is searching both for his origin and for the 'path of [his] being'. Yet this flight away from her and away from himself does not give man what he desires. Whilst man searches for his origin, woman measures how far man has travelled. She holds on to a thread to measure the distance and draws man back:

Imperceptibly, I wind you in, letting you believe you know the way on your own. I speak to you in silence ... Miming, without speaking a word, your next step. (EP 12)

Imperceptiblement, je te ramène, te laissant croire que, seul, tu connais le chemin. En silence, je te parle ... Mimant, sans mot dire, ton prochain pas. (Pe 13)

This quotation resonates with echoes of Freud's *Fort!Da!* account of the little boy who tries to master the absence of his mother; but Irigaray turns it upside down: in her narrative it is I-woman who holds the thread. You-man will not find the origin or goal of his being, he will not attain genuine subjectivity, if he does not acknowledge woman in this process. She is the one who gave birth to him, and must be recognized as a separate, female subject.

> And do I not still have to keep watch when you rush away from me? And have to measure how far you have leapt, keep track, so that each time I can hold fast the thread as it unwinds? And remind you of the distance you have travelled from yourself. (EP 12)
>
> Et ne faut-il encore que je te regarde quand, ainsi, tu t'élances pour t'éloigner? Et que, de ton saut, je prenne mesure et me souvienne pour, à chaque fois, retenir le fil de son déroulement? Et te redonner mémoire de la distance que tu as marqueé par rapport à toi. (Pe 13)

The (male) subject of philosophy loses track of himself when he abandons his bodily origins, his mother. When the language of philosophy becomes phallic, when culture is seen as continuously thrusting forward to intellectual and technological goals, man loses touch with his origin and thus with himself. Irigaray deftly subverts Freud's Fort!Da! account by combining it with the story of Ariadne's thread from Greek mythology, which can be interpreted as woman's thread of language which leads man out of his maze back to the real labyrinth which the maze mimics: the womb, origin of being. These connections between a maze and a womb, a thread and language, a man and a woman, are supported by other passages in Irigaray's work. The first is from 'When Our Lips Speak Together':

> Speak, all the same. It's our good fortune that your language isn't formed of a single thread, a single strand or pattern. It comes from everywhere at once. You touch me all over at the same time. (TS 209)
>
> Parle quand même. Que ton langage ne soit pas d'un seul fil, d'une seule chaîne, d'une seule trame, c'est notre chance. Il vient de partout à la fois. Tu me touches toute en même temps. (Cs 209)

Both the speaker and the addressee in 'When Our Lips Speak Together' are female. A woman's speech is likened to touch. Her language is not linear but fluid; like a densely patterned web 'it comes from everywhere at once'. It blurs rigid distinctions.

The same fluid touch, with a reference to women's lips and language, occurs in *Sexes and Genealogies* where Irigaray draws attention to the connection between female lips and a maze.

> The labyrinth, whose path was known to Ariadne, for example, would thus be that of the lips. This mystery of the female lips, the way they open to give birth to the universe, and touch together to permit the female individual to have a sense of her identity, would be the forgotten secret of perceiving and generating the world. (SG 101)
>
> Le labyrinthe, dont Ariadne par exemple connaîtrait le chemin, serait alors celui des lèvres. Ce mystère des lèvres féminines, de leur ouverture pour la génération de l'univers et de leur retouche pour la perception de l'identité à soi de l'individu féminin, serait le secret oublié de la perception et de la génération du monde. (SP 115)

Ariadne's thread, woman's thread of language, can lead man out of the philosophical maze in which he has lost himself, back to his origin.

This is arguably one of the aims of *Elemental Passions*: to create a better future for both women and men by subverting destructive binaries with a more fluid

Interpretative synopsis of *Elemental Passions*

approach, modelled on mutual flow in relationship. The 'forgotten secret of perceiving and generating the world' from the above quotation is reminiscent of the promise of the prologue, a promise of a new way of thinking and living. It echoes Empedocles' new world, born out of Love. Its condition was that our senses should become fecund through the working of 'an innocent potency' (*une puissance innocente*) on the elements of the senses. This *puissance*, which is associated with the becoming of a female subject, is crucial for Irigaray's project of sexual difference, in which a female and a male subject will become in relation to each other.

Woman's language incorporates both touch and silence. Silence plays an important role in this chapter. Its meaning shifts almost imperceptibly until by the end of the chapter it is virtually opposite to what it was at the beginning. At the beginning of the chapter, woman is silenced because man does not hear her speak. By the end of the chapter, woman has decided to use her silence as a strategy by which she can convey her message of mutuality to man. She will keep hold of the thread which connects them, and when he thrusts forward to ever escalating goals, she will try to draw him back to his origin. But will her attempts be successful?

Three: narrative

Chapter three introduces key events in the relationship between you-man and I-woman. In chapter two man tried to thrust his way into the future, leaving his maternal origin, his connection with woman, behind. Yet however far he went, she was still with him, holding the umbilical cord, the thread that is his security in the labyrinth. She draws him back.

Deep, deeper than the greatest depths your daylight could imagine, once again I caress you ...

Deep, deeper than anything you could dream of taking or giving beneath the surface of my skin, that is where I am (EP 13)

Très profond, et plus profond que le plus profond qu'a imaginé ton jour, encore je t'embrasse.

Très profond, et plus profond que ce que tu rêves puiser ou donner au-delà de la surface de ma peau, encore je demeure (Pe 15–16).

Woman said she would mime man's steps in search of himself, and imperceptibly lead him back to his origins. Where has she led him? She has taken him to a place that is 'deeper than the greatest depths your daylight could imagine' to a 'luminous night'. It is a place which follows its own rhythm, 'quickening in movements both expected and unexpected' (EP 13; *Qui bouge selon des mouvements attendus et inattendus*, Pe 15), which results in a force so strong that it cannot be measured, but only poured out in 'mortal ecstasy' (*une extase mortelle*, Pe 15). Where and what is this place?

At the first level of interpretation, I-woman has led you-man to sexual encounter, where he is received once again to her womb, and where, if they recognize one another as subjects in their sexual difference, they can come to mutual ecstasy (jouissance). Woman has taken man back to his place of origin, the womb, where movements and fluids follow their own rhythm. What is man's reaction to this? As Irigaray presents it, man does not accept the mutuality. Instead, he tries again to appropriate the woman, eating her alive, refusing her her own subjectivity and thereby also losing his own chance of mutuality. Although on the face of it woman takes man into herself, in fact it is man who absorbs woman.

You took me into yourself ... so that you could get back to that sameness whose origin remains a mystery to you. To get back to that sameness, you took me inside outside yourself. And so you continue to suck me up: my life. You continue to absorb me, inside you, turned inside out, in this cavern where I am still alive. Your body is my prison. (EP 14)

Tu m'as prise en toi ... pour retournée à ce même, dont tu ne connais pas l'origine. Pour faire retour au même, tu m'as prise dedans dehors en toi. Ainsi tu continues à me boire : la vie. Interne à toi, l'intérieur repassé à l'extérieur, tu m'absorbes encore, en cette cave où je demeure vivante. Ton corps est ma prison. (Pe 16–17)

But this is a tragedy for both man and woman. The woman is again violated, her subject position refused and unrecognized by the man. And the man, by refusing to allow her to be a subject in her own right but only a reflection of himself and his wishes, has ensured that there is nobody left to love him or to have a reciprocal relationship with him, since one can have a relationship only with another subject, not with a mirror image. The more you-man senses this, the more he tries to force I-woman's love, and the worse it all gets.

Thinking that she has now become one in your image, according to your model, you take fright at what you begin to sense: how enclosed you are, how unattainable to others. You strike, knock, cut, wound, rub raw this living body to rediscover the source of life ...

Do not strike so hard, you are paralysing her, stopping her flow. Those blows are only aimed at you. You are the one who needs to be opened up again. (EP 18)

Pensant qu'elle est maintenant une à ton image, selon ton modèle, tu t'éprouvantes de ce qui te devient ainsi perceptible : ton enfermement, ton dérobement à l'autre. Tu frappes, cognes, entailles, blesses, frottes jusqu'à l'écorcher ce corps vivant pour retrouver la source de vie.

Ne frappe pas si fort, tu la figes, la paralyses dans son flux. Ces coups ne s'adressent qu'à toi. C'est toi qui as besoin d'être rouvert. (Pe 21–2)

At a psychosexual level, the man's response to the woman's attempts at a subject position is a reaction of violence, using bodily force to reinstate his dominance and her position as a mirror to reflect himself. The fear of living without reflection is unbearable for a man, and he uses his sexual power to appropriate woman to his needs. She responds:

Interpretative synopsis of *Elemental Passions*

And I understand the mystery of your power. You get close to my gift, my renunciation of any limit, the intensity which floods out in the abandoning of all reserve, and you take it back into yourself. You limit it within the horizon of a skin which stretches, swells, and gradually expands. And you are erect: I am. Such is, being. And whoever cannot contain that force, is not. Outside you is nothingness. (EP 13–14)

Et je comprends le mystère de ton pouvoir. Tu touches à ce qui se donne dans le renoncement à tout bord, à l'intensité qui se profuse dans l'abandon de toutes réserves, et tu le reprends en toi. Tu le rebordes d'une membrane horizon qui s'étend, se gonfle, se déploie à mesure. Et tu t'ériges : je suis. Tel, l'être. Et qui ne dispose de quoi contenir la force, n'est pas. Hors de toi, le néant. (Pe 16)

Again, Irigaray uses sexual encounter both as a description of actual relationships between men and women and also as symbolic of structures of thought in philosophy and culture. Man's power comes from the appropriation of woman's gift; or, in philosophical terms, the force of structures of thought based on rigid binaries and boundaries is possible only because it covertly appropriates fluidity while overtly imposing precise distinctions. There are in French two words for power: *le pouvoir* and *la puissance*. As Gillian Gill notes (SG 12), the former is used by Irigaray for patriarchal power, the latter for power, ancient or new, associated with women. The 'mystery of man's power' [*pouvoir*], therefore, forces boundaries upon potentiality, limiting its flow and restricting its *puissance* to the categories imposed upon it.

In this passage Irigaray is revisiting the Cartesian cogito and its philosophical trajectory through Hegel to Sartre and Heidegger; and by putting it into explicitly sexual terms she shows its gendered nature. 'I think, therefore I am': 'You are erect: I am'. It is from the assertion of himself, whether in intellect or sex, that man imposes being on the world. The categories by which the world is structured come from himself; and whatever does not fit into these categories or cannot be contained by them is nothingness. Man asserts himself as one subject, sexually and philosophically: a unified One, in Hegelian terms, in which anything that is separated out as a distinction is reincorporated into a higher unity. In this process, woman or mother, the origin of man's being, is ignored or forgotten, just as is the earth and material reality and elemental passions in the quest for intellectual unity and technological mastery. Yet if only he could let go of his fear, man might be able to find that

a world's circular horizon always conceals the inner movement of the womb. The imposition of distinctions is the mourning which their bodies always wear. One + one + one … separated out. And the gathering of all into One will never amount to the living quality of a resting place which, always pouring out liquid, blurs boundaries. (EP 15)

l'horizon d'un monde toujours dérobe dans son cercle la membrane mouvante d'un ventre. L'imposition de la netteté, tel sera le deuil que portent leurs corps. Séparés : un + un + un … Et le rassemblement du tout en Un jamais reviendra à ce vivant d'un séjour qui, donnant toujours du fluide, mêle les bords. (Pe 18)

Elemental Passions

Man might think that the sexual has nothing to do with the philosophical, that reason can be separated from passion; but Irigaray shows how man's sexual behaviour is a paradigm for his philosophical constructions. The rigidity of Western philosophy with its neat boundaries and distinctions can be given a psychoanalytic interpretation as displaced sex.

The framework you impose and posit as a given, is your skin ... You forgot, left out of your economy whatever moves across boundaries from one to the other. For you, a limit exists, with some things under, some things over. (EP 16)

Le cadre que tu imposes, que tu fixes comme a priori, c'est ta peau ... Tu as oublié et laissé hors de ton économie ce qui passe de l'un à l'autre sans bords. Pour toi, il y en a l'en-moins et l'en-plus d'une limite. (Pe 19)

This limit must always be retained, because it gives unity, oneness, to reality. It is thus the place of man's dwelling, his property, carefully bounded: 'infinity is an aporia'. The allusions move freely from Heidegger to Marx and Derrida, and are sometimes opaque, but the central purport is clear: Western philosophical thinking with its rigid binaries is a masculinist projection of his sexuality. Since the latter is riddled with the elemental passions of love and strife, longing and fear, so also is the former, even though it is covered by a veneer of dispassionate objectivity (which is only another technology of repression).

To retain – contain the oneness of this whole, you push out to the limit whatever has the greatest denseness, will not be pierced or puts obstacles to any passage through, or, simply, between. You separate within from without, inside from out. You and the rest. (EP 17)

Pour retenir-contenir le un de ce tout, tu repousses vers la limite ce qui a la densité la plus forte, ce qui ne se laisse pas traverser, ce qui fait obstacle au passer outre, ou simplement, entre. Tu sépares l'intérieur de l'extérieur, le dedans du dehors. Toi et le reste. (Pe 21)

The 'rest', the other, is both feared and desired; if it is bounded and controlled then the needs expressed by both the fear and the desire are met. We are back with Lacan's analysis of mastery as an expression of the need to control the (m)other and anything that stands for her, back with the Fort!Da! of Freud's little Ernst.

But we are back also with Ariadne's thread. Unlike Freud and Lacan, Irigaray writes from the perspective of I-woman, the woman who is trying to enable a sexual relationship in which both man and woman are subjects. From this point of view, the 'other' cannot be so neatly separated out: 'Where and what has become of me?' (EP 17). Again using sexual encounter as paradigm, Irigaray suggests that rigid binaries are inadequate: there must also be room for fluidity.

Your skin and mine, yes. But mine goes on touching itself indefinitely, from the inside. Secreting a flow which brings the sides together. From which side does the liquid come? One or the other? Both? So which is one and which is other in that production? Neither? Yet it exists. Where does it come from? From both. It flows between. Not held or held back by a source. The source already rises from the two caressing (EP 15).

Ta peau, la mienne – oui. Mais la mienne se retouche indéfiniment de l'intérieur. Sécrétant un flux qui rapproche les bords. Qui a donné ce liquide? Un bord ou l'autre? Les deux? Alors, qui est l'un ou l'autre dans cette production? Personne? Pourtant elle existe. D'où? Des deux. Ça coule entre. Sans être tenu ou retenu à une source. La source provient déjà des deux qui s'embrassent (Pe 18).

The need and pleasure of fluidity in sexual encounter becomes in Irigaray's representation a model of a logic with room for undecidability, where the absence of boundaries is not a threat. 'Why should the solidity of an erection be more valuable than the fluidity of a flow between two?' (EP 16). Why should woman's sexual experience not be as central a paradigm of philosophical procedure as man's? It would generate very different modes of thinking from those which have dominated Western culture.

What does not pass through skin, between our skins, mingles in our bodies' fluids. Ours. Or at least mine. And as mine are continuous with yours, there is no fixed boundary to impose a definite separation. Except from you. Except by you. When you say: I am, or I exist. Or: you are this. (EP 16)

Ce qui ne passe pas à travers la peau, entre nos peaux, passe entre nos muqueuses. Les Nôtres. Ou, du moins, les miennes. Et, comme celles-ci continuent en celles-là, aucun arrêt n'est jamais fixé qui sépare définitivement. Sauf de toi. Ou par toi. Quand tu dis : je suis, ou j'existe. Ou : tu es cela. (Pe 19)

To put this in terms of the narrative structure of *Elemental Passions*, we find in this chapter I-woman drawing you-man back to his origins, back to an acknowledgement of the mother. In so doing he would also find freedom from his fear of the (m)other, now projected on to I-woman so that she is bounded and confined, unable to become a female subject in her own right. She tries to help him understand fluidity, but to no avail. He continues to assert his mastery, his boundaries: he strikes and wounds her body. And yet she knows that, much as he hurts her, his blows are really directed against himself. What can she do, to help both herself and him to become subjects of mutual encounter?

Four: narrative

As chapter four opens, we find I-woman returning to life after the violent sexual encounter with you-man at the end of chapter three. Her responses are typical of victims of trauma: she detaches herself from reality – the reality of you-man – and enters a world of her own.

Already I am further than the furthest you could imagine. Elsewhere ... I live in a space and time that are not yours ... I flee as soon as you say: come, or stay here now. When you call me to you, into you. Where I take on your consistency. A body-tomb? A shadow, double, reflection, mirage. Of your matter-substance. (EP 19)

Je suis déjà plus loin que le plus loin que tu imagines. Ailleurs ... Je n'habite ni ton espace

Elemental Passions

ni ton temps ... Je fuis dès que tu dis : viens ou reste là ici maintenant. Que tu m'appelles à toi, en toi. Où je deviens à ta consistance. Un corps-tombeau? Et une ombre, un double, un reflet, un mirage. En ta matière-chose. (Pe 23)

Yet even while she distances herself from man's violence, she recognizes both her own reality and the dependence of man upon her. 'I cannot be pinpointed', she says; 'I am stirred everywhere and all the time'. Woman cannot be halted and cannot be forced to stop moving, stop touching. Her fluidity overflows man's categories, whether sexual or philosophical: there are echoes here of Kantian preoccupations with the categories of space and time as structures of the phenomenal. Is Irigaray hinting that women have direct access to the noumenal? Or is she undermining the whole Kantian account? The fluidity that is suggested refers both to the fluids within a womb and to female sexual organs, woman's lips: in philosophical terms as different as could be imagined from the rigid categories of Kant's conceptual grid.

Woman is figured both as the forgotten ground of man's being (the womb, which offers him blood, and thereby food, air and water, the essential elements of life) and also as his reflection. I-woman relates how she made life possible for man by bearing him and surrounding him with love: it is a theme that is already familiar from chapter two, where I-woman used the thread to wind man back to his origin out of his labyrinthine confusion. Here the text is as follows:

Did you not realize? That I lived in silence, making it familiar and fertile for you. Did you not hear? Did you not sense that loving mist surrounding you with its tender nourishing embrace? That invisible presence bearing you, supporting you, there where you set up an opposing illusion of indifference as limit to your own desire. (EP 20)

Tu ne le savais pas? Que j'habitais dans le silence, te le rendant familier et fécond. Tu ne l'entendais pas? Cette nuée aimante qui t'encourait de son enlacement tendrement nourricier, tu ne la percevais pas? Invisible présence te portant, te supportant, là où tu opposais l'illusion de l'indifférence comme limite à ton propre désir. (Pe 24)

We find again the mention of silence and fertility (fécondité) already encountered in the prologue in relation to the need to rethink our relation to our senses and to the elements so that we will become productive in our construction of subjectivity and of sexual difference so that a new world can emerge. It is also a call to allow that difference to have an impact upon our philosophical method.

I-woman urges you-man to let go of his need to be reflected by woman in order to be confirmed in his uniqueness: it is a need so urgent that he feels he will 'die if I withhold myself from your exclusive desire' (EP 19) just as, earlier, he had wanted her to name him with names never spoken before. Rather than collude with this melodrama, woman asks man to acknowledge his mortality. It is indeed true that in giving birth to man, woman has also given him death, since death is the condition of all life. But man has been preoccupied with struggling against death, trying to overcome his mortality; and since he has identified woman with death he struggles also against her. But until he acknowledges both his origin and his mortality he will be alienated from himself and unable to accept either his own subject position or that of woman. So she says,

> I am returning this forgotten property to you: mortal. If you should die from this discovery, then you had not yet begun to be born. And dying from still carrying yourself, you would have found death in me. (EP 20)

> Je te redonne cette propriété oubliée : mortel. Si tu meurs de cette découverte, encore tu n'avais commencé à naître. Et, mourant de te porter plus longtemps, tu aurais trouvé la mort en moi. (Pe 25)

It is as if man thought that if only he had not been born of woman, if only he were independent of the body and matter and the elemental passions, then he would not be mortal. But of course those are the very conditions of life: without them he would not be a self at all.

The history of Western philosophy can be read as the attempts of man to refuse his mortality. We saw in Chapter 1 how far Parmenides' philosophy can provide the means for man to posit himself as immortal, unchanging, and 'forget' his mortality and the conditions of ordinary existence and experience in his ascent to the realm of logic. Yet this ascent occurred at the peril of a female subject within philosophy. It was at the expense of actual women in Western culture; and also at the expense of the fruitfulness possible when fluidity as well as rigidity is allowed a place in the philosophical imagination. This is why I-woman in *Elemental Passions* urges you-man to come back from his (Parmenidean) immortal heights and to incorporate within philosophy the (Empedoclean) material conditions of existence. Then he will be able to give up 'Truth' with a capital 'T' and return to truth, the reality of his own subject position. He will also be able to return to woman, seeing her not in terms of his womb, tomb and mirror but as a subject in her own right with whom a loving encounter is possible. And he will find that even death itself is less horrifying when it is acknowledged as a natural end of life.

> Take back this horizon: mortal, and consider that Truth has always been a lying mask for your truth. Death's most terrible aspect lies in the charades you have invented to separate it from you. And from me. (EP 20)

> Reprends cet horizon : mortel, et pense que la Vérité a toujours été le masque menteur de ta vérité. Ce que la mort a de plus horrible, ce sont les parades que tu as inventées pour t'en séparer. M'en séparer. (Pe 25)

There is here a significant reversal. In the previous chapter man has been violent towards woman, made her bleed out of the force of his need for her to reflect him. At the same time he has felt as though he would die if she withheld herself. Now, when she confronts him with his mortality, it seems that he is the one who is bleeding, and is terrified, thinking that blood means death. But woman suggests that the opposite is the case: bleeding is a sign of life, an

Elemental Passions

alternative to the bloodless artificiality of his pretence of immortality. By leading him back to his origin, his birth and his mortality, she has invited him to life and mutual relationship based on reality, not pretence.

> Do you bleed? Could it be that you are coming back to life? That this is your own way back? An end to that veneer of insensitivity which kept you captive? (EP 20–1)

> Tu saignes? Peut-être reviens-tu à la vie? Tel serait, pour toi, le chemin du retour? La fin de cette surface d'insensibilité qui te retenait captif? (Pe 25)

If man is able to respond to woman's challenging invitation, a whole new world of creative possibilities opens up, both philosophically and psychosexually. But can he do so?

Five: narrative

Chapter five develops further the themes of the two previous chapters, namely man's struggle with his fear of death, the notions of male violence and appropriation, and female resistance and movement. It reaches a breakthrough in the relation between man and woman.

The chapter begins with I-woman speaking tenderly to you-man, whom she calls her 'child of night'. He is inconsolable, filled with a 'bottomless anguish'. Man has been asked to take account of woman's womb, 'this first fleshly dwelling', the origin of his being, and to accept that he, like woman, is mortal. However, he struggles against this awareness, using oceans of ink, 'black tears', to write philosophical systems that try to deny mortality, rather than accepting mortality as a condition of being alive at all. Moreover he continues to behave violently towards woman. The same words are used as in chapter three: man pummels (cognes) and wounds (blesses) woman's living body (corps vivant) (EP 18 and 23/Pe 21 and 27). He continues to impose his framework (cadre) onto woman, enclosing her and shutting her away from the horizon of her own becoming.

In Irigaray's representation of man's behaviour there are pointers both towards actual marriage customs in Western culture, in which women are often confined to the home and to serving their husband's needs rather than their own, and also towards philosophical metaphors of framework, dwelling and property, especially as found in Heidegger and Marx.

> You supplant that horizon by the home and its institutions. Instead of ties which are always developing, you want fixed bonds. You only encounter proximity when it is framed by property. (EP 24)

> Cet horizon, tu y suppléés par la maison et ses institutions. Au lieu d'alliages toujours en devenir, tu veux des alliances définitives. Le proche, tu ne le rencontres que cadré dans le propre. (Pe 28)

Man's imposition of his framework can be understood as resulting from his need to impose his power onto woman and control her as the 'other', metonymically his origin and his death. It can take the form of an institutionalized relationship such as a marriage, or a fixed living space such as a family home. The earth too is appropriated and marked by man's frame. It is divided up. Man establishes himself as the proprietor of both the earth and the female body.

Man's frame, which can be interpreted in multiple ways – as his penis, his phallus, his language, his logic and his categories of space-time – seems indispensible to him. Yet it is ultimately an empty structure if it does not allow for living and developing subjects to exist. Ironically, although it is death against which man is struggling, his strategies of framing and control extinguish life, and thereby bring about precisely that which he most fears.

> Could it be that what you have is just the frame, not the property? Not a bond with the earth but merely this fence that you set up, implant wherever you can? You mark out boundaries, draw lines, surround, enclose. Excising, cutting out ... What remains is an empty frame. You cling to it, dead. (EP 24–5)

> De la propriété, n'aurais-tu que le cadre? De rapport à la terre, seulement cette clôture que tu poses, implantes, où tu peux? Tu fais des lignes, tires des traits, entoures, engrillages, enceintes. Par coupures, tranchant ... Reste – un cadre vide. Tu t'y retiens, mort. (Pe 29)

This emptiness and death-dealing, I-woman says, is the doing of you-man. He clings to his frame as a skeleton, as if it will secure his subjectivity: 'You need a frame as you need bones, a skeleton, clothes, bandages to hold you together' (*Tu as nécessité d'un cadre comme d'une ossature, d'un squelette, de vêtements, bandages, où te tenir ensemble*) (EP 25/Pe 29). Woman, however, is stifled and cannot live as a subject whilst enclosed by man's proprietal boundaries, man's categories of thought and meaning: she 'freezes and is paralysed' by them. An impasse is reached.

You-man loves I-woman. That is not in doubt. But his love is characterized as a love that appropriates and confines the other. I-woman proposes an alternative, a love that allows each their 'living becoming' (*devenir vivant*).

> Love can be the becoming which appropriates the other for itself by consuming it, introjecting it into itself, to the point where the other disappears. Or love can be the motor of becoming, allowing both the one and the other to grow. (EP 27)

> L'amour est le devenir qui s'approprie l'autre en le consommant, en l'introjectant en soi-même, jusqu'à sa disparition. Ou l'amour est le moteur du devenir qui laisse l'un et l'autre à leur croissance. (Pe 32)

These two forms of love may look the same; but whereas one love is premised on a mutual relationship between subjects who respect one another, the other tries to force the beloved into being an object for his own desires, whether sexual, or for security or domesticity, or as a reflection of his own ego, and not for her own development as a subject. Again Irigaray represents this in terms of the fluidity of sexual encounter.

> The only difference between the love which flows through the envelope-walls of skin or mucous fluids and the love which appropriates for itself in and by the same, lies in the 'through' which allows each one their living becoming. (EP 27)

> Entre l'amour coulant à travers les parois-enveloppes des peaux ou muqueuses et l'amour s'appropriant dans et par le même, il n'y a de différence que le à travers qui laisse à chacun son devenir vivant. (Pe 32)

For the love that includes this all-important 'through', this rejection of rigid boundaries and mechanisms of control, 'two lives should embrace and fertilise each other, without either being a fixed goal for the other' (Que deux vies s'embrassent et se fécondent l'une l'autre, sans fin arrêtée en l'un ou en l'autre) (EP 27 / Pe 33). It is clear from the French text that the embrace from chapter three is recalled, together with the fertilization mentioned in the prologue. This fertilization accompanied the promise of a new way of living. The embrace indicated a new way of relating to each other which also encompasses new forms of knowing and living. The words 'sans fin arrêtée', literally translated 'without final halt' or more freely 'without fixed goal', are recurrently used in Elemental Passions in the context of female sexuality and the development of female subjectivity. They exemplify fluidity and change without boundaries, as in the prologue where the mingling of breath and air was described as diffusion without limits (diffusion sans ârret).

A crucial feature of a love which allows becoming is that it respects and accommodates difference. Reading Irigaray's text as narrative, it seems that there is a breakthrough. You-man has responded to I-woman's invitation to a mutually empowering love rather than a love which controls and consumes.

> I see you in this way and you see me. At last I see myself when I see you in this difference which means that your existence can never be appropriated by me. (EP 28)

> Ainsi je te vois et tu me vois. Je me vois enfin de te voir dans cette différence qui fait que ton existence est à jamais inappropriable par moi. (Pe 33)

This does not magically make everything easy: difference can be frightening, like 'an abyss'. But you-man should be careful not to fall back into his old ways of projecting fear and fault on to I-woman. The abyss is not to be identified with her: 'not in me but in our difference lies the abyss' (EP 28). Moreover, love that is premised on freedom and respect rather than control is always a risk.

> We can never be sure of bridging the gap between us. But that is our adventure. Without this peril there is no us. If you turn it into a guarantee, you separate us. (EP 28)

> Nous ne sommes jamais assurés de franchir le pas entre nous. Mais cette aventure est la nôtre. Pas de nous, sans ce péril. Si tu me laisses en gage, tu nous sépares. (Pe 33)

One of the time-honoured tactics of the masculinist Western philosophical tradition is to look to God or to religion as a way of mitigating the risk represented by human freedom and natural contingency. Irigaray argues, however, that if God is conceived of as 'difference extrapolated to infinity' and man as simply the finite version of this God, made in God's image, then this effectively reduces all human difference to relative sameness. Humans could be 'distinguished only as more or less'; infinite difference would be located only in inaccessible transcendence (EP 28). This would eliminate the risk, but at the price of eliminating also all possibility of mutual relationship and fecundity between subjects who are different, different not only in degree but in kind: sexually different subjects.[1]

The refusal to allow an appeal to divinity as a means of mitigating the risk of difference is a hint towards the philosophical level of interpreting this chapter. A further hint comes with Irigaray's comment that if difference is not valued then the copula could no longer come into action. The places of affection become fixed according to definite attributes and immutable configurations (EP 28). The copula, in philosophical grammar, is the word that binds subject and predicate together: 's is p'. It immediately calls to mind the Aristotelian 'Laws of Logic' we discussed in Chapter 1: the Law of Identity (A is A), the Law of Non-Contradiction (A is not not-A), and the Law of Excluded Middle (Either A or not-A). It points, therefore, to binary logic with its rigid distinctions.

But of course 'copula' carries close associations with 'copulate'; and, as before, the sexual language is explicit, of lips and penis. In Irigaray's view, female sexuality has been defined in relation to man, so that, for example, woman serves as an instrument for male orgasm. Man is subject, woman (h)is object. Irigaray criticizes this view of female sexuality: 'my lips could never be reduced to subject or object, instrument of use or function' (EP 29) ([mes lèvres] *ne se laisseraient pas réduire en sujet ou objet, ni instrument d'utilité, d'usage* (Pe 35)). As we have seen, however, for Irigaray the sexual is a paradigm for the philosophical; and the refusal to allow female sexuality to be reduced to an instrument for male use can be read as a refusal to allow the hegemony of the philosophical logic of the copula.

In her earlier book *Speculum*, Irigaray had discussed the copula with reference to Descartes. The Cartesian subject erects himself through his rigid methodical doubting until he is left only with his own subjectivity: 'I think, therefore I exist'. Everything else is generated out of this self-thinking self. Ultimately, the 'I' is the foundation of his knowledge and of his subjectivity. He searches for himself, and reflects upon himself as if in a mirror, and in that reflection is coupled with himself. For Irigaray, such a copula disregards the material ground of his being, his embodiment and his relation to his mother. Speaking from the position of the Cartesian 'I' and alluding to Lacanian psychoanalytic theory, Irigaray writes,

I shall remain in ignorance of the fact that, in this embrace of truth that I covet above all else, I am seeking, in simplest terms, to be united with *an image in a mirror*. This is how I am. At last alone, copula. I-me, coupled together in an embrace (SpE 189–90; cf. Braidotti 1991: 253–5)

Et m'aura laissé dans l'ignorance que, dans cet embrassement de la vérité que je convoite par-dessus tout, c'est à l'irréductible d'une *image en miroir* que je tente de me conjoindre. Ainsi suis-je. Enfin seul, copule. Je-moi réunis en un accouplement (SpF 237)

---

[1] The question of why sexual difference should take priority over all other sorts of difference – race, age, ability, sexual orientation, and so on – here becomes insistent. We shall return to it in Chapter 6.

The copula as used in this passage is thus indicative of all that is misguided in the masculinist philosophical and psychoanalytic perspective.

In *Elemental Passions*, however, the copula seems also to be used more positively, with allusions not only to the Cartesian cogito but also to Aristotle's teaching of actuality and potentiality. Whereas in *Speculum* the copula locked the self-reflective subject in his own embrace, in *Elemental Passions* the copula unites two sexually different subjects: 'always at least two, and never the same' (*toujours au moins deux, jamais les mêmes*) (EP 29 / Pe 34). In such uniting, there is continuous potentiality, an undoing of any privileged configuration in favour of 'a becoming which keeps potentiality and action in disequilibrium. Potentiality in action, never ceasing' (Ibid.). There is room for change and movement, fluidity without fixed categories; for 'act that is never finished', in the Empedoclean cycles of generation and disintegration of the universe.

If this reading is correct, then, it is a significant further step in showing what a logic that allows room for fluidity is like. Irigaray protests against binaries and tries to destabilize them, yet at the same time she insists on difference – paradigmatically sexual difference – which she often refers to as difference between two. It is sometimes puzzling what she means by this: after all, what is the difference between binaries and 'difference between two'? Is the latter not just another binary? Is Irigaray not insisting in one breath upon the very thing that she rejects in the next?

The answer to this question shows the importance of fluidity for her thinking. Whereas binaries are defined strictly in terms of each other – not-A is precisely what A is not, neither more nor less – difference between two allows for all manner of variation and change, 'reserve, excess, source of movement' (EP 29). The 'other' is not defined in terms of the one; it is not the other of the same, but is genuinely different, in a difference which is allowed to grow, to become. There is continuous movement of potentiality, in act that 'is never finished. It cannot be constituted into a whole', a One, in opposition to which the other must be defined. Irigaray is using the paradigm of sexual difference as a real-life example of Derridean *différance*, where the 'truth' is continually different/deferred in endless fecund movement and interpretation. In further chapters we will see more of what the idea of fluidity brings to philosophical logic, but this emphasis on difference as 'reserve, excess, source of movement' is central.[2]

This chapter, then, can be read as a significant advance, both in her philosophical project and in terms of the narrative. I-woman shows you-man how his violence is a product of his fear, and invites him instead to take the risk of love, love which does not devour but which respects and cherishes mutual difference.

---

[2] It must be said, however, that Irigaray's insistence on the heterosexual couple as paradigmatic and normative of difference often appears to fall back into the same rigid binary logic from which she is trying to escape, leaving little room for other sorts of difference. We will consider this further in Chapter 6.

Interpretative synopsis of *Elemental Passions*

At the end of the chapter it seems that you-man is taking the risk, willing to let go of rigidity for fluid exchanges. I-woman muses: 'Our exchanges? An engendering through rare and always infinite fortune' (*Nos échanges? Un engendrement dont la chance serait rare, et toujours infinie*) (EP 29 / Pe 35).

At the end of chapter five the narrative makes way for two non-narrative chapters.

Six: interlude 1: image of a flower

In chapter six the narrative is interrupted by an interlude. It starts with a question that introduces its theme:

Do you make me become a flower? Then why do you fear that this flower will be taken from you, since it is you who gives it birth? Before you, there was the nurture of the plant. The blossoming of the flower belongs to you. (EP 31)

Tu me fais devenir fleur? Alors que crains-tu que cette fleur te soit enlevée, puisqu'elle naît par toi? Avant toi, le nourrissage de la plante. L'éclosion de la fleur te revient. (Pe 37)

Woman's body is likened to a plant; the flower is her sexuality. In chapter five we will consider more fully Irigaray's use of the flower as an image; so we will restrict ourselves here to the use of the image in relation to the story of I-woman and you-man and its philosophical implications.

At the end of chapter five I-woman and you-man have come together. But now it seems that man's relation to the flower is that he wishes her to flower just for him – a variation on his earlier desire for woman to reflect him through unique words. For him the open flower becomes an offered flower, as the French play on words indicates: 'La fleur ouverte: la fleur offerte' (Pe 37). Woman offers herself by opening herself. But if man's unique reflection is to be ensured, then this must be just for him; she must never be open in any other context. 'Do you want the flower to open only once?' (*Veux-tu la fleur une seule fois ouverte?*) (EP 31 / Pe 38). If it is only in relation to him that woman is permitted to flower, and not of herself or for her own sake, then once again woman becomes a means to man's achieving his own subjectivity while woman's becoming a subject would be halted. 'Its becoming would be arrested ... Growth suspended in ecstasy, the ideal flowering for you' (*Son devenir serait arrêté ... Croissance extasiée dans cette floraison idéale pour toi*) (EP 32 / Pe 38).

Man who looks at woman is a theme that recurs throughout this chapter. His gaze is an objectifying gaze, a look that appropriates woman's beauty and truth for himself and thereby prevents her from developing and from becoming a female subject. I-woman asks whether his gaze reduces her to

the projection of your history? The flower would grow and blossom simply to let you gaze at yourself and find your double in it? Simply to let you swoon in ecstasy as you contemplate this extrapolated reflection of yourself. (EP 32)

> Projection de ton histoire? La fleur pousserait et s'épanouirait uniquement pour que tu puisses t'y regarder, t'y redoubler. T'y extasier dans cette contemplation extrapolée de toi. (Pe 39)

The importance of the gaze in this chapter is a reminder of psychoanalytic theory of female sexuality. For Freud, as we discussed in Chapter 2, the fact that women's genitalia are not visible in the same way as are men's led him to his idea of the Oedipal stage and the castration complex. Woman is thought of as a hole, an empty nothing; and a little boy grows into a man because he is frightened that if he identifies with his mother he will be castrated and will become a nothing like his mother. Similarly in Lacan woman is emptiness, a lack, and knows nothing of her own sexuality and therefore cannot discuss it. Man is so preoccupied with his objectifying gaze that he does not take the trouble to listen to the actual woman, and then he mistakes his refusal to listen for the idea that she has nothing to say.

As far as man is concerned, the flower exists exclusively for him. However, a counter-current also runs through this chapter. Hidden from man's gaze, the flower's roots touch within the earth. Both the continual touching of its roots and of its petals indicate that the flower has her own subjectivity to develop, away from man's penetrating gaze. I-woman has her own potential to flower, her own connection to the four elements and their passions: why should she abandon them to become the precise sort of flower which you-man would find satisfying to his gaze?

> I also have roots and from them I could flower. Earth, water, air and fire are my birthright too. Why abandon them to let you appropriate them and give them back to me. Why seek ecstasy in your world when I already live elsewhere. Why spread my wings only in your sunlight, your sky, only as your air and your light permit? Before I knew you, already I was a flower. Must I forget that, to become your flower? (EP 34)

> J'ai aussi des racines à partir desquelles je puis fleurir. La terre, l'eau, l'air, le feu, sont aussi mon partage. Pourquoi les quitter pour que tu me les redonnes, appropriés par toi. Pourquoi m'extasier dans ton monde alors que, déjà, je vis ailleurs. Pourquoi ne me déployer qu'à ton soleil, dans ton ciel, selon ton air et ta lumière? Avant de te connaître, déjà j'étais fleur. Faut-il que je l'oublie pour devenir ta fleur? (Pe 41)

Interspersed in this meditation are motifs of earth and air, darkness and light, matter and intellect. Man treats woman as body, as womb, the darkness of his light, his tomb:

> I have become your exile. While you fall back, heavily, into matter. You sleep, in the dark. Submerged in thick black night. Drowned in a massive abyss. I am imprisoned in a celestial flight, you are buried under ground. (EP 36)

> Je suis devenue ton exil. Tandis que, lourdement, tu es retombé dans la matière. Tu dors, sans lumière. Immergé dans une nuit épaisse et noire. Noyé dans un abîme massif. Je suis enclose dans un survol céleste, tu es enfouie sous la terre. (Pe 43)

Interpretative synopsis of *Elemental Passions*

Philosophically, the point is that if intellect is so completely severed from the material elements, then matter, body, the earth will become foreign territory, the place of exile. Allusions and images are piled on top of each other in this Interlude: their meaning becomes clearer when they are taken in conjunction with those of the following chapter.

Seven: meditation 1: the light of reason

Chapter seven presents a meditation on the element of fire. It is full of references to flame, the sun, the sky, the clear horizon, flashes of lightning; and their contrasts: night, darkness, shadowy enclosure. There are multiple interwoven allusions to figures of myth and history: Icarus who made wings of wax which melted when he flew too near the sun; Narcissus, who drowned when he fell into a pool that reflected his own face; Heidegger, whose clear horizon may bring the flash of disclosure of Being. All of these strands (and many more) would be well worth tracing. To do so, however, would be a long and complex process which would distract from the theme which we have chosen to pursue through *Elemental Passions*: the becoming of woman as a sexually different subject as a paradigm for the development of a philosophical logic in which fluidity as well as stability has a place.

We have therefore chosen to follow only one strand of the rich web of allusions in this chapter, those which have resonances with Plato's cave allegory, a reading of which Irigaray had already presented in *Speculum*. Plato's narrative of the cave is in Book 7 of the *Republic*. Socrates asks his listeners to imagine that there are men who live in a cave which slopes downward, under the ground. Their bodies are shackled in such a way that they cannot move their heads but have to look straight ahead, to the back wall of the cave. Behind them, up the slope, burns a fire, the only source of light in the darkness of the cave. Between the fire and the men tied in the cave, other men walk on a road which passes through the cave. A small wall has been erected to separate the men on the road from the rest of the cave. The passers-by carry 'all sorts of artefacts, human statuettes and animal models carved in stone and wood' and hold these just above the small wall. These figures, projected by the fire from behind, become shadows on the back wall of the cave (Plato 1994: 241).

Who sees the true world in this situation? Socrates asks. The prisoners who are tied in one position think they do, since this is their whole experience, but they are mistaken. They see only shadows, and take it for reality. If one of them were to be led up the cave and then out into the light, what would his reaction be? Initially, he would be reluctant to get up and walk away from the only world he knew. Once outside, he would at first be blinded by sunlight. Only slowly would he be able to see properly. However, once he was used to the real world, he would not want to go back into the cave except to lead his fellow prisoners into daylight too.

In Plato's allegory, the cave symbolizes the material world of ordinary experience, including the physical body: the same world that Parmenides left behind him as unreality, mere appearance. The journey upwards to the surface of the earth and into the light of the sun symbolizes the philosopher's journey away from mere appearance in which ordinary people are bound and into the realm of true knowledge. The sun represents the source of all light and life, all knowledge and reality. Just as the prisoner freed from the cave does not want to return to it, so the philosopher does not want to return from the realm of knowledge, and descends only to teach his fellow mortals.

In *Speculum*, Irigaray gives a reading of Plato's myth of the cave which reveals its implicit gender connotations. The cave – in Plato's account the material world and the body – can be likened to the womb, and the prisoner's ascent through its narrow passage to birth. Seen in this way, the cave narrative describes not only biological birth but also a 'second birth' into philosophy. Only by leaving the womb, the body, woman, behind can a philosopher escape darkness and imprisonment and attain the realm of knowledge (SpE 243f.). Only by recognizing the primacy of light – the intellect – will he be able to gaze upon reality. Just as we have noted in *Elemental Passions*, so already in *Speculum* Irigaray challenges this concept of reason as light and the primacy for philosophy of the visual, the male gaze.[3] In *Elemental Passions* she asks:

Why should we not be illuminated by the night of our *jouissance*? ... For sight is no longer our only guide. Seeing within an expanse which is dazzling and palpable, odorous and audible. A night of sensation where everything lives together, permitting co-existence without violence. Before the brutal slash of discrimination assigns each their place. Already trapped in the form of a judgement which obstructs the mutual embracing of relationship ... An overarching vision exiled from feeling. (EP 37–8)

Pourquoi ce qui nous éclaire ne serait-il la nuit de notre jouissance? ... Le visuel n'étant plus notre seul guide. Voyant dans une nappe étincelante et palpable, odorante et audible. Nuit du ressentir où tout cohabite dans un laisser être sans violence. Avant le tranché brutal d'une discrimination qui assigne à chacun son milieu. Déjà pris dans la forme d'un jugement, qui fait obstacle à l'embrassement réciproque dans le rapport ... Survol d'une vision qui s'expulse du sentir. (Pe 46)

Of the position of the prisoners in the cave, Irigaray remarks in *Speculum* that the scene of representation can take place only when 'the face, the figure and the gaze' are forced into one direction (SpE 260). This results in a thinking of linearity: 'Chains, lines, perspectives oriented straight ahead – all maintain the illusion of constant motion in one direction. Forward ... A phallic direction, a phallic line, a phallic time, backs turned on origin' (SpE 245). Even when the prisoner is released from the cave, he maintains his linearity; reality is expressed and organized 'into a hierarchy' (EP 38). Irigaray attempts to disrupt this linearity, this self-protective

---

[3] Martin Jay comments that Irigaray's suspicion of the gaze is an example of a more widespread 'antivisual attitude' within French twentieth-century thought (Jay 1993: 15, 493–542).

organisation. In Elemental Passions she suggests that much is lost when mutuality is sacrificed to hierarchy, when a quest for intellectual mastery replaces the mystery and delight of 'sun-filled mornings': 'But such grace is too dazzling for you. You separate yourselves from it. Pushing the fire far away and keeping the measured clarity' (Mais cette grâce est trop éblouissante pour vous. Vous vous en séparez. Renvoyant le feu au loin et gardant la clarté mesurée) (EP 41 / Pe 51). The fire, here, and the tangible are similar in their purport to fluidity: all of them are metaphors that work against rigidity, linearity and the gaze. They suggest the four elements, the material, rather than disembodied intellect.

In language reminiscent of *Speculum*, Irigaray here suggests that even when they come out of the cave, Plato's prisoners have to impose binary categories of thought in order to cope with reality. They divide it up into manageable chunks.

The sun in their eyes seemed unbearable. It was too much ... That light which floods out in such a burning stream was making them lose their way. A separation had to be imposed ... They needed limits now so they could distinguish outlines, identify them, move them closer together or further apart, go from the one to the other without confusing them. (EP 40–1)

Le soleil dans leurs yeux sembla intolérable. C'était trop ... Cette lumière qui inonde d'un flux aussi brûlant leur faisait perdre leur chemin. Il fallait séparer ... Il leur fallait maintenant des limites pour percevoir les contours, les identifier, les rapprocher ou éloigner, se diriger de l'un à l'autre sans mélange. (Pe 50)

They need dichotomies, categories, in order to get a grip on the situation, to exert control. Irigaray's point is not that categories of thought should not exist. They have an important place. But when categories are fixed and rigid, when there is no room for fluidity and movement, then the result is impoverishment. In her paradigm, fixed categories have been instrumental in thinking about subjectivity in terms of 'one and not-one', male and not-male. But this has resulted in the oppression of the not-one, woman: she has not been permitted to develop a subject position in her own right. Extending this paradigm, the rigid categories of the intellect have resulted in the exclusion of all that was seen as its other: the body, the earth, the elements, the passions. Sight is unduly privileged over other senses in the construction of knowledge.

And, instead of moving inside that superabundance given to them, and letting themselves be directed by it without fear or a desire to seize hold, they began by wanting to understand – grasp the reason, the cause and the provenance. (EP 41)

Et, au lieu de se mouvoir dans cette surabondance reçue et de ce aussi agir par elle sans peur ni volonté d'accaparement, ils commençaient par vouloir comprendre – saisir la raison, la cause, la provenance. (Pe 50)

Thus the world is neatly organized; its contents made safe and predictable. Desires are met through technologies of control, and fear is kept at bay. And the price? The wonder and mystery of the world: *jouissance*.

Elemental Passions

Eight: narrative: backlash

The narrative picks up again in chapter eight. At the end of chapter five, before the meditation on flower and on light, I-woman and you-man had seemed to arrive at a breakthrough in which they could acknowledge their sexual difference and develop into subjects through love and mutual respect. Indeed it would be plausible to suppose that it was this breakthrough which opened up the possibility for the meditations of chapters six and seven. But the breakthrough is not sustained. Contrary to the reader's expectations, man imposes his grid of time and space, his categories of control, on to woman again. He positions her according to his needs. She says,

What you intend for me is the place which is appropriate for the need you have of me. What you reveal to me is the place where you have positioned me, so that I remain available for your needs. (EP 47)

Tu me destines la place qui convient à la nécessité que tu as de moi. Tu me découvres la place où tu m'as fixée pour que je demeure à portée de tes nécessités. (Pe 57)

The power relation between man and woman has reverted from mutuality to male dominance so that once again man determines the rules. Man meets woman where he wants to and as he wants to.

And you meet me only in the space that you have opened up for yourself. You never meet me except as your creature – within the horizon of your world. Within the circle of your becoming. (EP 47)

Et tu ne me rencontres que dans l'espace que tu t'es ouvert. Tu ne me rencontres jamais que comme ta créature – au sein de l'horizon de ton monde. Du cercle de ton devenir. (Pe 57–8)

Once again the difference between man and woman is not acknowledged by man as mutual difference deserving respect; rather he sees it as an opposition, constructing woman as his other. The power balance is such that man decides what woman's subjectivity is to be, how her subjectivity should be developed.

One of the ways in which he does this is by positioning her in a space – a dwelling or a domestic establishment – in which she is kept while he comes and goes as he chooses. Repeatedly, she is the one who is left, the one who is expected to be the place holder for him, hold his place for him.

This time, you have left. Once again. Once more. Once, endlessly. The pain of an interminable wrenching begins once more to seep into the darkest depths of my flesh. Once again it will be rent, fissured, torn asunder, perhaps destroyed. (EP 49)

Cette fois-ci, tu es parti. Une fois encore. Une fois de plus. Une fois, sans fin. La douleur d'un arrachement interminable va recommencer à sourdre au plus profond du plus obscur de ma chair. Ça va encore craquer, se fissurer, se déchirer, s'effondrer peut-être. (Pe 59)

I-woman is not allowed a subject position for herself; 'in the place where my being should take place there is at present nothingness'. Indeed it could become

Interpretative synopsis of *Elemental Passions*

even worse: 'if I do not take care, I am reduced to the state of object-utensil' (EP 50). And yet, precisely because of this, she is made to be utterly dependent upon man, so that if he left her permanently it would not mean freedom for her. It would mean disaster: disaster for her, but disaster for him as well, because he finds his own subject position by her mirroring of it to him.

> If you go away, how can ruin be averted? Your ruin? And where should I be when you live somewhere else? Pure transparency? Air without a horizon, matter without limits, a face without an outline? (EP 49)
>
> Si tu t'en vas, comment éviter la ruine? Ta ruine? Et où faut-il que je sois quand tu demeures ailleurs? Pure transparence? Air sans horizon, matière sans bords, visage sans contours? (Pe 60)

The theme of woman being confined by man's control runs through the whole chapter. Woman finds that she cannot speak 'gagged by your discourse' and that she cannot move. Complex and allusive as Irigaray's writings are, there are here (besides the obvious sexual meanings) indications of the gendered economic and political structures of Western culture, of a Lacanian psychoanalytic account of language, and of the gender assumptions of philosophy and religion. Man pretends that the source of his being is within himself, or extrapolated to God, the absolute or the Idea. Man positions himself as limitless, powerful and immortal just as we had seen him do in chapters three and five before the breakthrough. Once again, 'he does not acknowledge his source of life' (EP 64): the womb, the mother, the woman, the whole complex web of life previously illustrated by the figure of Ariadne. There is here considerable play on the associations between mother, matter, mother-nature, mother earth and their traditional binary opposites: father (God), form or intellect, culture, heaven or air/spirit, once again moving among the linked chain of opposites first set out by Pythagoras. The 'female' side of this table is severely restricted: in the narrative of sexual encounter it is presented as almost lethal. Within man's categories of thought woman cannot become a subject, can hardly move. Yet only if she keeps moving will she stay alive. But her movements remain unnoticed by man.

> While I keep moving in my repose. You cannot understand ... The way I move being too imperceptible for you. Experiencing as inertia what you cannot perceive, you believe you have to guide my destiny. Thinking as death the most living part of life. (EP 55–6)
>
> Moi, je reste mobile dans le repos. Tu ne peux comprendre ... La façon dont je me meus étant trop imperceptible pour toi. Eprouvant comme inertie ce qui ne t'apparaît pas, tu crois avoir à diriger mon destin. Pensant comme mort le plus vivant de la vie. (Pe 67–8)

The word 'imperceptible' occurs frequently in *Elemental Passions*. It describes woman's attempts to develop towards subjectivity, which remain unnoticed by man because they do not fit within his frame of reference.

The reader is left with a sense of sadness and disappointment. The narrative has returned to the situation that we saw in chapters two and three. There, woman speaks but is not heard. In this chapter she moves but is not noticed, and, as in chapter three, she barely survives.

Nine: narrative: breakthrough II

Even more surprising is the turn of events in chapter nine, which opens with you-man and I-woman in an embrace.

> You have come back inside me. Your affection has come back inside me ... And I guard you, I regard you without ever becoming you ... Not only have you returned to me, you have turned in to me. And I have turned in to you. (EP 57)

> Tu es retourné en moi. Ton affection est retournée en moi ... Et je te garde, je te regarde, sans jamais devenir toi ... Tu n'est pas seulement retourné en moi, tu es encore tourné en moi. Et je suis tournée en toi. (Pe 69)

Yet this turn/return, which the French play on words makes visible, is not the appropriation of the woman by the man which had been such a problem before. In the coming together of sexually different bodies which the first half of this chapter celebrates, the old notion of the female body as an instrument and object for man has become obsolete. This is poetically described as follows:

> If, in affecting you, I affect myself, the body-instrument opposition no longer holds. For the instrument which I am in order to affect you is itself affected as a body, just as your body, which I affect, is an instrument which affects me. (EP 58)

> Si, t'affectant, je m'affecte, l'opposition corps-instrument ne vaut plus. Car l'instrument que je suis pour t'affecter s'en trouve affecté comme corps, de même que ton corps que j'affecte est instrument de m'affecter. (Pe 70)

Woman's body is more than man's object; the body cannot be perceived as an instrument. In affecting woman, man's body is reciprocally affected; therefore neither woman nor man is understood any longer in a one-dimensional way. Similarly the idea that the female body is owned or controlled by the man is gone. It is replaced by mutuality, fluidity.

> I caress you, you caress me, without unity – neither yours, nor mine, nor ours. The envelope, which separates and divides us, fades away. Instead of a solid enclosure, it becomes fluid: which is far from nothing. This does not mean that we are merged. But our relationship to place, which maintained our hierarchical difference, takes on different properties. (EP 59–60)

> Je te caresse, tu me caresses, sans unité – ni de toi, ni de moi, ni de nous. L'enveloppe, qui nous sépare et nous divise, se subtilise. De clôture solide, elle devient fluide : ce qui n'est pas dire rien. Nous ne nous confondons pas pour autant. Mais le rapport au lieu, qui nous maintenait hiérarchiquement différents, change de propriétés. (Pe 72)

The mutuality that is thus enjoyed overcomes rigid binaries in the overflow of creative pleasure, enabling a joyous opening to one another. The subject position

Interpretative synopsis of *Elemental Passions*

of each is acknowledged and respected by the other, so that their differences become fecund.

In the second half of this chapter I-woman looks back and recalls the situation before she became a subject. It can be read as a summary of how things were before the breakthrough. She alludes to Plato's philosophy of matter and form, and philosophical tradition built on it (including Kant and his categories, and Marx's theory of property and production):

> You had form, I was matter for you. You were seeking the earth, taking pleasure in being back on your ground, in burying yourself in it, in using your labour as a measure of your work, your possession, your production. (EP 60)

> Tu avais la forme, je te servais de matière. Tu recherchais la terre, jouissant de retrouver ton sol, de t'y enfouir, de mesurer, par tes labours, ton travail, ta possession, ta production. (Pe 73)

She alludes to psychoanalytic theory, emphasizing that she did not have an existence other than as man's mirror or double. Again the paradigm is overtly sexual, as it is in Lacanian theory: woman's function was to serve as a mirror for man's reflection. She assisted man in his pleasure, forgetting that she too had desires. She was the material ground upon which his erections could stand; the lack upon which his desires could be premised; the hollow place where he could be fulfilled. But in all this she was only a projection for his wants, an 'unheard song' (EP 61).

The summary of this past state makes sad reading, and one might wonder why, if a genuine breakthrough has occurred, it is necessary to go over all the negative history yet again. Why not leave it behind and celebrate the present? Perhaps Irigaray's point is that it is only when woman is finally able to develop a subject position in a relationship of mutuality and respect that she is able to acknowledge and articulate the full difficulty of her previous state. Only when a philosophy that admits of fluidity begins to develop can we see the impoverishment imposed on our thinking by a logic that restricts itself to rigid binaries.

Elemental Passions could have ended at this point. The struggle between man and woman has been described, their differences recognized and acknowledged. The promise of the prologue has been fulfilled: the recognition of their sexual difference means that both woman and man can become subjects. Dichotomies of hierarchical opposites have become undone and a new way of thinking, loving and living has been opened up. Nothing more needs to be said.

Nothing more? It is true that it has been established that woman's becoming can only take place starting from the recognition of sexual difference. It is also true that the narrative chapters which remain do not add anything new but revisit themes from chapters two to nine, though in a somewhat different light. However, the book does not end at this point. A reason for this could be that the function of the narrative has been to open man (and the reader) up to the woman's voice, so that the remaining narrative chapters enable the same things to be heard, but more distinctly. This clarity is even sharper in the two non-narrative chapters which immediately follow the breakthrough of chapter nine. Moreover, in the remaining chapters the philosophical concepts which have been hinted at in the previous account are given greater prominence, explored from the perspective of a developing female subject. It becomes clear that her development will challenge and change the rigid categories of man's philosophy.

Ten: interlude II: lips and boundaries

Chapter ten presents the second interlude in *Elemental Passions*. In the first interlude of chapter six, woman's body was likened to a flower. Man wanted the flower to open just for him, to open up to him and in the end behave like a mirror in which his reflection – and thus his subjectivity – was given back to him, in a Lacanian interpretation of the master–slave parable. In chapter ten, female lips form the main image of the interlude. We shall explore this image more fully in chapter five; the theme we wish to emphasize here is that the image of the lips points to an alternative fluid way of thinking, communication and exchange. Thinking in terms of binary oppositions gradually becomes undone. For example, the opposition between open and closed is not a simple binary with regard to lips.

Two lips kissing two lips. The edges of the face finding openness once more ... But when lips kiss, openness is not the opposite of closure. Closed lips remain open. And their touching allows movement from inside to outside, from outside to in, with no fastening nor opening mouth to stop the exchange. (EP 63)

Deux lèvres embrassant deux lèvres. Les bords de la figure se redonnant de l'ouvert ... Mais l'ouvert, dans l'embrassement des lèvres, n'est pas l'opposé du fermé. Les lèvres fermées restent ouvertes. Et leur toucher fait passer du dedans au dehors, du dehors au dedans, sans qu'aucune boucle ni bouche jamais n'arrête cet échange. (Pe 77)

Lips remain open while closed. They touch and are touched simultaneously. They exchange fluids between them. And yet their closed openness cannot be represented in philosophy except as a contradiction, a self-cancellation that leaves zero, or in psychoanalysis except as a hole, a lack, which could be filled only by desire.

Openness permits exchange, ensures movement, prevents saturation in possession or consumption. But openness dwells in oblivion ... because it cannot be represented, nor made into an object, nor reproduced in some position or proposition. Who knows that the possibility of exchange is born from two lips remaining half open? (EP 63–4)

L'ouvert permet l'échange, assure le mouvement, empêche la saturation dans la possession ou consommation. Mais d'être non représentable, non objectivable, non reproductible dans quelque position, ou thème ... l'ouvert demeure dans l'oubli. Qui sais que la possibilité de l'échange naît de ce que deux lèvres demeurent entr'ouvertes? (Pe 78)

The fluid exchange between female lips – a paradigm for a reconsidered philosophy and psychoanalysis – forms a contrast with the male exchange of objects. The objects of exchange could be material: gifts, money or possessions, the whole market economy. They could also be human beings: as already noted Lévi-Strauss has argued that societies rest ultimately upon the exchange of women. And yet Irigaray points out that all these exchanges among men – whether of material objects, language or women – rest ultimately upon a much more fundamental exchange which is not of objects but of fluids: the exchange of fluids between man and woman at conception, and the exchange of fluids within woman and between woman and child during pregnancy, childbirth and infancy. These earliest and most fundamental exchanges, Irigaray argues, remain unspoken and unacknowledged within philosophy, economics and even psychoanalysis. Man erases from his consciousness the exchange of fluids upon which his very existence depends; he pretends that he erects himself by himself and pronounces himself a subject. And yet without fluidity man and his culture could not exist, either physically in relation to biological reproduction, or intellectually, since without the free flow of imagination all the rigid binaries in the world could never produce a truly human culture.

My lips are not opposed to generation. They keep the passage open. They accompany birth without holding it to a – closed – place or form. They clasp the whole with their desire. Giving shape, again and again, without stopping. Everything is held together and not held back in their fond embrace. (EP 65)

Mes lèvres ne s'opposent pas à la génération. Elles maintiennent ouvert le passage. Elles accompagnent la naissance sans la retenir dans un lieu ou une forme – fermés. Elles embrassent le tout de leur désir. Donnant et redonnant sans cesse contour sans jamais arrêter. Tout se tient et ne se retient pas dans leur enlacement. (Pe 80)

Irigaray is not arguing that there is no need for categories and distinctions, walls and separations. She is certainly not advocating the collapse of all into some kind of diffuse unity. Categories and distinctions are necessary; the question is, what should their nature be? Should they be designed to exclude, to keep things (and ideas, and people) apart, in rigidly designated structures? Or should they be intended precisely to admit and even encourage movement, passage between one and another? Continuing with her metaphor of lips, Irigaray writes,

The wall between them is porous. It allows passage. Of fluids.

Nothing there can be grasped with both hands. It filters through, a gift which slakes the whole body's thirst. (EP 66)

La paroi, entre elles, est poreuse. Elle laisse passer. Du fluide.

Rien ne s'y prend à pleines mains. Cela filtre à travers, et se donne à une désaltération de tout le corps. (Pe 81)

By contrast to this porous wall the categories and structures of male logic are

Elemental Passions

hard and rigid, made to exclude. Any movement or breakthrough between them requires violence.

For them, walls are solid. Even those of their body. They have to rub or strike hard to pass from the one to the other. There are thresholds to cross, doors to open, windows to knock through, thresholds to create. (EP 67)

Pour eux, les parois sont solides. Même celles de leurs corps. Il leur faut frotter beaucoup, ou frapper fort, pour passer de l'un à l'autre. Il y a des seuils à franchir, des portes à ouvrir, des fenêtres à percer, des seuils à pratiquer. (Pe 81–2)

Man's preoccupation would be to keep at bay that which he has repressed in the construction of these rigidities, the place of his origin. The womb, the woman – what Lacan had called a nullity or a hole – at once arouses and frightens him.

Their pleasure and their fear – holes. Below, above, in between. They construct or deconstruct on, under, around, along, across, between ... holes. They make and unmake holes: eternal architects. (EP 67)

Leur plaisir et leur crainte – les trous. En dessous, au-dessus, entre. Ils contruisent ou déconstruisent sur, sous, autour, le long de, à travers, entre ... des trous. Ils font et défont des trous : éternels architectes. (Pe 82)

But Irigaray points out that men need not think of women in such terms. In all their sexual difference, women can be approached with respect and understanding. The womb, the woman, indeed the whole world can be thought of and encountered with enjoyment that is not appropriation, with categories that are not rigid. In a passage moving between the (woman's) body and the world, and that explicitly affirms both sides of a seeming contradiction, she writes,

this bodily dwelling in which you can move or rest is not enclosed. It unfolds around you as you move, without need to search for windows or doors. You are not stopped by any opaque wall. The world belongs to us – does not belong to us. We live in it in all its width and breadth and in all its dimensions. (EP 68)

cette maison de corps où tu peux bouger et te reposer n'est pas clôturée. Elle se déploie autant que tu te meus, sans qu'il soit besoin de chercher portes ou fenêtres. Aucun mur opaque ne t'arrête. Le monde nous appartient – ne nous appartient pas. Nous l'habitons de long en large et en toutes dimensions. (Pe 83)

This dwelling without enclosure, belonging without appropriation, enjoyment without control is presented by Irigaray in relation to sexual difference; but once again sexual difference and encounter are presented as a paradigm for every sort of dwelling in the world, including economics, philosophy and religion.

Again there is far more in this chapter then we have chosen to comment upon; and as ever no commentary can be a substitute for a close engagement with the text. *Elemental Passions* shows that when the concepts of fluidity and fluid exchanges within and between bodies are accepted as a guiding metaphor, then a rethinking of embodiment becomes possible, and with it a rethinking of the major disciplines of Western culture. In this rethinking, the surfaces of bodies – or of ideas – are not rigidly demarcated or appropriated; they remain porous and open to the flow of mutual interaction. In *Elemental Passions* this is represented as endless touching, symbolized by the sound of the wind in an evocative passage in which Irigaray draws this chapter to a close:

> Leaves, and trees, and birds, and sky, and grass, all cross and brush each other continuously: a supple and mobile dwelling ... The whole murmurs so softly that the melody has room for the highest and the lowest note, the sharpest and the deepest ... If no sound is detached, the atmosphere remains full of music.
>
> Listen: nothing. The sound of silence. The rustle of air in the silence. The music of air touching itself – silently. (EP 69–70)

> Tout feuille, et arbre, et oiseaux, et ciel, et herbe s'effleurent et se croisent continûment : maison souple et mobile ... Tout bruit avec une amplitude si légère que cette mélodie laisse place au plus haut et au plus bas, au plus aigu, au plus grave ... Si aucun son ne se détache, l'atmosphère demeure musique.
>
> Ecoute : rien. Le bruit du silence. Le frottement de l'air dans le silence. La musique de l'air qui se touche – en silence. (Pe 85)

Eleven: meditation II: space, time, infinity and movement

Chapter eleven offers a meditation on the nature of time, space, infinity and movement. These categories, which man imposes on woman and on the world, have appeared throughout *Elemental Passions*, often with allusions to the Kantian conceptual grid by which man experiences and structures the phenomenal. In this chapter these categories are questioned and rethought from a woman's perspective, and the rigidity of their definitions are modified or balanced by fluidity.

According to Irigaray, man's concepts of time and space arise from a fear of that without boundaries or closure, '*ce sans arrêt*'.

> Origin and end, form, figure, meaning, name, the proper and the self: these are your weapons against that unbearable infinity. But, in addition, the construct which organises many – or at least three – points into an entity which exists in relation to the whole: your framing of time. (EP 71)

> L'origine et la fin, la forme, la figure, le sens et le nom, le propre et le soi...sont tes instruments contre cet insupportable infini. Mais, aussi, la constitution rassemblante de plusieurs points – au moins trois – dans une entité qui existe par rapport au tout : ton cadrage du temps. (Pe 87)

These categories, imposed as a struggle against '*ce sans arrêt*', structure the world. But the phrase '*sans arrêt*' has already occurred a number of times in *Elemental Passions*, for example in the prologue in relation to the images for woman's love, a song and a cloud. In fact, one characteristic of the female subject in *Elemental Passions* is precisely the '*sans arrêt*', the boundless: it is this which opens up the possibility for the continual development of woman as a fluid female subject.

Elemental Passions

Thus man's fear of the boundless is also (perhaps fundamentally) a fear of woman; and the imposition of rigid categories of space, time and the rest, while seeming to spring from philosophical necessity, are in fact not gender neutral.

Irigaray uses this meditation to probe the gendered nature and consequences of these concepts, beginning with the concept of infinity. For man, infinity means

> An uninterrupted sequence of projected points. With nothing linking them. Emptiness ... Points programmed as such indefinitely, on a background of absence. (EP 71)

> Une suite ininterrompue de points projectifs. Entre eux, pas d'articulation. Le vide ... Points programmés comme tels indéfiniment sur fond d'absence. (Pe 87)

The points are like disconnected atoms, stretching away into infinity, with nothing relating them one to another. Anything that could be put between them to hold them together would be just another point, and so the connection could not be made. The linearity of this sequence of points reminds the reader of Irigaray's critique of Plato's cave.

For woman, by contrast, infinity is a non-linear concept, something which indicates an ever-continuing development, as in the generation of the Empedoclean universe.

> For me infinity means movement, the mobility of place. Engendering time, yes. Always becoming. How can that future be brought to pass between your instants which are always already counted? (EP 71)

> Pour moi, l'infini signifie la mouvance, la mobilité du lieu. Engendrant du temps, oui. Toujours en devenir. Comment faire advenir ce futur entre tes instants toujours déjà comptés? (Pe 88)

The word *devenir*, to become, is used frequently in Elemental Passions in relation to becoming a subject, at times in conjunction with *puissance*, translated as potentiality. The infinity of becoming requires fluid movement from moment to moment as its potentiality is brought to reality; it is the very opposite of a linear sequence of disconnected points.

In relation to the category of time, man thinks of the infinity of points as eternity, an endless sequence of instants, each of them exactly the same as the one that went before. But Irigaray says that in relationships, the present, past and future cannot be thought of in terms of a conception of time based on the ticking of a clock in exactly equal segments detached from one another: 'that punctual quality of the instant is quite foreign to the dilation of time which persists in the present of our relations' (EP 72). Rather, some instants overflow their 'point in time': time is opened up; moments are fluid and pour into one another.

> Fluid density which overturns habitual space-time and yet always already takes place in it ... Giving back to time that volume, that light density, that absence of assignable limits which, however, is not eternity; that porosity which is not simply permeable to all, to everything; that touch ... (EP 72)

> Densité fluide qui bouleverse l'espace-temps habituel et pourtant y a toujours déjà lieu...Redonner au temps ce volume, cette épaisseur légère, cette absence de limites assignables qui pourtant n'est pas l'éternité; cette porosité non simplement perméable à tout, au tout; ce toucher... (Pe 88)

Irigaray is not suggesting that concepts of space and time as points or instants are wrong or valueless: they have their uses. But if they are the sole way in which space and time are allowed to be conceptualised, if everything – including relationships, intuitions, the experience of beauty – is reduced to a series of equal points, then their rigid categories have deprived us of much that makes life worthwhile.

In this chapter Irigaray uses a variety of metaphors to make her critique of thinking in terms of linearity and its goals, and to offer alternatives suggested by fluidity. For example, she writes:

> Within the venture of erection is its fall. Those who aspire to superiority create the abyss. Mountains are matched by deep ravines. Yet the sea remains: the fluid petrified in sublime rocks, still subsists as mass, surrounded by firm ground. (EP 73)

> La rechute est comprise dans le projet d'érection. Qui se veut supérieur, crée l'abîme. Aux montagnes, cooerespondent les gouffres. Reste encore la mer : le fluide, pétrifié en rocs sublimes, subsiste en masse, bordé par les terres fermes. (Pe 89)

Water, the marine element associated with woman, flows and keeps flowing: there are here many echoes of Irigaray's earlier book, *Marine Lover of Friedrich Nietzsche*. Again, fluidity without boundaries is an image both for subjectivity and for the mutual gift of relationship. In love, it is suggested, one can give oneself without goal, give without losing oneself.

> Giving oneself, that giving – a transition which undoes the properties of our enclosures, the frame or envelope of our identities ... Loving you, I am no longer the same; loved, you are different. Loving, I give myself you. I become you. But I remain, as well, to love you still. And as an effect of that act. Unfinishable. Always in-finite. (EP 74)

> Se donner, ce donner – transition qui défait le propre de nos clôtures, le cadre ou l'enveloppe de nos identités ... T'aimant, je ne suis plus la même ; aimé, tu es différent. Aimant, je me donne toi. Je deviens toi. Mais je reste, aussi, pour t'aimer encore. Et comme effet de cet acte. Inachevable. Toujours in-fini. (Pe 90)

In mutual love, man and woman can be subjects in an endless becoming, without fixed delineations between one and the other, without a fixed goal or categories of thought which constrict. Yet this can only be successful when both man and woman accept the notion of fluidity in a new understanding of time and space. In such an understanding – which has implications far beyond individual relationships – infinity comes to mean endless movement, becoming. And again woman's lips provide an image which illustrates this endless flow, porosity, and movement in the continual touching of her lips.

Elemental Passions

> For me there is no possible horizon. At least not a closed one ... My body closes and opens the horizon with a single gesture. Touching myself again and again, I bring my edges together. But the one is no more the end than the other is the beginning. (EP 75)

> Il n'y a pas, pour moi d'horizon possible. Du moins fermé ... Mon corps ferme et ouvre l'horizon d'un même geste. Me touchant-retouchant, je rapproche mes bords. Mais l'un n'est pas plus la fin que l'autre le commencement. (Pe 92)

Twelve: narrative: a vision of the future

Chapter twelve takes as its starting point a celebration of the differences between man and woman. These differences were accepted in the breakthrough of chapter nine, and opened the way to the meditations of chapters ten and eleven. Now those meditations are taken forward, as though woman and man are musing together after making love about their new relationship and its implications for the future. Once again the sexual encounter is a paradigm for rethinking philosophical categories. The concepts of being, embodiment and procreation are rethought, as if in answer to the prologue's promise of fertilizing our bodily senses. These concepts are no longer exclusively within the realm of male thought, but are refigured in relation to two sexually different subjects. Images such as the flower and the copula, as well as woman's gift of love, again form part of the poetry. Touch is re-emphasised as the form of contact between bodies, which enables the development of subjects:

> Our embraces redefining the constantly renewed outline of our bodies. Bringing us into the world once more. Making us appear, endlessly? (EP 79)

> Nos enlacements redéfinissant le contour, toujours nouveau, de nos corps. Nous remettant au monde. Nous faisant apparaître, sans cesse? (Pe 95–6)

A new birth into philosophy is anticipated. Yet this time it will not be a birth of man, isolated in his oneness and constructing the world according to the rigidity of his gaze. It will be a birth of two subjects irreducible to each other, through the fluidity of mutual touch.

As usual, there are many layers of allusion in this chapter to themes that have been prominent in the history of philosophy and psychoanalysis, and hints at how the refiguration will be different from the past. For example, the whole idea of mirroring and reflection and how it gives rise to language (as in Lacan's mirror stage) becomes reciprocal rather than exploitative, and thus enables the development of two mutually respectful subjects of language rather than one whose emergence is based on his mastery of the other.

> If being no longer belongs to you, if you are no longer devoted to it as you are to your language enclosure, if being means permanent advent between us, our bodies become living mirrors. Sense mirrors where the outline of the other is profiled through touch. No longer the site of a frozen, fixed appropriation – expropriation. Already a womb of the ideality. (EP 77)

Interpretative synopsis of *Elemental Passions*

Si l'être ne t'appartient plus, si tu ne lui es plus voué comme à ton enceinte de langue, si être revient à l'avènement permanent entre nous, nos corps deviennent miroirs vivants. Miroirs sensibles où se dessinent, tactilement, les contours de l'autre. Non plus lieu d'une appropriation-expropriation glacée, figée. Matrice, déjà, de l'idéalité. (Pe 93)

The womb, here, is no longer identified solely with the woman, but is the place of their shared creativity, the potential for the realization of their emerging ideals. This means that language itself will change, since there will be two speaking subjects whose differences will be a source not of threat but of fecundity. Irigaray gives no details about what such an ideal language would be like; but it is plausible to suppose that she offers her own allusive style as one of its possibilities.

The home, too, is reenvisaged: this could be the literal domestic home, or it could be the dwelling place in language and reality structured for himself by man. Irigaray suggests two ways of thinking about it:

In the home, it is possible to privilege the walls, the outline determining a place as closed off, or the atmosphere: the environment. (EP 77)

Dans la maison, on peut privilégier les murs, le pourtour déterminant un lieu comme clos, ou l'ambiance : le milieu. (Pe 94)

Obviously walls are necessary; without walls there is no structured dwelling place, either literal or conceptual. But what is within the walls, the atmosphere or environment and the way the walls permit movement between the spaces, determines whether the structure is a happy home or a prison. If the whole focus is on the walls themselves, erecting them ever higher and with greater rigidity, and no attention is paid to the atmosphere within their enclosure and the flow between the rooms, the result can only be disaster. If on the other hand the environment and atmosphere, the flow of air and breath, are attended to, then the walls offer an enclosure of safety and intimacy within which creativity can take place. Again, it is easier to see the force of this in relation to actual than to conceptual dwelling places; but Irigaray is referring to the gendered rigidity of conceptual structures (like the Kantian categories) as surely as to actual homes. In each case, what is looked for is not a separation of man from his environment but a subjectivity of both man and woman developed in relation to the elements.

Hovering behind all of *Elemental Passions* is the figure of Empedocles, but in this chapter he comes to the fore. Empedocles had spoken of love and strife as the passions structuring the universe. Irigaray, using the image of the copula, suggests that of the two, love is the more primordial.

The mysterious energy of the copula, rediscovering a buried source. Hidden before the separation of the elements? Before hatred? (EP 78)

Energie étrange de la copule, qui retrouve une source enfouie. Avant la séparation des éléments? Avcant la haine? (Pe 95)

Elemental Passions

It is this fecund love that is at the basis of all creativity. Engendering takes place in the *jouissance* of mutuality, whether of body or mind: 'Which is not limited to begetting a child' (EP 79). How can newness enter the world? How can ideals of creativity and joyful mutuality be brought to reality? The 'buried source' of love, more fundamental than strife, gives hope of its possibility.

Irigaray merges this idea with that of the gift: gift given freely and in love, not as object of exchange.

In the gift, what happens to me is not that I become a thing thanks to your offering, but that I touch you without any system of mediation-screens. In that touching, I become you, also. And I receive from you, of you, in giving myself. In that gift which touches, 'we' becomes a flow, fluid. (EP 79–80)

Dans le don, ce qui m'advient n'est pas de devenir chose grâce à ton versement, c'est de te toucher sans système de médiations-écrans. En ce toucher, je deviens, aussi, toi. Et je reçois de toi, du toi, en me donnant. Dans ce don qui touche, nous devient flux, fluide. (Pe 96)

The fluidity is connected back to association with Empedocles and the four elements: earth, air, fire and water. At the end of the chapter man is afraid that fluidity, water, will undermine his solid foundations, the womb-like rock or cave which gives him security.

Fire, air, water – are they thus to be dominated by the earth? The outline of a womb-like maternal body, based upon your need for solidity. For a rock-solid home. (EP 80)

Le feu, l'air, l'eau ainsi dominés par l terre? Le pourtour d'un corps matriciel, maternel, établi à partir de ton besoin de solide. D'une maison en dur. (Pe 97)

It is this need, this repressed desire and fear of the mother, which reactivates man's need for control, mastery. And yet the elemental passions can only show their creativity and beauty when they are freely celebrated, not seen as a threat.

Is fire not joy? Is burning with you not grace? The very lightest, dancing. The lightest, and the densest. The most whole? Most elemental? For you?

Why do you think of it as destructive, when it is life itself? (EP 80)

Le feu, n'est-ce la joie? Brûler avec toi, la grâce? Le plus léger qui danse. Le plus léger, et le plus dense? Le plus tout? Le plus originaire? Pour toi?

Pourquoi le penses-tu comme destructeur, alors qu'il est la vie même? (Pe 97)

For the new type of subjectivity achieved in the breakthrough and celebrated in these meditative chapters it is necessary that man abandons his desire to appropriate woman and to control the 'other' – woman, the earth, the body and its passions – through fixed categories of interpretation. The ending of this chapter anticipates man's fear and reluctance to do so. This leads to a backlash in the relation between 'I' and 'you' when the narrative continues in chapter thirteen.

Interpretative synopsis of *Elemental Passions*

Thirteen: narrative: backlash II

In the resumption of the narrative, we find that you-man has given in to his fear and re-exerted his mastery, erecting himself as the sole knower who constructs the world according to his own categories of domination. Man again proceeds to 'live in conceptuality', 'magisterially spelling out your Truth', using woman to do so while at the same time obscuring her role. We are back to the beginning, or even worse.

I-woman seems to give up. After the joyful hope of the future which the breakthrough of the previous chapters had promised, she is met once again with control and refusal of mutuality, and is in despair.

Instead of the feelings I had, an unseizable void ... And through your declaration, have I not become blind, deaf, paralysed, numb? ... An opaque blank, instead of what I saw with you yesterday. And the music I heard no longer reaches me. A neutral, frozen barrier shuts me off from it ... (EP 81)

Au lieu de ce que j'éprouvais, l'insaisissable d'un vide...Et ne suis-je devenue aveugle, sourde, paralysée, insensible, en ta déclaration?... En place de ce que j'ai vu hier avec toi, l'opacité d'un blanc. Et cette musique que j'entendais, ne me parvient plus. Un infranchissable neutre et glacé m'en sépare... (Pe 99)

I-woman has maintained throughout that her gift, the gift of life and love to you-man should not be seen as something which he should appropriate and claim as his property, but should be incorporated in reciprocal subjectivity. But now in her discouragement she says that man may as well take it and feign that he is masterful: the manner reminds the reader of Irigaray's attitude to Lacan.

Take, master, this product is yours. And no voice will utter a word about the destruction on which it is based. Let there be silence about that act.

And while you magisterially spell out your Truth ... your nothingness has not lost what it feeds on. Of course it is buried beneath your showy speeches. (EP 82)

Tien, maître, ce produit. Et sur quelle destruction il se fonde, nulle voix ne le proférera. Silence sur cette opération.

Et, tandis que tu articules magistralement ta Vérité ... ton néant m'as pas perdu sa subsistance. Certes enseveli sous la parade de tes discours. (Pe 100)

Once again, woman finds that her speech, the condition of her subject position, is taken away from her. In a subtle variation upon the earlier instance where she speaks but is not heard, the following words are used to describe woman's sense of being cut off from herself.

...I still exist. And my mouth is kept open. And I speak. But the gag of your nothingness prevents me from feeling what I say. (EP 81)

...encore, j'existe. Et ma bouche est tenue ouverte. Et je parle. Mais la bâillon de ton néant m'empêche de sentir ce que je dis. (Pe 100)

Yet even while man is silencing woman, he is once again using her to establish his own ascendancy, both intellectually and physically. He returns to her, domestically, sexually, and psychologically, when he requires nurture of his body or his ego, and then leaves her again for his public or conceptual spaces, 'repeatedly, creating a place from which you draw my substance so that you can experience yourself' (EP 83). This appropriation of woman (and of the fluid, and all that it stands for) is absolutely necessary for man and all his physical and philosophical activities, though he represses his own consciousness of what he draws from her.

What is the rigour of your thought? The superb confidence of someone moving inside a fleshy fabric borrowed from the other ... The implacable, systematic quality of an organisation which has already taken from living organisms the elements it needs to be sustained and developed unreservedly. A sovereign power, miming and undermining the whole of the resources from which it draws. (EP 82)

La rigueur de ta pensée? Superbe aisance de qui se meut dans un tissu de chair emprunté à l'autre...Systématicité implacable d'une organisation qui a déjà enlevé aux organismes vivants de quoi s'entretenir et se déployer inconditionnellement. Puissance souveraine, mimant et minant le tout de ce qu'elle y prend comme ressources. (Pe 101)

On the basis of this appropriation, man is able to effect 'an assiduous and scholarly erasure', make brilliant speeches, drink 'the milk of the honours awarded to your work' (EP 83–4).

But this time I-woman has had enough. Her reaction is clear and definitive. She tells you-man to leave. She will no longer tolerate his comings and goings, using her to meet his needs and then abandoning her as it suits him.

Go. And do not come back to measure the strength of love's effects. Go. Do not return to your birthplace in the embrace. Leave me the opportunity of continuing to become. And of being something for you other than a tomb in which you endlessly seek what you need to sustain that oblivion which underpins your elevation. (EP 84)

Va. Et ne reviens plus mesurer l'ampleur des effets d'un amour. Va, ne retourne plus au lieu de ta naissance dans l'étreinte. Laisse-moi la chance de devenir encore. Et de n'être pas, pour toi, tombe où tu recherches sans fin de quoi entretenir l'oubli qui soutient ton élévation. (Pe 103)

The decisiveness of woman's dismissal is somewhat at odds with what has gone before, in that woman can tell man to leave only if she does have at least some level of language, some kind of subject position. Moreover she seems to expect to continue to develop without him. Earlier in this text, as well as in her earlier writings, Irigaray had suggested that woman had no subject position, no voice of her own, because of male control. Now, however, woman has found within herself the resources to assert her independence. 'I would rather march towards a new dawn. And bring one more child into the world' (EP 84).

However, for man this will not prove to be a solution. Man can leave the place where he was born and grew up; he can also leave woman, if she no longer allows him to use her for his purposes. However he cannot completely forget woman-mother because his very existence is proof of his origin. Once again as in chapters three and four man tries in vain to leave woman behind and to be oblivious to his origin; and once again this proves impossible for him.

And thus the cycle of return is brought to perfection: born of the flesh, the gaze emerges from it and extends the horizon of its domination, but then returns to it, only to come up against an icy transparency. A fluid frozen because the body which gave it birth is hated or forgotten? (EP 88)

Ainsi advient le parachèvement du cycle du retour : né de chair, le regard en émerge et déploie ses horizons de domination, mais y retourne, se heurtant à une transparence de glace. Fluide figé par l'oubli ou la haine du corps dont il a pris naissance? (Pe 107)

Man seems to have rejected mutuality and returned to domination. If he is ever to become a subject without fear either of the (m)other or of the differences between subjects, man has to rethink his debt to the (m)other, and thus to woman. This will involve recognition of the unwarranted prioritising of the gaze over the flesh, and allowing fluidity and movement its scope. Instead, by his attitude rigidity is reimposed, the fluid is frozen, we are going round the same old circle.

At the level of psychosexual narrative all this can be readily understood. But how is it a paradigm for philosophy? Suppose one were to try to develop thinking from a purely 'feminine' position; in other words keep all concepts fluid, use no binaries, no fixed constructs. It is hard to see how that could result in anything but vague indefiniteness. Perhaps the point, however, is that just as fluidity requires structures to channel and contain it, so also rigidity loses its purpose and origin unless it allows for movement. It is as though man has concentrated so hard on constructing a cup that he has forgotten about the water it was meant to hold. Or, in philosophical terms, there has been so much focus on logic and epistemological constructs that it has been forgotten that these structures are there to aid and channel creative thinking, not to stifle it. If newness is to enter the world, then the fluidity of imagination and creativity cannot be repressed. Structures and movement need one another, in mutual fecundity.

Fourteen: narrative: backlash continued

This chapter continues the narrative and explores man further, offering more hints about the implications of the psychosexual paradigm for philosophy. Although woman has asked man to leave her, he does not let her go. He retains his control of her; but yet at the same time he does not allow her to develop her subjectivity or her speech.

When I am speaking to you, I sense something like a dark and frozen chasm capable of engulfing everything. Slippery and bottomless. The fall of a night without illumination?

Elemental Passions

The disappearance of the sun. That of your intellect? Of your understanding? (EP 90)

Quand je te parle, je sens comme un abîme noir et glacé qui avalerait tout. Où ça glisserait, sans fond. Tombée d'une nuit sans lumière? Disparition du soleil. Celui de ton intelligence? De ta compréhension? (Pe 110)

Man does not understand what woman is trying to say. Perhaps he does not want to understand. He freezes her in his gaze.

Your order freezes the mobility of relations between. It produces discontinuity. Peaks, pikes, fissures. Energy no longer circulates. Is hoarded in forms that create closure ... It is taken, circumvented in a morphology whose outlines are overvalued. (EP 90)

Ton ordre fige la mouvance des relations entre. Il produit du discontinu. De pics, des piques, des cassures. L'énergie ne circule plus. Se thésaurise dans des formes clôturantes...Elle est prise, circonvenue dans une morphologie dont les contours sont surfaits. (Pe 111)

Man and his categories of meaning, his concepts of appropriation and propriety, cannot recognize the movements which occur 'imperceptibly' within the 'world of the senses', because he has excluded such movement from his philosophy. These movements do not fit within rigid categories of thought, for 'only an attentiveness that is not rigidified within formal frameworks can detect this kind of movement' (EP 91). Once strict categories are imposed, the moving flow is impeded. The imperceptible movements, which require attentiveness rather than unbending frameworks, have been a theme of the developing female subject throughout Elemental Passions. Time after time Irigaray returns to love and strife and to the elements in order to think differently and create the space for a female subject.

As this subject develops, she increasingly resists man's insistent control: we saw in the last chapter how she told the man to leave her and not come back. The result of this, however, is that man asserts his mastery even more strongly: the female subject, 'in its struggle for liberation, will necessarily bring about aggression, violence, rape' (EP 90). The violence might be physical or it might be intellectual. Its aim is to master difference, and thereby to achieve oneness, perfect infinity that is also immortality, since the complete resolution of tensions is forever deferred.

When you become the place where tensions are capitalised, tensions whose purpose is always deferred to some future perfection, to an omnipotent infinity, tensions which you cannot contain without the threat of explosion, you take me as a place of relaxation. You wound my living skin to safeguard your claim to some divine ideal. You abolish the edges of our bodies to turn yourself into a God. The only theophore? (EP 92)

Quand tu deviens lieu de capitalisation de tensions dont la finalité est toujours reportée à une perfection future, à un infini tout-puissant, tensions que tu ne peux contenir sous peine d'explosion, tu me prends comme lieu de détente. Tu blesses ma peau vivante pour sauvegarder ta prétention à quelque divin idéal. Tu anéantis les bords de nos corps pour te faire Dieu. Seul théophore? (Pe 112–13)

Interpretative synopsis of *Elemental Passions*

Man's quest for dominance is ultimately a quest for omnipotence, trying to make himself an all-powerful God who is a projection of his idealized self.

In response to man's imposition of order and desire for ultimate power, woman urges man to 'return inside yourself'. Rather than aspire to infinity and immortality, woman asks man to take measure of himself and to let go of his pretensions and illusions. If instead of trying to master and overcome difference he were to welcome it, recognizing that even his own origin is rooted in difference, then a whole new way of becoming divine is opened up, based not in some future immortality but in vibrantly shared life.

> Once returned in this way inside yourself, you can offer yourself, radiate yourself. You can at last be received. Without excessive pretensions. Without promises that cannot be kept. Without semblance erupting in my flesh. This letting go will bring a share of heaven if it is not made into some far-off goal, unattainable by you today. At every instant Heaven is created. Even if it extends before and after us, it is also our own achievement. (EP 92–3)

> Ainsi retourné en toi, tu peux apporter toi, irradier toi. Toi enfin recevable. Sans excessive prétention. Sans promesse intenable. Ni irruption de semblant en ma chair. Cet abandon aura sa part de ciel s'il ne se veut quelque au-delà inatteignable par toi aujourd'hui. Le ciel se crée à chaque instant. S'il s'étend avant et après nous, il est aussi notre œuvre. (Pe 113)

If man can let go of his fear, and become 'permeable without mastery', then together and precisely in virtue of their difference man and woman can become 'creators of new horizons'. If he cannot, then he will exert his power in a bid to master his fear, project an omnipotent deity (God, Truth, technology, money) as a source of his security, and see woman always as a threat to be controlled.

Irigaray suggests that to deal with his fear man constructs his world into binary opposites, 'two props to shore it up', his 'doublings'. One of these is the 'Omnipotent': God, or whatever stands in for God. The other is the 'impotent', the powerless, woman. Neither of these correspond to reality; they are masculinist projections not-A to man's A. Nevertheless man exerts himself to realize his projections, investing ever more power in his gods of religion, science, or economics, and keeping woman from her own subject position. God and woman are constructed as opposite to one another, 'a good doubling and a bad one'.

> The celestial envelope of the God from whom all comes and to whom all returns. And the infernal one, which robs the origin and the end of their middle and surround. A God in whom the whole of what is created finds its place and is kept on the right course. A God in whom is contained the perfection of the whole. And the other, turning away from that absolute. Another who would be like God. (EP 94)

> L'enveloppe céleste du Dieu de qui tout vient et à qui tout revient. Et l'infernale, celle qui dérobe à l'origine et la fin leur milieu. Un Dieu en qui a lieu l'ensemble du créé et qui le garde de dévoiement. Un Dieu qui contient la perfection de Tout. Et l'autre, qui détourne les yeux de cet absolu. Un autre qui se voudrait semblable à Dieu. (Pe 115)

As long as man insists on constructing the world according to these binaries, there is little that woman can do. She will be projected as god-like or demonic, the angel or the temptress, but not related to simply as a sexually different subject in her own right. If, however, he were to overcome his fear and return to his origins none of this would be necessary; he would not need to 'defer to Infinity' the life which he could live in the present. Rather than preoccupation with death, he could engage with woman in life here and now, creative, in a new dawning of the world.

Fifteen: epilogue

As the prologue of Elemental Passions began with a song, so the epilogue begins with a sunrise. But it is a 'sunrise-forgotten' – forgotten by man who forgets his place of origin in the womb/cave and lives only in the full glare of the sun. Woman, however, thinks of the sunrise and its possibilities:

The first outline of forms emerging. A world being born. Not yet caught within a defined horizon ...

The sun rising – rays alighting upon things, lightly touching them all over and gradually revealing them, bringing them out of the enveloping mist.

This unveiling of the morning's beauty is renewed daily. (EP 95)

Le contour des formes qui se profilent. La naissance d'un monde. Et non encore sa prise dans un horizon déterminé ...

Le soleil levant – les rayons qui touchent les choses et, les effleurant de partout, les découvrent peu à peu de leur enveloppe de brume.

Ce dévoilement de la beauté matinale recommence tous les jours. (Pe 117)

Although the man/philosopher seems to have become oblivious to becoming and instead concentrates on the hard outlines of being, there is still the possibility of change. The sun rises again and heralds the birth of a little girl, of an other who is truly irreducible to man's self-same. Her birth is described as

Another – the other – being brought into the world. A dawning as powerful as that of the Greeks ... the revelation of the end of a unique truth. Not as the advent of chaos, but as the possibility of the copula – in the sun. (EP 95)

La venue au monde d'une autre – de l'autre. Geste d'aube aussi puissant que celui des Grecs...la manifestation de la fin d'une vérité unique. Non comme avènement du chaos, mais comme possibilité de la copule – dans le soleil. (Pe 117–18)

The copula between two, in full visibility of the light of reason reconfigured to allow for fluidity as well as rigidity, heralds the beginning of a creative thinking, feeling and living in which sexually different subjects can grow and become.

Yet after this almost utopian, visionary introduction, I-woman recounts how you-man did not hear her speak or call out to him. It was not through speech or through the gaze but through touch that two subjects emerge. It is not the glare of daylight that makes them into subjects, 'that cold lucidity which freezes each one with a sealed identity' but rather 'attentive vibration picking up the imperceptible tremor of your approach' (EP 98). The mutual development as subjects is characterized as a mingling for which the now-familiar images of lips, a cloud, a song and a flower are used.

Once again, Irigaray appeals to Empedocles. The elements are held together in the flow of the passions; the material and sensory is given its due weight and not displaced by the conceptual.

In golden light you flow. Firm density, so light. Before the separation of earth and sky, sea and continents, light and dark. A mixture of rock, fire, water, ether. Where violence can still espouse gentleness. The heroic body overflowing with tenderness ... Which blurs all sharp distinctions and brings all divisions back to their original nuptials. An alliance in which the opposing parties unite in intense intermingling. (EP 102)

En lumière dorée, tu coules. Densité ferme et si légère. Avant la séparation de la terre et du ciel, de la mer et des continents, du clair et de l'obscur. Mélange de roc, de feu, d'eau, d'éther. Où la violence épouse encore la douceur. Le corps héroïque débordant de tendresse... Qui confond toutes distinctions tranchées, et reconduit toutes divisions à leurs noces originelles. Alliance où les partis opposés viennent s'unir en une intense mêlée. (Pe 125)

In spite of such positive, even visionary passages, it must be said that the epilogue is undecidably ambiguous. It contains passages of beauty and fulfilment, in which it seems that the creative breakthrough really has taken place, such as the above or the following:

I was created by you, still faithful to what I was. A fruition of my becoming that did not remove me from my past ... Espousing you, like the whole which is offered without closure ... Mingled, and so calm and so vast – yet I was careful to allow you your heaven. We were intermingled and returned to ourselves. An eternity, and I knew that tomorrow it would become more eternal still. (EP 100)

J'étais créée par toi, fidèle encore à ce que j'étais. Epanouissement de mon devenir qui ne m'enlevait pas à mon passé...T'épousant, tel le tout qui se donne sans clôture...Mêlée et si calme et si large, et pourtant attentive à te laisser ton ciel. Confondus et rendus à nous-mêmes. Eternité, dont je savais que demain elle serait plus éternelle encore. (Pe 123)

In such passages it would seem that man has overcome his fearful need to control; binary logic and rigid categories of meaning are replaced by returning to the elemental with the concepts of a flow and of mingling. Thus both woman and man together become subjects in love.

Running through the chapter, however, is also a recognition of the difficulties inherent within this process. From the start, man is presented as the one who has forgotten the sunrise: woman says, 'I was calling you, but my cry did not reach your ears' (EP 96). This depressing strand is interwoven with the more optimistic strand right until the end, when there is again the recognition that rigid categories of meaning still obstruct communication.

> How many words to prevent or forbid closeness! ... Attestations, quarrels, protestations, disputes over identity or the identical, distancing us, dividing us without any crossing of these barriers being possible. We are separated by so many similar things that the flow which attracts us to each other is exhausted as it beats against these obstacles. It no longer flows, held back by boundaries that are too watertight. (EP 103–4)

> Que de mots pour empêcher ou interdire le proche !...Les attestations, querelles, protestations, disputes quant à l'identité ou à l'identique, nous éloignant, nous écartant sans franchissement possible de leurs frontières. Tant de semblables nous séparent que ce flux qui nous attire l'un vers l'autre s'épuise en déferlement sur ces obstacles. Il ne coule plus d'être arrêté par des limites trop étanches. (Pe 127–8)

Finally, woman says, 'I opened my eyes and saw the cloud'. Is she waking up from a utopian dream, realizing that it is impossible? Or is she once again finding in the cloud an image of mingling, of new hope? In the very last sentence, she says that having become aware of this 'resistance of air', she 'felt something akin to the possibility of a different discovery of myself' (EP 105). Is this a new beginning? Or is it despair?

We do not consider this final ambivalence or the recognition of difficulties to be a weakness in Irigaray's presentation, but rather an honest indication of the problems of becoming subjects in a different way, and of the on-going process of mutual becoming. The open ending of *Elemental Passions* is faithful to the open-endedness of relationships, forever fluid. There is no finality, no closure; only the invitation of an endless embrace.

CHAPTER 5

Images for a female subject

Introduction

Elemental Passions has given us an insight into a new way of thinking, using images of fluidity which reconfigure sexual difference and thereby subvert the rigidity of the binary logic of traditional philosophy and psychoanalysis. In this chapter we would like to select some of the most important of these images which have emerged in the commentary on Elemental Passions and look at them in more detail. We suggest that these unaccustomed images of fluidity could usefully supplement the more familiar metaphors regularly used in philosophy: metaphors of groundwork, foundation, erection, attack and defence. By paying attention to the woman subject and her development, it becomes clear that sexual difference is itself not a question of binary opposition. This difference then becomes a paradigm for understanding other sorts of difference in fluid terms rather than in terms that set them up as oppositional. It is a commonplace of psychoanalytic theory since Lacan that images and metaphors play a central role in constructing and reinforcing the ways in which we think. It is therefore a task of great importance to develop images that subvert or supplement rigid logic and show the emergence of the woman subject.

Irigaray has used vivid imagery from the very beginning of her writings. A few of her images, in particular that of the lips, have become famous in feminist writings: it will quickly become apparent why this has been so. However, many of the other images that occur in Elemental Passions have hardly been considered before, either in relation to the development of sexually different subjects or in relation to binary logic. We have therefore chosen to begin with the more familiar imagery of the lips, and then select several of her other important images of fluidity for discussion. We would stress again, however, that there is far more in the text of Elemental Passions than we comment upon here; and that the allusive and poetical nature of the text is open to a range of interpretations beyond the ones we offer.

Lips

The Irigarayan exchange of fluids between lips can be taken as a model for exchange between subjects. In the literature on Irigaray, female lips are commonly regarded as her most significant image for woman and female sexuality (see Gallop 1988: 91–100; Braidotti 1986; 1991: 249). This is demonstrated for example by the following quotation from Braidotti:

> The now famous image of the lips of the female sex – close together and yet apart – stands for the multiplicity, the excess and the unique combination of plurality and singularity which characterizes the bodily sexed reality of the female experience. (Braidotti 1986: 9)

Lips are characteristic of women for Irigaray from early in her writings, and continue to play a central role in the imagery of *Elemental Passions*. The significance of Irigarayan lips lies in the fact that although two lips are not one, neither can they be neatly separated into two; they certainly cannot be construed as binary opposites. The opposition 'touched' and 'touching' for example, does not apply because the lips touch each other all the time. This is true of the lips of the mouth, which both sexes experience; it is also true of female genitalia. Woman touches herself in the movement of her genital lips; these lips are always already two. In touching, the lips touch each other and it is not possible to distinguish neatly between what is touched and what is touching, between object and subject, known and knower, passive and active.

In Chapter 2 we noted how Freud applied the dichotomy of active/passive and subject/object to the relationship between woman and man. In the essay 'This Sex Which Is Not One' Irigaray counteracts Freud's argument as follows:

> As for woman, she touches herself in and of herself without any need for mediation, and before there is any way to distinguish activity from passivity. Woman 'touches herself' all the time, and moreover no one can forbid her to do so, for her genitalia are formed of two lips which embrace each other continually. Thus, within herself, she is already two – but not divisible into one(s) – that caress each other. (TS 24)

This quotation illustrates how Irigaray undoes the binary opposition of activity–passivity that has been of significance not only for psychoanalytic construction of sexuality, but also for its gendered construction of subjectivity and language. If the active–passive opposition is not valid in the construction of subjectivity, then the whole Lacanian argument on language as well as sexuality needs to be rethought. That, of course, is one of Irigaray's aims.

In *Elemental Passions* Irigaray takes the imagery of lips further. In the previous chapter we characterized the second interlude (chapter ten) as taking 'female lips' as its theme, though it occurred frequently elsewhere in the text as well. The interlude begins as follows: 'Proximity? Two lips kissing two lips. The edges of the face finding openness once more' (EP 63). The whole chapter is a plea for openness, for never-ending fluid exchange, and for the absence of enclosures: an openness which will eventually lead to a philosophy of sexually different subjects.

In this, it contrasts with one of the activities of you-man in *Elemental Passions*, the activity of enframing. As Irigaray presents it, man imposes his (Kantian) spatio-temporal grid upon what he takes to be previously unformed matter (cf. Grosz 1989: 173–6). Irigaray argues that in thus structuring and marking matter, man imposes a patriarchal structure upon reality which prevents woman from becoming a subject. Her point is of course not that we could dispense with concepts or frameworks with which to make sense of reality, but that we should recognize them for what they are: even the term 'framework' is a metaphor. By supplementing these rigid metaphors with fluid ones, new possibilities are opened up for thinking.

In Irigaray's imagery, the (male) enclosures of the (female) earth correspond to the male intrusion of the female body in, for example, the breaking of the hymen. The words which describe both processes are 'viole et vole', 'rapes and steals'. In chapter five man's empty frame is imposed on matter. It 'rapes' and 'steals' (*il viole, vole*) (EP 24). The second time these words are used is in connection to the hymen:

Exchange between men [*entre hommes*] is sealed by the gift of a virgin. And the rite of breaking and entering, of raping and stealing the hymen [*du viol et vol de l'hymen*], represents a denial of what was always already offered: exchange within woman and between women [*en elle et entre elles*]. (EP 64)

The parallel between the earth and the female body goes further than a similar usage of words. As we have noted, earth is the central element of *Elemental Passions*. In relation to Empedocles, Irigaray figures the elements as female. This is connected to her aim both to re-think our relation to materiality and to re-value that which philosophy has excluded. One theme that resurfaces throughout *Elemental Passions* is that like women's bodies, the earth itself is exploited, with destructive consequences for both men and women. In contrast, and using the imagery of the lips, Irigaray develops a notion of openness:

Openness is not reflected, not mimed, not reproduced. Not even produced. Openness: ... A space, not demarcated, not enclosed. Outside any possible symmetry or inversion. (EP 63)

L'ouvert ne se réfléchit, ne se mime, ni se reproduit. Ne se produit même pas. L'ouvert: ... L'éclaircie sans pourtour, ni encerclement. Hors symétrie et inversion possibles. (Pe 77)

The whole meditation on space, enclosure and framing is written with reference to Heidegger's concept of *Lichtung*, 'clearing' or 'opening', within which nevertheless Heidegger wishes to build and dwell (see Chanter 1995: 127–70). It is a set of images which Heidegger himself had developed with great insightfulness from the Kantian ideas of space and time; Irigaray ponders the associations which Heidegger's metaphors raise, including their implicit masculinist bias, and in so doing offers new images and allusions which allow for the emergence of sexually different subjects.

Elemental Passions

In *Elemental Passions*, lips are an image which represent Irigaray's ideas of openness in multiple ways: we will mention four. Firstly, woman's lips touch continually; yet in their touching they remain open. As Irigaray puts it,

> For me there is no possible horizon. At least not a closed one. My body closes and opens the horizon with a single gesture. Touching myself again and again, I bring my edges together. (EP 75)

> Il n'y a pas, pour moi, d'horizon possible. Du moins fermé. Cercle fini, clôture. Mon corps ferme et ouvre l'horizon d'un même geste. Me touchant-retouchant, je rapproche mes bords. (Pe 92)

Irigaray argues that a woman's lips guarantee that her body is never completely closed. For Irigaray, female closed lips do not mean an end to communication. This is true in the first place in relation to speech. Indeed, Irigaray argues elsewhere that closed lips are a feature of a girl's language:

> It may be that for girls to keep *their lips together* is a positive gesture. In the positive sense, closed lips do not exclude the possibility of either song or speech. (SP 114–15)

Putting it another way, if the lips were held constantly open, talking would be impossible: we are only able to speak because our lips move together, opening and closing. Nor is a person whose lips are always open pleasant to look at. The same fluidity and movement is true also of the genital lips: they can be touching one another, closed, without being locked or debarring sexual communication.

Secondly, the lips of woman and man touch in a kiss. Irigaray writes that: 'When lips kiss, openness is not the opposite of closure. Closed lips remain open' (EP 63), or, in French, 'l'ouvert, dans l'embrassement des lèvres, n'est pas opposé du fermé. Les lèvres fermées restent ouvertes' (Pe 77). The lips that meet do not close. The kiss allows exchange to take place without demarcations. It becomes impossible to distinguish whose fluid is which, or where it comes from. This means that it is very different from the concepts of ownership and property. There can be no sense of possession or mastery if the kiss is to remain one of mutual openness and vulnerability rather than domination of one by the other.

Thirdly, in heterosexual intercourse, woman's lips give form to man's penis in a way that allows it to grow:

> Is your penis substance to which my lips give form? In a becoming [*devenir*] which keeps potentiality [*la puissance*] and action in disequilibrium. Potentiality in action, never ceasing [*Puissance en acte, sans arrêt*]. My lips drawing the outline, without end, of the act. (EP 29; Pe 34)

This allows both for the mutuality of desire and pleasure, as well as for the conception of new life between man and woman, literally in the creation of a child, but also in the creativity that can come to both through the mutual giving and receiving of love.

Fourthly, the female lips are involved in giving birth.

They accompany birth without holding it to a – closed – place or form. They clasp the whole with their desire. Giving shape, again and again without stopping. Everything is held together in their fond embrace. (EP 65)

Elles accompagnent la naissance sans la retenir dans un lieu ou une forme – fermés. Elles embrassent le tout de leur désir. Donnant et redonnant sans cesse contour sans jamais arrêter. Tout se tient et ne se retient pas dans leur enlacement. (Pe 80)

The child who emerges from the lips is still held by the mother; and her lips speak to the child and welcome it into the world.

In all four interpretations, Irigaray shows a different mode of exchange from that of domination and possession common among men and celebrated by anthropologists such as Lévi-Strauss. Between the lips, exchange is possible whether they are closed or open. Woman's lips caress each other when closed. This carries the additional suggestion that woman, unlike man, does not need an object or an 'other' to lead her back to her origin. Lips which kiss remain open to each other; genital lips in intercourse or during birth suggest an unending source of becoming and desire.

It has already been mentioned that, for Irigaray, the exchanges of adult life are founded upon the earlier exchanges between a woman and her child. This first exchange involves closeness, touch and bodily fluids such as milk and blood, produced by the mother. Philosophy forgets this when, as Irigaray writes with reference to Plato's cave: 'morning is flooded with light', reason takes over from the senses and boundaries are distinguished and drawn (EP 64). However, Irigaray argues in chapter ten of *Elemental Passions* that this closeness should be recovered:

What is said silently, not said at the beginning but held back, not shown in the distance, that is the nearness that is so close that no name can reveal it nor release it from its shelter.

Before morning is flooded with light, before noonday life is set on fire, the whole is held together in a tender embrace, not yet open to allow anything to be seized in its presence. Departure, the severing of the one from the whole has not yet happened, an appeal for its return home to a surrounding proximity is not needed. (EP 64–5)

Ce qui se dit en silence, ce qui se tait au commencement, se retenant de se montrer dans le lointain, c'est le si proche qu'aucun nom ne peut le dévoiler, le libérer de son abri. Avant que le matin ne s'illumine, avant que la vie au midi ne s'embrase, le tout se tient dans un tendre enlacement, qui ne s'ouvre pas encore pour qu'une chose se laisse appréhender dans sa présence. (Pe 79)

This 'nearness', this 'tender embrace', Irigaray argues, should be retrieved and incorporated within philosophy through love and the copula, illustrated in lips that kiss and petals of a flower that touch.

Flower

In Elemental Passions lips that touch each other in a caress are invoked in the image of petals which fold together. The following quotations, on lips and petals respectively, illustrate this:

What my lips were keeping is put into motion, into action – edges which touch each other, communicate with each other, without privileging the one or the other. (EP 29)

Ce que gardaient mes lèvres est mis en mouvement, en acte mobile – des bords qui se touchent, se renvoient, sans privilège de l'un ni de l'autre. (Pe 34)

Two petals which meet and embrace endlessly ... The engendering ... of one petal by the other, the engorging of the petal, at the same time for both. Not the outpouring from one to the other, nor even from the one into the other. (EP 78)

Deux pétales qui se croisent et s'enlacent sans fin ... L'engendrement ... d'un pétale par l'autre, le remplissage du pétale, en même temps pour les deux. Et non le versement de l'un à l'autre, ni même de l'un dans l'autre. (Pe 94–5)

The fluid feature of lips discussed above also applies to petals of a flower. Here, too, exchange takes place without rigid boundaries. It is not possible nor indeed desirable to distinguish between one petal and the other. Engendering takes place without appropriation.

Irigaray's imagery of the flower is most fully presented in chapter six of *Elemental Passions*. 'Do you make me become (*devenir*) a flower?' is the question with which this chapter opens. The word for 'become', '*devenir*', is significant here. It is used by Irigaray to refer to woman's subjectivity, often in conjunction with 'puissance' (potency or power). When used together, 'puissance' (power) and '*devenir*' (to become) hold a promise for becoming a subject and point to the future, as we have also seen, for instance, in the closing sentences of the prologue. This becoming must be undertaken in freedom. 'Do you *make* me become a flower?' therefore suggests to the attentive reader that there is something wrong. For Irigaray, 'becoming' (*devenir*) is typically something that a man or woman should do or be allowed to do for themselves, and should not be made to do. 'Do you make me become a flower?' gives rise to the question of who makes whom become what and why? What would you-man want? Perhaps what man wants is a flower which offered itself to him in full bloom, like lips that were perpetually open? The French plays on words: 'La fleur ouverte: la fleur offerte' (Pe 37). But this is grotesque.

Irigaray suggests that the flower is an image with multiple resonances for woman in relation to man. The visible flower would be that in which man in Lacanian fashion wanted to find himself reflected: 'The flower would grow and blossom simply to let you gaze at yourself and find your double in it?' (EP 32); 'La fleur pousserait et s'épanouirait uniquement pour que tu puisses t'y regarder, t'y redoubler' (Pe 39). This flower would be an object for man as the following description makes clear:

Images for a female subject

Spread out, spread-eagled, exposed, no longer embracing, no longer embracing itself. No longer a brazier? (EP 32)

Ecartée, écartelée, dans son exposition, elle n'embrasse plus, ne s'embrasse plus. Ne s'embrase plus? (Pe 39)

In this quotation Irigaray's wordplay and seductive questioning style is apparent. The language used indicates a connection or at least an association between a flower, the display of its petals and display of the female body for purpose of the male gaze. We could interpret the reference to the exposing of woman's body as a comment on the use of women's bodies being spread-eagled in advertisements for clothing and in pornography. In these instances woman's body can be said to function as object for male lust. Yet *Elemental Passions* explores the possibilities for woman to become a subject; and Irigaray shows that the metaphor of the flower can be reconfigured to enable this becoming. After indicating that man requires the flower to blossom for his gaze, Irigaray points out that there is more to the flower than meets the eye. The flower also knows a different way of being, better found in the vocabulary of vegetation, of growing and flourishing:

... the petals spreading and coming together, that other growth, that other potentiality, which is not arrested in one actuality. (EP 32)

L'éloignement et rapprochement des petals, cette autre croissance, cette autre puissance, sans arrêt dans un acte. (Pe 39)

The flower knows of a way to be in which the production of blossom is not the main goal and in which there is no finality. Linear thinking is contrasted with a cyclical development in which petals fold and unfold endlessly. The word for 'that other potentiality' which marks this 'other growth' is once again 'puissance'. Of this potentiality it is said that it is 'sans arrêt dans un acte' (not arrested in one actuality) (EP 32; Pe 39). This recalls the passage of the prologue where I-woman's words are described as a song which is 'diffusion sans arrêt' (spilling out without a break) (Pe 8; EP 7). Woman's lips were said to safeguard the 'puissance' in the act of making (heterosexual) love: 'potentiality in action, never ceasing' (*puissance en acte, sans arrêt*) (EP 29; Pe 34). In all these instances the words 'sans arrêt' (literally 'without stopping') describe female sexuality and connect the images of a flower, song and lips.

A flower which blossoms just once, because you-man wants it to reflect himself, obscures woman's own becoming: 'Touching is hidden away ... beneath the earth' (EP 32) 'Enfouissement du toucher ... sous la terre' (Pe 39). In this way the flower indicates that woman's subjectivity does not follow the rhythm of growth that man dictates, nor does it follow the rules laid down by men for male subjectivity. This should not come as a surprise: the dichotomous structures of subjectivity have been designed by men, Irigaray suggests, precisely to exclude women from becoming subjects in their own right. In this economy they are meant to be objects of male desire, sexual and domestic. However, woman can only become a female subject if she is not forced to be something merely for man. When she is nevertheless forced to function solely for him, she wilts: 'A flower cut off from itself, in itself, by the erectness of the gaze' (EP 33).

The imagery of the flower shows the paralysing effect of the male gaze upon woman. What is at stake is that when you-man refuses I-woman-flower to grow and blossom for herself, then 'the flower has no reason other than your desire to bloom again and again for you' and loses her own 'puissance' (EP 35). Eventually, however, the flower is not content with merely waiting upon man. I-woman asserts herself to ask:

You want to make me into a flower? I also have roots and from them I could flower. Earth, water, air, and fire are my birthright too ... Let me flower outwards too. Free, in the air. Come out of the earth and blossom, following the rhythm of my growth. (EP 34)

Et tu veux me faire fleur? J'ai aussi des racines à partir desquelles je puis fleurir. La terre, l'eau, l'air, le feu, sont aussi mon partage ... Laisse-moi aussi fleurir vers le dehors. A l'air, libre. Sortir de terre et m'épanouir selon le rythme de ma croissance. (Pe 41–2)

I-woman asks why she should remain content with being a function for you-man, being the flower which is 'your destiny for me'. The double irony in this is that of course the possibility of becoming in the first place is intrinsically dependent upon woman. The mother initially gives the son the possibility to exist by letting him grow and mature in her womb. She is the source of his life, 'the flower which I have already given you'. Also, women among themselves have a relation before man breaks in: initially to their mothers, and eventually to their daughters and sisters, biological and chosen. 'Before I knew you, already I was a flower. Must I forget that, to become your flower?' (EP 34).

In other words, does woman have to let go of the kernel of her subjectivity planted in her by her mother, in order to enter into a relationship with man? Was Freud right? Or would it be possible for her to become a subject in relation to man, as she already is in relation to her mother and other women? If indeed women and men are to find mutual subjectivity, rather than domination and exploitation, then the 'path in between' that refers to Plato's forgotten path from darkness to light, from the unconscious to the conscious, from woman to man, needs to be rediscovered: 'what passages are there from the one to the other?' (EP 36).

Man's desire to be reflected by woman-flower has the following result: 'Unable to avoid the gaze, until then it [the flower] must bend, fold, close up again to safeguard some hope of rebirth' (EP 33). The French again plays on words: 'Ne pouvant se soustraire au regard, jusque-là elle doit se, *replier*, *renfermer*, *refermer* pour se garder une chance de renaître' (Pe 39, emphasis ours). The Irigarayan promise of better times, most explicit at the end of *Elemental Passions*, is invoked in this quotation. The flower droops and wilts and seems to die under its domination; but in fact it reassembles itself out of sight, far from the male gaze. Deep within her roots, woman, like a flower, will preserve her strength and promise of becoming until the opportunity for sexual difference will present itself and intersubjectivity will get a chance to develop.

Song

In *Elemental Passions* song is an image which appears only a few times. However, the places where it appears are highly significant. Song plays an important role particularly in the first and the last chapters, which we have characterized as respectively the prologue and the epilogue. In these places Irigaray's song defies dichotomies and boundaries through its fluidity.

Song is an image for woman's utterances when she cannot speak. In the beginning of *Elemental Passions* woman is withheld from speaking by man. Man, it is said, has 'stopped her speech or tongue'. The only way of expressing herself left to woman is singing. And sing she does. Her melody rises up to the clouds and mingles with the air. It envelops those who are near. This, however, does not mean that those who hear it actually understand. The first reaction of man to woman's song is one of ignorance and oblivion: he prefers speech to song, and cannot respond to her singing. 'You do not hear. So many words divide us. Divide us from the song' (EP 7). If such misapprehension occurs in the prologue, it is echoed and elaborated in the epilogue:

> How many words to forbid closeness! ... Attestations, quarrels, protestations, disputes over identity or the identical, distancing us, dividing us without any crossing of these barriers being possible. (EP 104)

> Que de mots pour empêcher ou interdire le proche! .. Les attestations, querelles, protestations, disputes quant à l'identité ou à l'identique, nous éloignant, nous écartant sans franchissement possible de leurs frontières. (Pe 127)

The aim of the song is to provide a 'way between', a bridge over the abyss of which Heidegger had written (1971: 92), an abyss that in the first instance separates man and woman (though that was not Heidegger's concern). As Irigaray presents it, too many words and philosophical arguments prove to be solid barriers rather than bridges towards a change in thinking about subjectivity. At the end of *Elemental Passions*, after all the struggle and small glimmers of hope for change it can still be doubted whether the goal of female subjectivity has come any nearer.

Still, the solution to the impossibility of closeness between man and woman is to be found within I-woman's song: 'And I shall sing all day long' (EP 104). This song is characterized as a shelter: 'Sonorous home in which I shelter you'. It is the dwelling, the shelter which refigures both the womb and language. As Margaret Whitford has argued, women, like men, need a covering, a house of language within which to dwell. Women's lack of a (linguistic) shelter has resulted in the fact that women make use of artificial coverings such as make-up. Yet these are not adequate to provide a basis for a female subject. The lack of shelter is

Elemental Passions

illustrated, Whitford maintains, in Irigaray's reference to Ariadne. After Ariadne saved Theseus from the Minotaur, Theseus left her behind, stranded on the island of Naxos. Although Ariadne had provided Theseus with the means to find his way back to the entrance of the maze, leading him back to her and to himself, Theseus in turn abandoned Ariadne and left her without a shelter (Whitford 1991b: 78). Transposed to an Irigarayan–Lacanian setting, the myth shows how even though woman-mother enables man by her embodied support to become a subject, bringing him forth from her womb, he in turn denies her the possibility of a dwelling in language.

In describing a womb as a 'sonorous home' the connection is thus made between song, sound and shelter. The meaning of 'sonorous home' is multi-layered. In *Elemental Passions* Irigaray evokes several further images for the womb. For example, the womb as a 'supple home', a 'protective shell', 'that airy and radiant house with neither door nor windows', a 'bodily dwelling' is contrasted with rigid enclosures and fixed boundaries (EP 15, 47, 48, 68, 16). The fluidity of mucous tissue and blood is contrasted to regulated exchange. However, the womb at times also appears as a constricted space, for example as an 'airy vacuum' which imprisons (EP 55). But at the end of *Elemental Passions* the womb is evoked as an image which describes a way of being together without constrictions imposed by each other:

I find you once more in the interweaving of the whole of space. The invisible mucous tissue which unites us day and night. Inhabits us and shelters us. (EP 101).

dans l'enlacement de tout l'espace, je te retrouve. Tissu muqueux invisible qui nous réunit jour et nuit. Nous habite et nous abrite. (Pe 124)

that enclosure which shelters and yet has no boundaries. (EP 104)

cet enclose, abri, et pourtant sans limites. (Pe 126)

One of the positive characteristics of the womb is thus its fluidity. It offers shelter without end, limitless, a dwelling within which there can be singing. This song as shelter without marked boundaries is at the end of *Elemental Passions* depicted as follows:

Childhood's cradle, where any rapture is given free play. An attentive hymn, which does not falter and is not interrupted. And whose tender fragility is never breached by fixed duration. (EP 104)

Berceau d'enfance, où toute ivresse s'ébat librement. Hymne attentif. Qui ne faiblit ni ne s'interrompt. Et dont nulle durée n'entame la tendre fragilité. (Pe 128)

Elemental Passions could be performed as this attentive hymn, a text to be read aloud: I-woman's incantation of the elements and passions, invoking love in human relations, analysing the hate and violence currently present, and developing a different view of proximity and property. It is an aria that consists of a theme and variations. The theme is the fluid exchange which is necessary for a female subject and for a love which allows subjects to become and develop in mutuality. The variations are the meditations: lips, flower, cloud, song.

Images for a female subject

The abyss and the mirror

The female subject who struggles to become in Elemental Passions is not a subject in isolation. She is not like a subject which erects itself by itself, like Descartes' subject in his Meditations. We have seen in the preceding chapters that Irigaray is critical of a subject in isolation. Both philosophy and psychoanalysis have been criticized by her for the construction of a solitary male subject who does not acknowledge his primary material dependence on woman. In Elemental Passions, a female subject becomes in relation to another subject. Both man and woman continue to develop as sexually different subjects, in contrast to the Freudian–Lacanian account in which female development is seen as lesser variant of the normative male pattern.

When discussing the mother–child, most commentators on Irigaray focus on her mother–daughter relationships (see for example Braidotti 1991: 259–61; Whitford 1991b; Boulous Walker 1998). The argument usually presented is that the mother–daughter relationship has been devalued, and that it is through a re-valuation of this relationship that women will be able to develop their subjectivity. In Elemental Passions, however, Irigaray also refigures the mother–son relationship. Whereas philosophy and theology have frequently emphasized a 'second birth', a birth for the male which is not from the mother but from Truth or God and which occurs by the ministrations of other men (Socrates as midwife; priests as administering the sacrament of baptism), Irigaray presents philosophy as something one can enter *with* the mother. A 'second birth' is then not necessary.

The philosophy into which such a maternal entry is possible is a philosophy in which love is part of its subject matter. This is illustrated by the following quotation from Elemental Passions in which the night refers to woman, the unconscious and materiality and the day refers to man, the conscious and thought.

And why should night and day be so radically divided? Is there anyone for whom loving and thinking are lived as different beginnings? (EP 34)

Et pourquoi le jour et la nuit seraient-ils aussi radicalement divisés? Pour qui l'amour et la pensée se vivent-ils comme avènements différents? (Pe 41)

The above quotation illustrates Irigaray's concern that binary oppositions rule our thinking. Night, associated with the feminine domain of love, and day, associated with the masculine illumination of reason, are constructed as binary oppositions. In Elemental Passions, these binary oppositions are radically questioned. Night is to be understood as valued in its own right, not merely as the absence or opposite of day (A and not-A); love and reason are not opposites but are different and mutually creative.

The distance between one and the (m)other and the enforcing of boundaries between one and the (m)other are subtly undone. The first contact between mother and son is recalled:

> Living inside me inside this mucous fabric he possesses me – my life. Surrounded by this warm and supple home, he sucks me up: my life. He is touched and touches himself – at first – inside this living flesh. (EP 15)
>
> C'est de l'intérieur d'un tissu muqueux qu'il m'habite, qu'il me prend – la vie. Entouré de cette maison souple et chaude, il me boit : la vie. Il est touché, se touche – d'abord – dans cette chair vive. (Pe 17)

In this quotation, attention is called to flesh and touch. Touch is the first sense we experience and Irigaray wants to bring this back within our thinking.[1] The foetus 'is touched and touches himself' at the same time. It is touched by the inside of the womb whilst it touches itself. Clear boundaries of touching and touched cannot be drawn. As was the case with respect to female lips, touch is here central to Irigaray's development of a female subject.

In her womb, woman gives part of herself to the unborn child: air, blood and body-warmth. As we have seen in the commentary on the text, it is Irigaray's contention that though he does not admit it, the adult man continues to feed off the woman-mother. Man's original debt to the mother is not acknowledged. Instead the (m)other is repressed and excluded from man's realms of thought and language. Yet man continues to rely on the (m)other for sustenance and material support. This dependence on woman also remains unnoticed. This means that woman supports man in being, but that this support is neither acknowledged nor reciprocated. For Irigaray, woman's lack of language, the silencing of her song, results in a lack of female subjectivity. She exists for man.

In contrast to the 'warm and supple home' that the mother offered the son, the son grown into a man offers woman fixed enclosures: a family home and the institution of marriage. Irigaray suggests that in the womb, the son could move about. In contrast, woman's mobility is halted in man's enclosures. She is paralysed in her becoming (EP 18). As a result, the enclosed woman loses her voice. She wears 'the covering of your choice' (EP 62); she lives by man's desires in terms of her dress, her make-up, the house he buys, and even his surname: first the father's and then the husband's. We have seen that the woman in *Elemental Passions* reacts to this covering in two ways. She first cries out in despair that man's coverings obscure her and her speech:

> And how could I cry out that I was living inside you? That I spoke through your mouth? That your love was mine just as much as yours? (EP 26)
>
> Et comment crier que j'habitais en toi? Que je parlais par ta bouche? Que ton amour était aussi bien le mien? (Pe 31)

But then, later in the book, when her best efforts have failed, she urges him to leave: 'Go ... Leave me the opportunity of continuing to become' (EP 84).

Interwoven within these outcries of desperation is the motif of change. In his

---

[1] As mentioned earlier, this was also a project of Maurice Merleau-Ponty, though he did not consider it in relation to sexually different subjects.

Images for a female subject

fear of difference, man forces woman into a place. He represses her difference. Yet *Elemental Passions* shows that this is not a fruitful solution:

But this difference creates an abyss. And is there anyone who does not fear the abyss? How can there be attraction between different beings in spite of the abyss? What risk is there in attraction through difference? Not in me but in our difference lies the abyss. We can never be sure of bridging the gap between us. But that is our adventure. Without this peril there is no us. If you turn it into a guarantee, you separate us. (EP 28)

Mais cette différence fait abîme. Et qui ne craint pas l'abîme? Comment a lieu l'attrait entre les différents, malgré l'abîme? Quel risque contient l'attrait dans la différence? Ce n'est pas en moi, mais dans notre différence, que gît l'abîme. Nous ne sommes jamais assurés de franchir le pas entre nous. Mais cette aventure est la nôtre. Pas de nous, sans ce péril. Si tu me le laisses en gage, tu nous sépares. (Pe 33)

The abyss, the fear of difference lies not within woman. The gulf between her two lips, the unfathomable dark gap should not give rise to fear and violence by man: as woman says: 'Not in me but in our difference lies the abyss'. The challenge for Lacan's son and mother, for Parmenides' one and other, is to face the difference between them instead of to bury and 'forget' it. It requires violence to repress differences and force people into a mould of the self-same. In Chapters 1 and 2 of *Forever Fluid* we saw examples of the violence which is unleashed when the 'other' refuses to obey the rules of the 'self-same' and insists on his/her difference. When the 'other' refuses to be seen in terms of the self-same, for example when woman refuses to be seen as not-man, man has to recognize that he himself is an 'other' too. He has to acknowledge that woman and man are distinctly different subjects. This means that one, man, cannot be taken as a norm for the other, woman.

In the third chapter of *Elemental Passions*, we saw that man reacts violently when woman refuses to be defined in his terms only. When woman establishes herself and says 'I', she is in fact 'returning this forgotten property to you: mortal' (EP 20). She, the 'other', asserts herself and reminds man that he, like she, is finite. Man's reaction to woman's difference is to repress it; but the recurrent denial of sexual difference results in a return of an 'abyss' between man and woman. How can this abyssal difference be resolved? Irigaray refigures this dangerous divide and makes it into a challenge for lovers to overcome:

But I take pleasure and you take pleasure in these differences, in this difference, as in an overabundance of riches. Experiencing you, experiencing me, espousing you, espousing me, we are more than one. And two. The accounts overflow, calculation is lost. (EP 58)

Mais de ces différences, de cette différence, je jouis et tu jouis comme d'un en-plus de bien. T'éprouvant, m'éprouvant, t'épousant, m'épousant, nous sommes plus qu'un. Et deux. Les comptes se débordent, les calculs s'y perdent. (Pe 71)

I caress you, you caress me, without unity – neither yours nor mine, nor ours. (EP 59)

Je te caresse, tu me caresses, sans unité – ni de toi, ni de moi, ni de nous. (Pe 72)

Elemental Passions

Irigaray takes love as the motive to acknowledge and respect difference. For Irigaray, the image of making love illustrates the possibility for two subjects to be different *and* together at the same time. She rejects the idea of a (sexual) union as a fusion because, she argues, a fusion would mean that woman would lose herself as a subject. Difference for Irigaray presents the opportunity for intersubjective relations to develop and ultimately functions as a safeguard against appropriation of one by the other. In the above quotation, we see a fluidity in the caress that the other images we have considered also display: 'you' and 'I' come into being together, both of them as subjects. In the caress, boundaries are blurred and 'accounts overflow'.

Irigaray distinguishes two kinds of love: a love that appropriates the other and a love that allows the other to become. She advocates the second kind:

> Love can be the becoming which appropriates the other for itself by consuming it, introjecting it into itself, to the point where the other disappears. Or love can be the motor of becoming, allowing both the one and the other to grow. (EP 27)

> L'amour est le devenir qui s'approprie l'autre en le consommant, en l'introjectant en soi-même, jusqu'à sa disparition. Ou l'amour est le moteur du devenir qui laisse l'un et l'autre à leur croissance. (Pe 32)

A love that allows the other to develop acknowledges the abyss of difference between two subjects. This abyss may give rise to fear, but is necessary for each subject to grow. Since both subjects develop in their own way, the outcome of this relationship in love is uncertain. The aim of *Elemental Passions* is not to provide a defined goal but to evoke this fluidity of becoming.

This new way of looking at the abyss also reconfigures Lacan's imagery of the mirror. Indeed in Irigaray's formulation, it becomes possible to see the resonances between the image of the abyss in philosophers of modernity such as Heidegger, and the mirror imagery of Lacanian psychoanalysis. Irigaray says,

> If being no longer belongs to you, if you are no longer devoted to it as you are to your language [*langue*] enclosure, if being means permanent advent between us, our bodies become living mirrors. Sense mirrors where the outline of the other is profiled through touch. (EP 77)

> Si l'être ne t'appartient plus, si tu ne lui es plus voué comme à ton enceinte de langue, si être revient à l'avènement permanent entre nous, nos corps deviennent miroirs vivants. Miroirs sensibles où se dessinent, tactilement, les contours de l'autre. (Pe 93)

Instead of a flat, silver mirror, which can freeze and fixate the images it reflects (*glace* means both mirror and ice), Irigaray develops the concept of 'living mirrors'. These living mirrors or sense mirrors are bodies, which touch, for example in the embrace of lovers. These mirrors do not reflect a lonely, solitary subject, nor a subject who is intent on mastery of the (m)other and control of its passions. Instead, it enables subjects to become in relation to each other. In this formulation, the mirror, no longer restricted to linear gaze but now also alive with touch, reflects both man and woman back to one another. No longer is woman the object of the male gaze, the one on whom his identity of mastery depends. Rather, the bodies of each reciprocally profile the other. The rigid binary of subject/object is replaced by mutuality which flows between them.

Indefinitely, I embrace you, you embrace me. And it is not in the mirror's shining silver that I seek you, endlessly.

But I find you once more in the interweaving of the whole of space. The invisible mucous tissue which unites us day and night. (EP 101)

Indéfiniment, je t'embrasse, tu m'embrasses. Et ce n'est pas dans la brillance du tain que, sans cesse, je te cherche.

Mais dans l'enlacement de tout l'espace, je te retrouve. Tissu muqueux invisible qui nous réunit jour et nuit. (Pe 124)

Irigaray thus uses the images of an abyss and a living mirror to develop the concept of love between two subjects, male and female; and instead of a flat surface where the shine is only on the surface, she uses the idea of a fluid image, like that of still deep water which reflects the beauty of its surroundings.

Irigaray's images intertwine with one another; so for example the mirror and the abyss are also closely related to that of the copula. The copula has already been mentioned as describing the lost proximity between man and woman. But what exactly is it? It is analogous to the 'living mirror', 'the path in between', which is also the umbilical cord. It brings two subjects together without obliterating their differences:

the copula ceaselessly undoes the privileging of any figure ... Always at least two, and never the same. Thus undermining any model appropriated. Remodelling our difference. (EP 28–9)

la copule défait, sans cesse, le privilège d'une figure ... Toujours au moins deux, jamais les mêmes. Déjouant ainsi tout modèle approprié. Remodelant notre différence. (Pe 34)

At the same time it refers to the bodily act of making love in a way that shows respect for bodies: the bodies of both man and woman (EP 79). Irigaray argues that too often the body has been 'reduced to erogenous zones, objects of attraction and manipulation, and ground for exploitation. Tool-machine for producing *jouissance* or children' (EP 79). The body when used as an object for pornography or for procreation ignores the potential for developing subjectivity, present in the embrace or copula. Irigaray claims furthermore that woman's body has been exploited in the same way as the earth has. So long as woman/earth is not respected, relations between men and women, and indeed the act of loving, will not be fruitful. The copula as an image indicates restored respect for bodies and points to the possibility of the development of a female subject. In the epilogue Irigaray paints a promising picture:

A new East – the sun accompanying the birth of a little girl. Another [*une autre*] – the other [*l'autre*] – being brought into the world ... You are witnessing the revelation of the end of a unique truth. Not as the advent of chaos, but as the possibility of the copula – in the sun. (EP 95)

Nouvel orient – le soleil accompagnant la naissance d'une petite fille. La venue au monde d'une autre – de l'autre ... Tu assistes à la manifestation de la fin d'une vérité unique. Non comme avènement du chaos, mais comme possibilité de la copule – dans le soleil. (Pe 118)[2]

A little girl is born. Not a little boy-Christ, nor a little girl who really should be a little boy, but a little girl who claims her position as other/*autre*. The 'unique truth', the truth of man and his reflections, is undone. In its place comes the copula, the (sexual) embrace, in the sun, which is also the mirror and the abyss. It is not hidden away from the light of reason. The material, corporeal conditions for life are openly acknowledged. And touch becomes the sense which takes prevalence over sight.

Virginity

In the images discussed so far, woman's subjectivity and morphology are intricately linked. This is also highlighted in Irigaray's interpretation of the significance of virginity for a woman. Irigaray contrasts the exchange between female lips to the exchange of a virgin between men in an economy where women are chattels. The tearing of the hymen of the virgin (*viol et vol*) forms a contrast with the unseen, unrecognised and unvalued exchanges which take place prior to this exchange: the exchanges within woman (*en elle*) and between women (*entre elles*) (EP 64). Within a woman fluid is continually exchanged between her lips; and within a pregnant woman, fluid and air are exchanged between herself and the foetus.

These exchanges, Irigaray holds, are lost within masculinist language, which is founded upon a male subject who takes the virgin as his object/property. Yet Irigaray argues that this masculinist mastery would not be possible unless there were a prior exchange, exchange between women and between mother and child. We saw in the previous chapters how the exchange of communication between mother and daughter which takes place before the daughter enters language is undervalued. Irigaray, however, maintains that these unrecognized female exchanges make the exchanges between men, exchanges of women and of language, possible. These are the unseen but necessary foundations of male exchange. Following on from the quotation about the exchange of virgins between men cited above, she says:

[2] In the following chapter we will address the question of Irigaray's failure to address differences other than sexual difference, as here in her use of 'the East' as an image of that which is 'not West': an uncontextualized orientalist appropriation rather than genuine engagement with Eastern practices and Eastern women.

Images for a female subject

without the prerequisite openness, without those lips always leaving a passage from inside to outside, from outside to inside, and staying in between as well, the place of exchange would not be so secure. It is the closed-open lips of the woman which make it practicable for them. (EP 64)

sans le préalable de l'ouvert, sans ces lèvres laissant toujours passage du dedans au dehors, du dehors au dedans, demeurant aussi entre elles, le lieu des échanges ne serait pas assuré. Les lèvres fermées-ouvertes de la femme, tel est leur practicable. (Pe 78)

The 'passage from inside to outside, from outside to inside' in this quotation, is crucial for the exchange between lips. It is analogous to the path in Plato's cave which Irigaray maintains is forgotten; and parallel, also, to the forgetting of air or breath.

In addition, Irigaray makes links to the development of christendom, in particular to the enormous importance that has historically been attached to the idea that Mary was a virgin when she gave birth to Jesus. It could be argued that a husband's right to penetrate his wife was secured by the male Christian God: Mary did not have sexual intercourse yet the male God saw to it that she conceived. Her fertilization was still under (divine) male control. Irigaray maintains that in the prevalent interpretation of Mary's role in the Annunciation, Mary's virginity is seen purely in terms of the hymen, whose status determines the woman's value to men. If on the other hand virginity could be seen as a woman's property, not a possession of men or part of an exchange value, then one could argue that the multiple debates about whether or not Mary was a virgin when she was pregnant with Jesus would be irrelevant. Elsewhere Irigaray re-interprets Mary's role in the Annunciation as follows:

In my view, respecting Mary's virginity does not mean forcing a Father-logos upon her whose son she conceives outside of her female body, as is all too often taught; rather, it means not touching her body without asking her if it is what she wishes or desires. What we celebrate in the name of the Annunciation would then be the time of shared words between a man and a woman prior to any carnal act or conception. (ILo 123)

Dans ma perspective, respecter la virginité de Marie ne revient pas à lui imposer un Père-logos dont elle concevrait un fils en dehors de son corps féminin – comme cela s'enseigne trop souvent – mais cela signifie ne pas toucher à son corps sans lui demander si elle le souhaite ou le désire. Ce que nous célébrons sous le nom d'Annonciation seriait le temps d'un partage de paroles entre un homme et une femme avant tout acte charnel et avant toute conception. (Jat 190–1)

In Irigaray's interpretation virginity stands for an inherent quality of woman's being. She argues in 'When Our Lips' that the idea of becoming a woman through losing one's virginity only makes sense from a male heterosexual perspective in which a woman is seen as a (sexual) object which can be 'owned' (TS 210–11). In Irigaray's economy of sexual difference, the term 'virginity' describes the physical and moral integrity of a woman. Irigaray says in an interview:

This meaning of the word 'virgin' is to be distinguished then from the assimilation of virginity to the conservation or non-conservation of a corporeal hymen. It is a question of a becoming spiritual aiming at the maintenance of the integrity of the self and the other. (Pluhacek and Bostic 1996: 353)

Thus, for Irigaray, virginity is not something which can either be held on to or lost once and for all, but an aspect of womanhood that should be preserved and protected by law throughout a woman's life (1993b: 86–8). If at any time a woman's virginity, her integrity, is taken against her will, she should be able to take legal action. The hymen loses its importance as something which simply marks a rite of passage, something that can be kept intact or can be broken through by force. What is wrong is *any* violation of a woman's integrity: in *Elemental Passions*, therefore, virginity is yet another image for the female subject and the possibility of fluid mutuality. Once again, Irigaray's interpretation subverts linear thinking which operates through dichotomies. In relation to Irigaray's concept of virginity, there is no clear 'before' or 'after', there is no violent rupture or break-through; instead, woman's virginity, understood as her integrity, evolves over time.

In relation to the image of a flower discussed above, this means that a woman cannot be 'deflowered' by a man. The concept of 'deflowering' loses its meaning. The flower in *Elemental Passions* which blossoms once and once only, so that man can find his reflection in it, conveys the idea that a man's bride should be a virgin so that he and only he break her hymen. In such a case, the relation between man and woman is not a relation between sexually different subjects but between a male subject and his property. A female subject cannot become in these circumstances: the flower dies. In Irigaray's rethinking of virginity, however, the exchange of an object, a woman, between men is replaced by the exchange within a subject, a woman. The exchange of fluids within a woman takes place between her lips which touch continuously. It is this which enables a woman subject to engage in mutual exchange with a man. Thus in relation to male and female subjects, the exchange of an object is replaced by endless exchanges, shown by multiple images. Both a male and a female subject are in continual development, in relation to each other; neither of them is a 'possession', let alone an 'opposite' or binary other; both of them are in an endless process of growth, forever fluid.

The images in *Elemental Passions* are not the images usually found in philosophical texts. All of them are crucially related to fluidity; all of them point towards the becoming of sexually different subjects and away from the rigid binaries of traditional philosophy and psychoanalytic theory. Because of the great potential of Irigaray's work for rethinking discursive and material reality, and because *Elemental Passions* is relatively unknown, we have chosen to offer our commentary without intruding critical remarks. There are, however, problems in Irigaray's work which must be confronted, and we turn to them in the following chapters.

PART III

Critical identities

CHAPTER 6

Multiple subjects and fluid boundaries

The development of mutually affirming sexual subjects, different but not oppositional, and thereby the destabilizing of traditional binary categories of oppositional logic, is simultaneously highly innovative and has far-reaching consequences. Because of the significance of Irigaray's work in this regard, and because until now there has been no detailed study of *Elemental Passions*, our strategy in the first two sections of this book has been to present and explicate Irigaray's text with a minimum of critical comment. However, the act of thinking about mutual subjectivity and developing images of women who are subjects, and replacing a rigid binary system of thought with a rationality that allows for fluidity, is not just an abstract academic exercise. It affects lives. It is therefore important to consider to what extent Irigaray achieves her aims and what the consequences are.

In this section, therefore, we will subject Irigaray's methods and contentions to critical scrutiny. In Chapter 6 we will present a critique of Irigaray's method and her claims regarding the development of a female subject. In the final chapter we will revisit the idea of fluidity in relation to logic, to see what difference it can actually make. Our argument in both cases is that although there are serious problems with Irigaray's account, nevertheless useful insights can be taken from her work for thinking through alterities and the consequences of alterity for logic. Although we find certain problems in the ideas Irigaray presents in *Elemental Passions*, it is nonetheless a highly creative work which gives us the necessary signposts to direct us beyond its own limitations.

Who are you?

When Irigaray in another context considered the question of who she would like to have as her reader, she wrote as follows:

The only response one can make to the question of the meaning of the text is: read, perceive, experience ... *Who are you?* is probably the most relevant question to ask of a text, as long as one isn't requesting a kind of identity card or an autobiographical anecdote. The answer would be: *how about you?* Can we find common ground? talk? love? create something together? (SG 178)

> La seule repartie qui puisse être donnée à la question du sens du texte, c'est : lisez, percevez, éprouvez ... Qui es-tu? serait une question plus pertinente, à condition de ne pas retomber dans la demande de carte d'identité ou l'anecdote autobiographique. La réponse serait : Et toi? Pouvons-nous nous rencontrer? nous parler? nous aimer? Créer quelque chose ensemble? (SP 192)

The questions this quotation raises for us are perhaps slightly different and more literal than Irigaray intended. Who is Irigaray? – not, indeed, in 'identity card' or biographical terms, but rather in terms of the question: from what subject position does she write? And who is the 'you' to whom she addresses herself and with whom she engages? Who does Irigaray read? Who does she hope will read her?

The questions indicate a tension in Irigaray's thought, a tension which was already present in her earlier writings and which recurs in Elemental Passions. Irigaray largely accepts Lacanian psychoanalytic theory whereby woman has no language, no subject position of her own: indeed it is precisely this which she says is constitutive of Western culture and especially of philosophy. Women are inscribed in the Name of the Father; the ruling symbolic is masculinist, and women have no voice with which to speak. But then what about Irigaray herself? Is she not a woman? And does she not speak, in this book and in her others? We are not the first to raise these questions: they have been of concern to her readers from the publication of Speculum onwards. Soshana Felman articulates them well in her review of Speculum:

> If 'the woman' is precisely the other of any conceivable Western theoretical locus of speech, how can the woman as such be speaking in this book? Who is speaking here, and who is asserting the otherness of the woman? If, as Luce Irigaray suggests, the woman's silence, or the repression of her capacity to speak, are constitutive of philosophy and of theoretical discourse as such, from what theoretical locus is Irigaray herself speaking in order to develop her own theoretical discourse about women's exclusion? (Felman 1997: 120)

If we are all steeped in and structured by the masculinist symbolic, then how can Irigaray step outside of it and analyse it? In terms of Elemental Passions, how (and in whose voice and language) can I-woman address and challenge you-man? It is on the face of it self-contradictory to complain on the one hand that 'you have stopped my tongue' (EP 7) and on the other hand to continue to speak and write a whole book in a woman's voice, thereby assuming the very subject position whose possibility she denies.

Whatever may be the case for her earlier books, by the time Irigaray writes Elemental Passions she has found a way out of this performative contradiction. Although she still sometimes writes as though woman has no voice, more often her complaint is not that women cannot speak but that man refuses to hear. 'You did not hear. Nothing from outside the place where you already are reaches you anymore' (EP 10). So I-woman uses various strategies to try to get you-man to hear. She sings. She uses imagery. She writes in a poetic, allusive style so that the reader can make something of it only by actively engaging with it.

But if this is the case, if women (including Irigaray) can speak after all even if in a different style from men, then it must also be the case that as speaking women, they already are subjects. Only subjects can speak. So it is not possible for Irigaray to write in a woman's voice, to allow that women can speak, and at the same time to argue that women have no subject position. What she *can* do, of course – and we would suggest that this is how *Elemental Passions* should be read – is to show how men keep refusing to listen, keep trying to silence women and in so doing circumscribe and suppress women's subjectivity, imposing male needs and desires, male domination and enclosure. Only if the book is read in this way does I-woman's repeated effort to get you-man to listen and respond to her make sense and avoid performative contradiction.

This interpretation is consistent with other things Irigaray has written, especially her exhortation to women to refuse patriarchal domination and to take responsibility for ourselves, not only in terms of speech but also culturally and politically. Irigaray argues in This Sex Which Is Not One that women are in a unique position on the borders of patriarchy (TS 191). We should utilize this position to critique the symbolic system we take part in, so that we become subjects of exchange rather than objects which are exchanged. Thus as she says again in an interview, 'Women are committed to two gigantic tasks: assuming consciousness of the order of language and of one's tongue as sexualized and also of creating a new symbolic morphology in which she can say: I, sexual being, woman, assert such and such, take such and such action and so on' (Mortley 1991: 72). Irigaray's insistence on women's responsibility for language and for our own subject position is however not without problems. Her assertions here seem to bypass what she elsewhere protests: the fact that as a consequence of our patriarchal society and its social and economic injustices many women do not have the means to take action or even to protest at their silencing. Irigaray sometimes writes as though all women are as privileged as she is, and seems unconscious of the situations of deprivation in which many women find themselves. Exhortations to women from whom the basic means of livelihood are removed are at best pointless and at worst callous. We would argue that it would be more appropriate to recognize differences *among* women – an issue to which we will return – and to urge those of us who are sufficiently privileged to be able to work for responsibility for our own language and subject positions to work also for justice and empowerment for others. In other words, the question 'Who are you?' must be confronted not only in relation to sexual difference but also in relation to social and material differences and their causes. We will come back to this.

The question of difference among Irigaray's possible addressees is closely related to her choice of discussion partners. Who does Irigaray read; with whom does she engage? If we begin from the assumption that at least some women – in the first place Irigaray herself – do find themselves able to speak and to take up subject positions, even though it is a struggle, then there is no reason to think that Irigaray is unique in this endeavour. If Irigaray can make a place for herself outside the patriarchal symbolic, or even adopt a critical position towards it, then so can other women: indeed if they could not, her exhortations would be futile. Yet Irigaray does not seem to write in a way that invites contributions from other women: could they not have significant contributions to make to the development of language and female subjectivity? Penelope Deutscher has pointed out that especially in Irigaray's later work she tends to adopt the position of a teacher who delivers a theory to her pupils: her aim is one of making herself clear rather than entering into a dialogue with readers who might have opinions of their own (Deutscher 1998: 172–3).

This is not entirely fair to *Elemental Passions* (or indeed to *Marine Lover*), in which a reader must engage with the text and actively interpret the images and allusions: it is impossible to read this text as a passive recipient of information or theory. Nevertheless, even *Elemental Passions* is entirely spoken by I-woman addressed to you-man, either directly or in meditation on images. Nowhere in the text does Irigaray leave room for other voices; nowhere does I-woman look for help in her efforts to communicate with you-man to other women and the strategies they might have developed. Is there scope for the creation of something new only in the ways Irigaray envisages it or in other ways as well? For all the questioning and elusiveness of *Elemental Passions*, the voice we hear is *one* voice and the female subject created is *one* subject. Are there perhaps other female subjects besides this one? What might they wish to say? Can they speak? The text comes perilously close to reinscribing the very silencing of women which it is intended to overcome.

The problem here is connected to the fact that Irigaray develops her philosophy of the female subject primarily in relation to a male philosophical and psychoanalytical subject and in relation to a male canon. There is virtually no indication in *Elemental Passions* and very little elsewhere in her work that Irigaray reads women writers. It is true that we have the occasional counter-example: she writes 'Equal to Whom?' as a review of *In Memory of Her* by the contemporary American feminist theologian Elisabeth Schüssler Fiorenza; and in *Je, tu nous* she comments on the French intellectual Simone de Beauvoir and her book *The Second Sex*. In addition, she discusses female psychoanalysts in 'Psychoanalytic Theory: Another Look' in *This Sex Which Is Not One*; and she interviews a female biologist in 'On the Maternal Order' in *Je, tu nous*. But that is about all. Even those texts, moreover, are relatively brief and are not nearly as intricate and exciting as Irigaray's close readings of male philosophers and psychoanalysts. Why? There is by now a considerable body of feminist work in philosophy and psychoanalysis, much of it addressing similar concerns to those of Irigaray, yet she virtually ignores it. According to her own theory it is crucially important that women develop engaged communication amongst ourselves; yet in her writings the voices of women are effectively silenced, and there is as little evidence that Irigaray is listening to them as there is that Freud or Lacan or Heidegger took women's voices seriously.

Critical identities

One could argue in mitigation that in order to create a space for a female subject within philosophy, Irigaray *has* to address what Braidotti calls the 'masters of philosophy' (1994a: 129). Nobody can do everything. Irigaray has done so much; it is churlish to complain that she has not done even more. On the other hand, however, one could also argue that by choosing to interact exclusively with male canonical philosophers and psychoanalysts, Irigaray perpetuates the very canon she is trying to destabilize; and by ignoring feminist philosophers she reinforces their marginalization and deprives herself of their insights into the issues with which they, like Irigaray, are concerned.

A 'secondary problem'?

Moreover, it is not surprising that since Irigaray pays attention chiefly to male thinkers, the primary difference she sets up between herself and her dialogue partners is sexual difference: it is indeed the only difference that arises in *Elemental Passions*. Her valorization of the male canon could perhaps begin to explain why Irigaray sees other differences as secondary. In a notorious passage in *I Love to You* Irigaray reiterates her argument about the importance of sexual difference, and adds that this constitutes the primary difference between people:

> Sexual difference is an immediate natural given and it is a real and irreducible component of the universal. The whole of human kind is composed of women and men and of nothing else. The problem of race is, in fact, a *secondary problem* – except from a geographical point of view? ... Sexual difference probably represents the most universal question we can address. Our era is faced with the task of dealing with this issue, because, across the whole world, there are, there are only, men and women. (ILo 47; our emphasis)

> La différence sexuelle est un donné immédiat naturel et elle est une composante réelle et irréductible de l'universel. Le genre humain tout entier est composé de femmes et d'hommes et il n'est composé de rien d'autre. Le problème des races est, en fait, un problème secondaire – sauf du point du vue de la géographique? ... La différence sexuelle représente probablement la question la plus universelle que nous puissions aborder. C'est au traitement de celle-ci que notre époque est affrontée. En effet, dans le monde entier il y a, il n'y a que, des hommes et des femmes. (Jat 84–5)

The passage bristles with difficulties. In what sense is sexual difference naturally – let alone universally – given? In the light of the work of Judith Butler (1990) and others, how can Irigaray possibly assert a rigid binary of 'men and women and nothing else'? – does this not run contrary both to the empirical reality of blurred boundaries and to Irigaray's own investment in fluid logic? To what extent is Irigaray reinforcing compulsory heterosexuality? And can other differences – of race, class and privilege – be so easily dismissed as 'secondary'?

In a recent interview, Irigaray was asked to explain this particular passage. The question and response are as follows:

Q. In what sense is sexual difference the most appropriate content for the universal? How do you respond to those who see this privileging of sexual difference a luxury due to a class, racial or cultural privilege?

A. Sexual difference is a given of reality. It belongs universally to all humans. Being interested in it cannot, in any case, result from any privilege, but forgetting its importance can. (Pluhacek 1996: 357–8)

We would argue, however, that this response is inadequate. While we of course agree that the question of sexual difference is hugely important, we would argue that even on Irigaray's own terms it is urgently necessary to consider *multiple* differences. It is not the case that 'woman' and 'man' (or even male and female) are 'naturally given' and universally the same. Nor is it the case that sexual difference is always primary and that other concerns are secondary, less urgent.

To show this we begin with race. In our view, the significant question to ask here is: for *whom* is race a 'secondary problem'? Who could be writing about the development of a female subject in philosophy and think that race is a secondary factor in the constitution of that subjectivity, a factor that could perhaps be deferred for later consideration? Such a perspective is possible only for someone who can afford to remain unconscious of racial privilege because she is not confronted with its oppressive realities in daily life. But what about those whose very lives depend day by day on observing the rules laid down by the dominant racial or ethnic group? If one's racial identity constantly excludes one from positions of power or even equality in terms of health, education, housing or the basic necessities of life, if one experiences regular definition of oneself as 'other', deviant from the norm, 'not-A', then it is impossible to put race on hold as a factor which could be sorted out later, once sexual difference has been dealt with. There are many instances: the apartheid regime in South Africa or the Nazi era in Germany, the Tutsi–Hutu conflict in Rwanda, the Palestinian–Israeli conflict. In each case and many others it could be argued that racial difference is more important than sexual difference with regard to survival and self-preservation: or, better, that sexual difference is simply undefinable without reference to its inextricable connections with race.

Nor is it enough to say that while this is unfortunately true in the examples we have mentioned, it is largely not true for white Western feminists, for whom sexual difference is central. Though we may remain unconscious of it, whiteness defines us as surely and as deeply as blackness or Jewishness defines black and Jewish women respectively. In Chapter 1 we presented Dyer's argument that whiteness is constructed as neutral in our society. White, he argued, is not perceived as a colour, while black is. If one belongs to the privileged group, if one is white, then it is possible to ignore the difference whiteness makes and to take the privileges whiteness confers as 'normal'. One can choose when and whether to consider race. But if one is oppressed because of one's race, then that choice is foreclosed, as we discussed above. As feminist standpoint theorist

Nancy Hartsock showed, those who belong to oppressed groups need to be aware of two perspectives in order to survive: their own, and that of the oppressor. The oppressors can suffice with their own perspective and even consider it to be neutral and universal (Hartsock 1987).

Hartsock argues for a struggle on the part of the oppressed to become aware of the dimensions of their oppression and to do all they can to resist and overcome it. We entirely agree with the necessity of this struggle. We would argue in addition, however (as would Hartsock) that it is vitally important that those who belong to the oppressive groups also bring this to consciousness and unite with those who are oppressed to bring about social change. Irigaray takes this strategy for granted in relation to sexual difference. Women are to become conscious of our exclusion from language and subjectivity and work to overcome that exclusion; and part of the strategy is to make men aware that their allegedly neutral and universal subject position is in fact one which silences and oppresses women. In *Elemental Passions* I-woman tries repeatedly to get you-man to see exactly this point. Nor would you-man be able to evade the issue by saying that he was not aware of doing anything to oppress women, that he intended no such thing, that some of his best friends were women, that he loved his wife... Even when all those things are true (and often they *are* true) it does not change the fact that in a language and culture dominated by the Name/Law of the Father, men belong to the privileged group. Indeed it is precisely for that reason that they can remain unaware of it, posit themselves as neutral and universal. But as Irigaray shows in *Elemental Passions*, true mutuality of sexually different subjects is possible only when men abandon that position of universality, and recognize and renounce their own (often unconscious) complicity in the dominance of their sex.

Now, surely the same must be said for other sorts of difference, including race, economic status, sexual preference, and dis/ability. The fact that in these cases (some white) women are part of the privileged groups rather than being oppressed in these respects does not change the argument a jot. Just as men who, without necessarily intending to oppress women or even without being conscious of their own privilege, nevertheless are part of the dominating group and need to become aware of it, so also white feminists who want to work for social justice need to recognize how fully our own identity is bound up with our whiteness. Failure to become conscious of this amounts to reinscribing racial injustice by complicity. These points have often been made before; the interlocking nature of oppression has been ably analysed by writers such as bell hooks (1994), Patricia Hill Collins (1991) and Val Plumwood (1993). It is an unfortunate consequence of Irigaray's lack of attention to feminist writers that she does not notice how her own writings can hardly escape being read as complicit with racial oppression from a perspective of assumed neutrality.

It is all the more unfortunate because, we would argue, Irigaray's own tactics could be used to recognize and celebrate multiple differences, not only the sexual difference upon which she concentrates. Who will take part in the construction of female subjectivities, and on what basis? Assuming that the invitation is open to all women, irrespective of race, sexual orientation, ethnicity, class, age and health, how exactly will the diversities among women be recognized?

One might begin one's reasoning by summing up all the factors that could be important for one's identity: thus for example we could say that we are white, female, Western academics. Such an acknowledgement of perspective has become something of an expectation in feminist writing; and it has a purpose in helping both author and reader to recognize the point of view from which something is written. But if we leave it at this and proceed to develop our theory of subjectivity as if we were speaking for all women, then the summing up of the above characteristics serves as little more than an excuse. It could amount to saying, 'I know I am influenced by these factors; so are we all; now let us theorize as usual'. Yet this 'as usual' could imply theorizing about other subjects as though our own subject position were universal: a subject who turns out to be white, Western and academic. This is no better than a female counterpart of the familiar traditional male subject: it is precisely the subject with which Irigaray herself seems to end up.

This is obviously not the way to go. It is not enough neatly to separate out, and then add or subtract, factors that make for oppression. One needs to take these characteristics seriously as interlocking to form a specific frame of thought, which can 'enframe' and constrict as surely as does that of you-man in *Elemental Passions*. Just as Irigaray's male subject has to learn that he is not universal, that his maleness is a factor in his point of view, so we, white women, have to learn that our whiteness (and other forms of privilege) shapes our own perspectives. Analogous to Irigaray's valorization of sexual difference, a case can thus be made for racial difference, indeed for multiple differences. Just as woman has been defined culturally as not-man, 'not-A' to man's 'A', so also within Western culture the term 'black' has been used as a repository for all the characteristics that white people did not want to attribute to themselves: wild, primitive, sexually aggressive, prone to criminal behaviour and the like. Just as woman requires to define herself in her own terms, not simply as what man is not, so also differences of race and ethnicity, ability and sexual orientation must be valued for themselves, not simply as opposites to an assumed norm.

What Irigaray attempts in *Elemental Passions* is to develop mutuality between subjects characterized by sexual difference; and this mutuality is enabled by loosening up and listening. By sustained efforts of communication, what had seemed like rigid categories can become fluid. Thus one aspect of the male subject in *Elemental Passions* is that he has to learn to listen in a different way, while one aspect of the developing female subject is that she has to learn how to speak of herself as a subject. These two movements encourage each other. Images of fluidity destabilize rigid polarities and enable mutuality where each is no longer defined by what the other is not. Together they create something new. The same process, we would suggest, can be followed with respect to multiple differences. Those in positions of privilege and power need to open themselves up to listen to voices that they were not hearing before, and by this listening help to create a space in which it is safe for those who are not so privileged to speak. In this way barriers that divide can be replaced by fluid boundaries that allow for mutuality between subjects with multiple differences.

I-woman and you-man

There is another way in which all this can be approached, and that is by revisiting the question of who I-woman and you-man might be in *Elemental Passions*. Although it is easy to read the text as though these terms stand for all women and all men in a false universalism, there are also indications that point to a more nuanced reading.

This could be the point at which to enter into a discussion of terminology and the related vexed question of essentialism. What is the difference between the terms 'female', 'femininity', 'woman' and 'women', for example, and how do these relate to corresponding French terms? What about Irigaray's own use of them? Is it true that Irigaray links the category of 'woman' so closely to sexual morphology that she ends up in sexual essentialism, thus reinforcing the very dualism which she is striving to subvert? Interesting and important as these questions of terminology and essentialism are, however, we propose not to enter into them directly, for two reasons. First, in relation to Irigaray's earlier work they are already well rehearsed (see Whitford 1991b, Burke et al. 1994). Secondly, we think that it will be more interesting to see whether *Elemental Passions* can widen the discussion of Irigaray's insistence on sexual difference.

The first clue comes from what appears to be a rigid distinction in the text itself. Throughout *Elemental Passions*, at least as we have interpreted it, I-woman is represented as loving, giving, unselfish, and making all the effort in a relationship in which she is silenced, abused, shut in, and kept from growth by you-man. He in turn is represented as violent, fearful, insecure, and constantly needing woman to bolster his ego. He doesn't seem even really to try to understand what she is saying, whereas she keeps on singing, trying to help him and shelter him, until the last page filling 'the air with the joy of you in me, of me in you' (EP 104) despite all the frustrations and setbacks. Life is not like that. If I-woman and you-man are supposed to represent empirical women and men, then the whole text collapses into caricature. One can almost see the cartoon: a nauseatingly self-righteous woman facing a violent but terrified little man. Many men are in fact decent and loving, and try their best to do their part in mutual relationships with women. And no woman is loving and wonderful all the time: women easily become manipulative, moody or selfish.

Everybody knows this; so how is the text to be read? We make the following suggestion, though somewhat tentatively. Irigaray was profoundly influenced by Lacan, as we have discussed in Chapter 2, and although she had very deep disagreements with him, he remains one with whom she is in constant conversation in her writings, implicitly or explicitly. Now, central to Lacan's discussion of sexual difference is his claim that the phallus is the universal signifier, and that in consequence language and subjectivity are male: this is exactly what Irigaray struggles against. Lacan says,

> The Phallus is a signifier, a signifier whose function in the intersubjective economy of analysis might lift the veil from that which it served in the mysteries. For it is to this signifier that it is given to designate as a whole the effect of there being a signified, inasmuch as it conditions any such effect by its presence as a signifier. (1982a: 79–80)

'Phallus', here, stands for 'desire/gratification', and as such is essential for entry into the symbolic which is inseparable from the chain of desires. However, Lacan repeatedly denies that 'phallus' equals 'penis'. 'Phallus' is meant to designate not anatomical structure but desire as such.

Now, Lacan's distinction between 'phallus' and 'penis' is unconvincing to say the least; indeed his insistence on the masculine nature of the symbolic actually requires their identification (see Jantzen 1998b: 51). But what interests us here is Lacan's attempt to keep them apart, to distinguish conceptually between the signifier (phallus) and the anatomical structure (penis). Might Irigaray be making the same sort of move between 'I-woman' and actual women? Thus in *Elemental Passions* 'I-woman' is not a quasi-name for all women, but rather acts as a signifier?

But a signifier of what? The first impulse is again to say that it can only signify women, and that 'you-man' must signify men; but that impulse obviously leads us straight back into the difficulties we were trying to overcome. We propose an alternative. Perhaps 'I-woman' could be taken much more broadly than as a simple signifier or 'name' for a particular woman or a group of women or even women in general. What if Irigaray's 'I-woman' were read as a signifier of *difference*, in the way that Lacan (at least sometimes) intended 'phallus' to be read as a signifier of desire?

To read 'I-woman' as a signifier of difference would have immediate advantages. In the first place, it would overcome the objection of caricature – the too-good-to-be-true woman pleading with the struggling, violent man, in a gendered variant of Hegel's famous rendition of the master–slave encounter. If 'I-woman' stands for difference, then there is no need to suppose that actual women are always wonderful or that actual men are dreadful. Rather, 'I-woman' is portrayed as generous and loving because in the encounter of difference, that is the role which 'I-woman' represents, while 'you-man' represents the role of dominance.

A second advantage, even more important than the first, is that if what is signified is difference (rather than empirical women and men) then this opens the way for multiple differences. The encounter between 'I-woman' and 'you-man' is then an encounter that seeks to establish mutuality in a relationship of two subjects, whether the two are sexually different, racially different, ethnically different, and so on. The struggle for mutuality is a struggle between two subjects, one of whose subjectivity is repressed and kept from flourishing by the other's strategies of dominance. Thus any such difference could be signified, not only sexual difference. Reading 'I-woman' in this way would therefore deal with the objection we raised above, that sexual difference is represented as the primary or the most important difference, when in fact there are situations where racial difference (or other kinds of difference) are at least as crucial, or are so thoroughly interlocked that there is no possibility of dealing with them separately. If 'I-woman' and 'you-man' are read as signifiers of difference as such, rather than as exclusively sexual difference, then the text of *Elemental Passions* is available for consideration of multiple different subjects.

These are enormous advantages. There are, however, also major difficulties with this reading, some of which could be overcome but others which seem to us less tractable. Beginning with the former, it must be said, first, that Irigaray herself never addresses issues of multiple difference. Indeed, as we have already discussed, when she has been questioned about issues of race, culture or privilege she has relegated them to secondary consideration and insisted on the primacy and universality of sexual difference. Whereas in Lacan's writings it is explicit that 'phallus' is not intended by him as a signifier of 'penis' but as a signifier of desire as such, the parallel move cannot be made in the case of Irigaray's stated aims. In terms of Irigaray's intentions, as evidenced both in *Elemental Passions* and throughout her other writings, there is little to indicate that she herself thought of 'I-woman' as a signifier for difference itself.

But this objection, we believe, is not insurmountable. Although it is of course not appropriate to attribute to Irigaray herself intentions which there is no evidence to show that she entertained, it is legitimate to show that her concepts and strategies can be extended beyond the ways in which she used them. This is especially the case when such an extension overcomes problems inherent in her own use. Thus we suggest that extending 'I-woman' and 'you-man' from their use in her text as tied to sexual difference, so that they are signifiers of difference as such, is a valid move even though Irigaray herself did not make it.

A second problem arises with the parallel to Lacan. In Lacan there is one signifier, the phallus, which is meant to signify desire as such. We suggested that, similarly, 'I-woman' in *Elemental Passions* could signify difference as such. So far so good; but of course in *Elemental Passions* 'I-woman' is always represented in relation to 'you-man'. Even in the meditations on the images, 'I-woman's' reflections revolve around that relationship. So are there two signifiers, rather than one? And if so, then what does 'you-man' signify?

These, however, we suggest, are the wrong questions, generated by a partially faulty presentation on our part. Although initially we suggested that 'I-woman' could be read as a signifier of difference, in our exposition of that claim there has already been a slide towards seeing 'I-woman' and 'you-man' *together* as the signifier of difference. We think that this slide should be welcomed, not resisted. After all, how could a single term by itself signify difference when difference is always between (at least) two? We would therefore propose that 'I-woman' and 'you-man' are separate signifiers only within the relationship of difference, but that together they signify difference itself. This makes the parallel with Lacan less exact, but it does more justice to the way in which the two terms function in *Elemental Passions*. We again emphasize that we are not attributing our reading here to Irigaray's intentions, though we believe that our reading is a creative extension of her text.

This brings us to a third, more difficult, problem, which can initially be expressed by again drawing the parallel with Lacan. As we have said, his attempts to dissociate the phallus from the penis are unconvincing: his discussion of language, subjectivity and the symbolic are implicitly – and often explicitly – masculinist. Might the same be true in *Elemental Passions*: that is, that even if we try to read 'I-woman' and 'you-man' as together a signifier of difference as such, they are in fact so closely tied, in direct comment and in allusion, to empirical women and men in Western culture that they cannot be disentangled, cannot actually be used as signifiers of difference as such? Certainly 'I-woman' and 'you-man' in the text of *Elemental Passions* are recognizable as a woman and a man in Western culture, with the physical and psychological characteristics typical of each: she bleeds, has a womb, is silenced by his mastery; he uses her as an object of exchange or a mirror for his esteem and resorts to violence and tactics of control. If these are stereotypes or even caricatures, they are nevertheless all too accurate in their portrayal of women and men in our society. Moreover, in her Introduction Irigaray makes it perfectly clear that she means them to be read as such.

This, we think, cannot be fully overcome. The most we could do would be to suggest that the text could be creatively extended and modified so that 'I-woman' and 'you-man' would carry allusions to other sorts of difference as well as sexual difference. Possibly this could be done, but even if it could, we would have to acknowledge that it would be a different text, not the one we have. We therefore have to admit that our suggestion that 'I-woman' and 'you-man' in *Elemental Passions* be read as a signifier of difference as such ultimately does not work. The text itself does not permit it.

But this does not mean that the suggestion was a waste of time, for ultimately it points beyond the text of *Elemental Passions* to issues of multiple difference, multiple subjects. We have argued above that the strategies of *Elemental Passions*, strategies of mutually vulnerable listening and communication, can be extended from the encounter between sexually different subjects to other sorts of difference. In this way the becoming and flourishing of many kinds of subjects can be respected and empowered. The narrative *events* between 'I-woman' and 'you-man' in

Elemental Passions are events dealing with sexually different subjects and cannot be forced to stand for other sorts of encounters; but the *strategies* of attentive listening, renunciation of a will to dominance, willingness to try and try again for communication and mutuality are strategies that have wider application. In this respect, the development of mutual subjectivity in sexual encounter can serve as a paradigm for other sorts of encounter as well.

However, this still leaves the question of whether sexual encounter can in fact bear the whole weight that is placed upon it. It seems clear that its strategies can be extended to other sorts of difference with good effect. In our exposition of the text we interpreted Irigaray as operating on more than one level. In terms of narrative, she is presenting the possibility of mutuality between sexually different subjects, and the vicissitudes of their development in relationship. But it was our contention that through the representation of this narrative a philosophical theme emerges, with links back to Empedocles, a theme that challenges the binary logic of Western philosophy. If the most important encounters of our lives, those encounters which enable us to develop and flourish as subjects who are nevertheless different from each other in important ways, require that we allow rigid binaries to be subverted by fluid logic, then Irigaray's text operates not only as a narrative of the encounter between 'I-woman' and 'you-man' but also as a subversion of the dogmas of Western rationality. If a system of thought that purports to be universal, as does standard binary logic, in fact cannot account for the most significant events of our lives in our development as subjects, then that system of thought is seriously flawed. Or put another way, if these events point to a fluid logic, then it is important that we investigate what such fluidity comes to, not only in the poetics of sexual encounter but in logic and rationality itself. This investigation is the task of our final chapter.

CHAPTER 7

Fluid logic

What could be meant by 'fluid logic'? What would be its characteristics? What difference would it make to philosophical or psychoanalytic theory if it took fluidity seriously and allowed it to destabilize the binary system of traditional logic? What would be its creative possibilities, and what would be its difficulties? These questions have been growing ever more insistent as we have explored *Elemental Passions*. We wish to use this final chapter to begin to address them.

Fluid logic and Irigaray's project

As we have interpreted *Elemental Passions*, the challenge of fluidity to philosophical logic has been the subtext of the whole book. Yet it must be said that Irigaray never addresses this issue directly. In terms of narrative structure, *Elemental Passions* is from beginning to end an address of I-woman to you-man, in which she tries to find her voice and language, and thereby become a subject in mutual relationship with him. Yet in that effort, as we have seen, ideas and images of fluidity play a central part. There is direct appeal to the fluids of sexual encounter and of giving birth: sperm, mucus, blood, placental fluid. Without these fluids there could be no life. There are images in which fluidity is significant even if also partly metaphorical: lips, flower, air. None of these can be held by rigid boundaries; all depend more or less literally or metaphorically on a flow from one to another or from one state to another. Most importantly of all, if an encounter is to take place between subjects of sexual difference, if there is to be mutuality between these subjects, then rigid boundaries must give way. It will not do for the man to be designated as the One, the universal or unmarked term, and for woman to be the bearer of the marks of difference, whatever the One is not, the other of the Same. In Irigaray's words,

> Giving oneself, that giving – a transition which undoes the properties of our enclosures, the frame or envelope of our identities. I love you makes, makes me, an other. Loving you, I am no longer the same; loved, you are different. Loving, I give myself you. I become you. But I remain, as well, to love you still. And as an effect of that act. Unfinishable. Always in-finite. (EP 73–4)

Se donner, ce donner – transition qui défait le propre de nos clôtures, le cadre ou l'enveloppe de nos identités. Je t'aime fait, me fait, autre. T'aimant, je ne suis plus la même; aimé, tu es différent. Aimant, je me donne toi. Je deviens toi. Mais je reste, aussi, pour t'aimer encore. Et comme effet de cet acte. Inachevable. Toujours in-fini. (Pe 90)

And in another passage, where Irigaray returns to the idea of the gift, fluidity is again to the fore:

In the gift, what happens to me is not that I become a thing thanks to your offering, but that I touch you without any system of mediation-screens. In that touching, I become you, also. And I receive from you, of you, in giving myself. In that gift which touches, 'we' becomes a flow, a fluid. (EP 79–80)

Dans le don, ce qui m'advient n'est pas de devenir chose grâce à ton versement, c'est de te toucher sans système de médiations-écrans. En ce toucher, je deviens, aussi, toi. Et je reçois de toi, du toi, en me donnant. Dans ce don qui touche, nous devient flux, fluide. (Pe 96)

Moreover, Irigaray sees the encounter between sexually different subjects as the most important issue to be addressed: important for ethics, for politics, for social justice. And this encounter cannot be thought without fluidity. As we argued in the last chapter, we find Irigaray's insistence on sexual difference too narrow; and we suggested that her strategies should be extended to multiple differences. Although the fluids of sexual encounter could hardly be so obviously appealed to as metaphor and model for the encounter of racially or ethnically different people, nevertheless here too it is obvious that rigid boundaries are inappropriate. The hitherto dominant group must acknowledge and renounce its assumptions of universality and normativity, and engage instead in listening to the other; and the hitherto oppressed group must continue its efforts to speak and find its own voice and subject position(s). Thus the importance of fluidity, of a back-and-forth flow between them, is as great here as it is in the case of sexually different subjects.

Irigaray's project is to make the case for (and enable the development of) sexually different subjects in philosophy, in psychoanalytic theory, and in Western culture generally. This is true not only of *Elemental Passions* but of all her writings from *Speculum* onwards. Although she never tackles systems of logic directly, let alone develops any *theory* of fluid logic, it is clear throughout her work that philosophy can never accord sexual difference the place it deserves as long as it continues in a 'business as usual' mode. Its canons of rationality and logic will have to be modified, and modified far more drastically than by simply adding women on to existing ontology or epistemology. Philosophy, according to Irigaray, has been structured and governed by a male imagery, especially in its model of rationality that bases itself on exclusion (A as excluding not-A) (see Whitford 1991b: 73). This, she argues, needs to be systematically disrupted.

We need to listen ... to its procedures of repression, to the structuration of language that shores up its representations, separating the true from the false, the meaningful from the meaningless, and so forth ... its syntactic laws or requirements, its imaginary configurations, its metaphoric networks, and also, of course, what it does not articulate at the level of utterance: *its silences*. (TS 75)

In her early work Irigaray focuses more on the disruptive than on the creative effects of such feminist listening, 'jamming the theoretical machinery' by 'suspending its pretension to the production of a truth and of a meaning that are excessively univocal' (TS 78). By the time she writes *Marine Lover* and *Elemental Passions*, however, it is clear that disruption and creativity are inseparable; indeed in the development of her poetic and allusive style and the dense imagery of these books, creativity has become central. And key to that creativity is a fluid logic that supplements and in some senses replaces the masculinist binary logic based on an imaginary of exclusion.

Thus the logic of fluidity is indispensable to Irigaray's project as a whole, and nowhere more so than in *Elemental Passions*. Yet she never presents it directly, or deals with its characteristics or how it functions. Within the terms of her own efforts towards sexually different subjects, perhaps she does not need to do so. But if her ideas about fluid logic are to be of use to feminist philosophers, if they are to serve as more than a mantra, then it is important to present and investigate them more fully than she has done, and to see them against the broader context of philosophical logic. This is what we try to do in what follows. We wish to stress, however, that although we have done our best to interpret Irigaray correctly, and we hope that our presentation is consistent with her views, our discussion of fluid logic is indeed ours, not hers. We have taken her ideas and images and tried to work out more systematically than Irigaray did what they come to. How do they challenge traditional logic, and what creative possibilities do they open up? As we develop these themes, we will try to be clear about when we are presenting Irigaray's ideas and when we are using them as a springboard for our own development of a logic of fluidity.

Irigaray and the Greeks

In earlier chapters we stated that *Elemental Passions* can be read as one of a series of books dealing with the four elements: earth, air, fire and water. It takes some of its reference points from Empedocles, who emphasized these elements as the building blocks of reality, and who saw Love and Strife as the primordial forces or passions which determine the interaction of the four elements. We also discussed, in the first chapter, how Empedocles' thought begins to suggest alternative patterns of rationality to the binary logic that characterized the system of Parmenides and Pythagoras. In that respect Empedocles is a congenial starting point for attempting to find a way forward.

But immediately it is necessary to make two qualifications. The first is that there is little scope for confidence about the precise meanings intended by the Greek philosophers in question. No writings survive from Pythagoras himself; his teachings are known only through the works of others, often far removed in space and time from Pythagoras himself. Even to some of these early witnesses Pythagoras and his teachings seem distinctly odd; and by the time of Ovid's representation of Pythagoras in his *Metamorphoses* the old philosopher had become a figure of fun. It is anybody's guess whether the table of opposites which Aristotle attributes to Pythagoras (odd–even, good–bad, light–dark, male–female, and so on) really did come from him. The case is a little better with Parmenides and Empedocles. Although no complete work of either of them survives, there are substantial fragments in their own voices. Moreover, there is extensive commentary by philosophers who are more nearly contemporary with them than is the case with Pythagoras. Nevertheless, it is impossible to be completely sure of their teachings at many points, partly because of the fragmentary nature of the sources and partly because their allusive, poetic style often permits more than one interpretation. This being so, is it really appropriate to blame or credit these Presocratic philosophers for the subsequent structure and development of Western logic? Is this not a disproportionately heavy weight to expect them to bear?

The second qualification, which to some extent mitigates the first, is that Irigaray herself does not offer *Elemental Passions* as in any sense a commentary on Empedocles or a refutation of Pythagoras or Parmenides. She does not so much as mention their names (or the names of any other writers), and she gives no references. She expects her readers to engage with her text in the context of familiarity with the canon of Western philosophy from classical Greece through Kant and Hegel to Heidegger, Sartre and Derrida. If a reader is immersed in this literature she will find frequent allusions and echoes: we have drawn attention to some of these in our commentary in Chapter 4. But Irigaray herself offers no help. Her approach in *Elemental Passions* is in this respect quite different from that in *Speculum*, for example, where she offered a close reading and line-by-line comment on writings of Freud, Plato, Descartes and others. It is only in a heavily qualified way, therefore, that *Elemental Passions* is linked to Empedocles. Its relation to Empedocles is much looser than, say, *Marine Lover* is linked to Nietzsche, or *Forgetting the Air* to Heidegger. At most, Empedocles offers Irigaray useful strands of ideas on elements and passions out of which she weaves her own web.

Although these qualifications must be made, however, they should not be taken to imply that Irigaray's allusions to Greek thought are casual or merely convenient. We pointed out in Chapter 6 that Irigaray conducts her philosophical work within the context of the male-dominated canon of the Western tradition. The texts with which she engages are those which would appear in any standard survey of the history of Western philosophy with a bias towards continental rather than English-speaking writers: Plato, Aristotle, Plotinus, Descartes, Kant, Hegel, Nietzsche, Heidegger, Derrida, Levinas. She takes their concerns as hers, and destabilizes them by raising the question of sexual difference. Although she is often sharply critical, she also owes much to these thinkers.

Now, one of the striking things about all these philosophers from Hegel onwards is their preoccupation with Greek thinking, especially with Presocratics. As Irigaray notes in an interview,

> We are witnessing ... a modification in the use of language by certain philosophers who are turning back toward the origins of their culture. Thus Nietzsche and Heidegger, but also Hegel before them, interrogated their foundations in ancient Greece, and in religion Levinas and Derrida are interrogating their relation to the texts of the Old Testament (Jardine and Menke 1991: 101)

and to the Greeks as well. In one way or another, each of these writers looks back to the Greeks – or to some of them – as a well-spring of thought which subsequent philosophy has contaminated; and they try to get back to a purer origin. This is perhaps clearest of all in Heidegger, who suggests that the West has forgotten the meaning of Being, something which he believed the early Greeks understood. When Irigaray argues that Heidegger has also forgotten something, has missed the significance of sexual difference in his efforts to remember Being, she is issuing a profound challenge to his thought, but not one which in any way minimizes the significance of his attempts to return to the Greeks. As Tina Chanter points out,

> It is not by chance that Irigaray, in her rehabilitation of the elements, draws on the very philosophers that figure so prominently in Heidegger's analysis of the history of Being – namely, the Presocratics ... Irigaray's reconstruction of a feminine morphology appeals to the material elements and seeks to expose the limits to which the male philosophical tradition submitted when it lost interest in the sustaining elements of the Presocratic world view. (Chanter 1995: 163)

Central among these was Parmenides, with his account of Being as that which excludes all change and becoming. Irigaray cannot ignore Heidegger's reliance on Parmenides in her insistence on the becoming of sexually different subjects.

In this connection it is significant that Levinas, another of her partners in conversation, had also explicitly challenged the logical structure of Western philosophical thought, which he attributed to Parmenides. In his *Time and the Other* (1987: 42) he specifically stated his intention to 'break with Parmenides', in particular in relation to the unity of Being and the logical structure which this imposed upon Western thought. In *Otherwise than Being* (1981) and *Totality and Infinity* (1979) Levinas carries this project forward, and explicitly appeals to sexual difference as crucial to his understanding of the face-to-face relation to which he appeals as the basis of philosophy. As we shall see below, Levinas' thought is of great importance for the development of a logic of fluidity; and in spite of the fact that Irigaray is in some respects sharply critical of him, she owes much to Levinas' thinking. Irigaray's use of the Greeks as reference points must therefore be taken seriously, even though she prefers allusions and associations of ideas rather than direct reference or quotation.

Critical identities

The story of Western philosophy is often told by English philosophers as though it is a story of steady progress, with rationality and logic developing from Presocratic origins through Plato and Aristotle: this is the impression given, for example, by the standard English work on the history of logic, William and Martha Kneale's massive *The Development of Logic* (1962). They move smoothly if briefly from Pythagoras to Plato, and then to Aristotle whose work they present in detail as foundational to Western logic. Continental philosophers such as Heidegger and Levinas are much more aware of the differences and disagreements among Presocratic philosophers; and aware, too, that the 'development' of logic and Western rationality rested on a series of choices and exclusions. These choices, they insist, could have been made otherwise. It would have been possible, for example, to valorize Heraclitus more than Parmenides, or to give Empedocles much greater weight, or to read Plato or Aristotle differently.

What impact such choices would have had on the logic that emerged it is not now possible to know. Indeed our thinking itself, our ideas of what counts as rationality, have been structured by the writings of those philosophers who were given prominence, so that when Heidegger or Levinas try to excavate alternative possibilities it is hard for them and for their readers to think otherwise. Nevertheless, these continental philosophers insist that the choices that were made were not inevitable. By going back to the origins of Western rationality, they argue, it is possible if not to start again, at least to make some urgently needed shifts in what counts as rationality. This also is Irigaray's project, especially in connection with sexual difference, as we have seen: a project which, if successful, also calls for major rewriting of a logic which has heretofore been structured according to rigid binary opposites.

What is logic for?

Logic is regularly presented as concerning itself with correct thought as contrasted with error. Parmenides, as we saw in Chapter 1, was told by the goddess that her teaching was the way of truth, while the masses who were not initiated into logic and who followed the way of opinion were 'two-headed', in perplexity with 'minds astray' (Coxon 1986: 54). This idea of logic as crucially involved with truth and with the correct thinking which will result in truth has been repeated many times in the history of Western thought. One of the philosophers who influenced logical theory most forcefully in the twentieth century was Gottlob Frege, who began his famous essay 'The Thought' by saying:

> The word 'true' indicates the aim of logic as does 'beautiful' that of aesthetics or 'good' that of ethics ... To discover truths is the task of all sciences; it falls to logic to discern the laws of truth ... Rules for asserting, thinking, judging, inferring, follow from the laws of truth.
> (Frege 1967: 17)

Frege continues by emphasizing that these laws are not subjective or psychological. Rather, 'the meaning of the word "true" is explained by the laws of truth' (18). We have here the closed circle which characterizes much modern logical theory: logic is defined by truth, but truth itself is defined by logic.

Logic and its methods are therefore presented as central to rationality, enabling thought and protecting from error. It does so in large part by evaluation of the validity of arguments and the logical truth of statements. Susan Haack begins her work on *Philosophy of Logics* in the spirit of Frege and of formal logic since his time:

> A central concern of logic is to discriminate valid from invalid arguments; and formal logical systems, such as the familiar sentence and predicate calculi, are intended to supply precise canons, purely formal standards, of validity. So among the characteristically philosophical questions raised by the enterprise of logic are these: What does it mean to say that an argument is valid? that one statement follows from another? that a statement is logically true? (Haack 1978: 1)

These 'sentence and predicate calculi' which fill many textbooks of symbolic logic are closely akin to algebraic formulae: many a newcomer to philosophy who approached the subject hoping to think about issues of human nature, the world, and God has found herself in astonished despair that her elementary logic class seems more like a continuation of mathematics by another name. Yet logicians insist that these systems of formal logic are vitally important to help us think clearly and to discriminate true claims from false ones and good arguments from bad ones (Grayling 1982: 20). Indeed 'good' and 'bad' here have resonances with praise and blame, as P.F. Strawson acknowledges when he writes,

> When a man [sic] says or writes something, there are many different ways in which his performance may be judged ... If you call a discourse logical, you are in some degree commending it. If you call it illogical, you are, so far, condemning it. (Strawson 1952: 1)

Although Strawson hastens to add that he is not suggesting this to be a moral appraisal, there is nonetheless a strong evaluative undertone: it is *better* to be logical than illogical.

Better for what? Better for whom? What is logic for? It is safe to assume that most people want to think clearly and do not want to be deceived; and it is common for logic to be presented as an essential tool for these purposes, as we have seen in the above examples. But having made perfunctory appeal to the desire for clarity of thought, Haack, Grayling and Strawson (and many others like them) fill the pages of their books with the notations and formulae of predicate calculi which are certain to confuse rather than clarify the subject for all but the most persistent readers. In this these authors are only following the lead of some of the most highly regarded logical texts of modernity: Frege's *Begriffsschrift* (1879/1970), Russell and Whitehead's *Principia Mathematica* (1910), and Wittgenstein's *Tractatus Logico-Philosophicus* (1961) to name three of the most influential.

Whether or not they intend to be elitist (and many of them would deny that they do) their writings illustrate the same contempt for ordinary mortals and their concerns – including their concerns for clarity of thought – that we have already found in Parmenides' description of the 'two-headed' masses.

This is so not only because they employ complicated symbolic systems and formal notation. If this were all, then the response might well be that they are not intended for the novice, and that this is no more a fault than it would be in the case of advanced astrophysics: a certain level of specialism and sophistication in the subject is a legitimate prerequisite to reading advanced texts. The issue is rather that central to the systems of logic I have mentioned is their purely formal nature. As we saw in the case of Frege, logic is defined as aiming for truth, and truth is defined by the laws of logic. These laws can be set out in purely formal terms without reference to content: the Law of Identity, for example, states that A is A, and the Law of Non-contradiction that A is not not-A; and these laws hold whether A is an apple or an albatross. The same quality of form without content applies to the entire system of symbolic logic. Indeed it is considered a virtue of the predicate calculus that it is purely formal; that it is entirely empty of content.

Now, this makes for fascinating intellectual gymnastics for those who are amused by such things. It may also have interesting implications in the field of advanced theoretical physics or mathematics. But to suggest that it enables 'us' to think clearly and to avoid deception could hardly be true unless 'we' are mathematicians or logic buffs. It does not – and does not pretend to – deal with the concerns of ordinary life. As Andrea Nye has said,

> The problems of logic, historians of logic seemed to insist, are logic's own; they are unrelated to conflictual relations between men and women, between men, or between men and the natural world, unrelated, that is, to all that might have made them understandable (Nye 1990: 3)

or indeed useful. As Nye points out, logicians may illustrate their writings with examples from ordinary life, but these are strictly irrelevant.

> In the midst of mortal life, the logician clears a supra-worldly space that he maps with the eternal patterns of logical relations. (3)

Part of these patterns, allegedly, are rigid binaries, articulated by the Law of Excluded Middle: anything is either A or not A. Formally, this law like the rest is empty of content. But as with other aspects of logic, it is not as innocent as protestation of its formal nature would make it seem.

The idea that logic is empty of content might make it irrelevant or of interest only to specialists, but in itself that is not a failing as long as it does not pretend to be about ordinary life. We could simply shrug and say that some people have strange hobbies. Indeed it is in part precisely its formal structure that enables authors such as the Kneales (1962) to trace its history as an orderly development: they present the story of Western logic as a narrative in which successive thinkers see ever more clearly what is involved in the pure rationality that is logic. Moreover, these thinkers, though presented chronologically and in relation to each others' thoughts, are not otherwise contextualized: their cultural and political stance, their motivations and their lives are not deemed relevant to the progress of pure thought.

And yet that approach, though in many respects it derives from Parmenides, also misses an important facet of his poem. For Parmenides, it was *desire* that prompted him to make the journey to the goddess, desire that urged him on as far as his heart would go. Although his quest for truth seemed to leave ordinary life and ordinary embodiment far behind, it was nevertheless passionately motivated. Now, desires do not come from nowhere. They are rooted in our bodily and sexual being and our social and political context. Passions are, as Irigaray insists, elemental. They are not avoidable, nor can they be superceded. We cannot attain a desireless state, nor should we wish to; and all human activities, including the activity of developing a logical system, take place only because they are somehow motivated.

Contemporary practitioners of logic might concede this, but still argue that although at some level every human activity is of course motivated, this has nothing to do with the logic that results. The laws of logic hold whether anyone wants them to or not. No matter how much someone might wish the Law of Noncontradiction not to apply to a particular occasion – might wish to have their cake and eat (not have) it too – it still applies, and no amount of passion or desire could make it otherwise. Indeed part of the point of logic is to cut through the desires and passions which too easily distort our thinking, and thereby to enable us to confront stark truth.

While this sounds initially plausible, however, especially when what is under consideration is an individual law such as the Law of Identity or the Law of Noncontradiction, it becomes much less persuasive in relation to the complex systems of logic that have been built upon them, the systems which the Kneales describe in their *Development of Logic* and that result in the quasi-mathematical propositional calculi of modern symbolic logic. In fact, a very different account can be given of these systems than a narrative of benign progress, an account which investigates the motivation behind some of these systems and the functions that they have been made to serve. Andrea Nye, in her important book *Words of Power* (1990) has begun such an investigation. She explains how systems of logic have been developed and used as technologies of control, and are intertwined with political motivations of dominance. Plato's methods in the *Sophist*, for example, are methods which remove reciprocity from a discussion, making one party (in this case Theatetus) a docile respondent while the other (the Stranger) controls the conversation.

The laws of noncontradiction and excluded middle force Theatetus' replies and also his thought, into approved channels. They structure a drill by which Theatetus can learn, not

> to think, but to repeat what his teacher says. The logic of the Stranger's argument is the exercise of that authority. It is logical necessity itself that denies Theatetus' futile attempts at response. (Nye 1990: 34)

Again, Aristotle's logic, developed in several of his books and still emphasized today as foundational for systems of logic, was not constructed in a neutral or dispassionate context.

> The debates for which Aristotle's logic was a handbook were not between a few leisured aristocrats disinterestedly contemplating eternal truths, but between men intent on winning and preserving power, privilege, and wealth. (43)

Similarly, the logic developed by the Stoics and promoted by Cicero was a logic that enabled the governance of the vast Roman Empire; the logic of Ockham served to separate church and state and thereby provided a model which could be used in the development of Protestantism and secularism; even the complex modern systems of totalizing logic developed by Frege were formed within a fascist context and played into Nazi hands.

It is of course possible to object to the implications of Nye's work by showing that some of her historical observations are mistaken; or by saying that the use of a system for bad ends does not invalidate the system itself; or by insisting that no matter how evil the motivation of a philosopher (and she is not attributing evil motivations to them as individuals) this does not render their claims untrue. All this must be granted. Even so, it is impossible to read Andrea Nye's book without being forever disabused of the idea that logical systems are neutral or benign, or that there can be an apolitical narrative of the development of logic. Logical systems are technologies of power, systems to structure thought. As her book shows, that power has regularly been used in oppressive ways; and it is always gendered. In every case that she investigates, one of the effects of logical systems has been to silence women, whether because the 'logos spermatikos' is quintessentially male, or because the nominalist logic of Ockham leaves the radical contingency of the universe to be governed by God's (male) surrogate, and on and on. Her book gives background to Irigaray's cry at the end of *Elemental Passions*:

> How many words to prevent or forbid closeness! Space mobilized, immobilized, preoccupied in order to make encounter possible. Attestations, quarrels, protestations, disputes over identity or the identical, distancing us, dividing us without any crossing of these barriers being possible ...
>
> I look at you, identify you, recognize you in that distance which constitutes us, distinguishes us, and paralyses us in the certainty of being ourselves. (EP 103–4)
>
> Que de mots pour empêcher ou interdire le proche! Espace mobilisé, immobilisé, préoccupé pour rendre impossible la rencontre. Les attestations, querelles, protestations, disputes quant à l'identité ou à l'identique, nous éloignant, nous écartant sans franchissement possible de leurs frontières ...
>
> Je te regarde, t'identifie, te reconnais dans cette distance qui nous constitue, nous distingue et nous paralyse dans la certitude d'être nous-mêmes. (Pe 127–8)

If these oppressive barriers are ever to be crossed, then logic as a technology of power will need to give way to a logic of communication and mutuality. Putting this another way, if, with Irigaray, it is possible to develop mutuality between sexually (or multiply) different subjects, then in so doing we will also have pointed the way to a revision of the logic which had kept the barriers in place.

Feminist strategies of logic

But how can we proceed? Even if logical systems have often been used as technologies of control, it remains the case that most people (including most logicians) do want to think clearly and do not want to be deceived. Nor should we assume that logic, and its structuring of rationality, is utterly useless and has provided no tools for careful thought. In particular, it would be perverse to draw the conclusion that logic is of no interest to feminists, and even more perverse to fall into the patriarchal trap of ascribing unemotional rationality to man and irrational emotions to women. What we need to do, rather, we suggest, is to take a hard look at some basic ideas of logic and reconsider them in the light of where we have come in this book, so that we may indeed 'go where [we] have not yet arrived' (EP 25). For this, we offer the following considerations for discussion, in the hope that others will take them up and carry them further.

First, we propose to observe more carefully the distinction between the basic laws of logic on the one hand – the Law of Identity, the Law of Noncontradiction, and the Law of Excluded Middle – and on the other all the complicated systems of formal and informal logic that have been built upon them. Although it is important for feminists and other philosophers who have been intimidated by these complex structures to see how they are in fact technologies of power, we also need to see that we cannot do without the fundamental laws upon which they are based. Even if we challenge the usefulness or motivation behind the complexities of the predicate calculus, it is less easy to see how we could challenge the laws of logic themselves. Our communication – the very act of writing and reading these sentences – depends upon the assumptions that the sentences mean what they say: not their opposite, and not both. In other words, communication presupposes all three fundamental laws.

Secondly, however, we suggest that it is important to reconsider the question of precision in relation to these three laws. Although there is a sense in which they underlie the very possibility of thought and are presupposed in all communication, it may still be the case, as Irigaray is suggesting, that they are too rigid, and need to be modified in order to enable the flow of thought rather than setting up barriers for it. We divide the investigation into two parts indicated by the following questions: first, is binary logic adequate on its own terms? Second, are there other forms of thought which binary logic might exclude?

What about drizzle? Rigid binaries and fluid images

The images of *Elemental Passions* are images which do not fit neatly into a binary structure. Images of lips, of the blossoming flower, of the song are images which suggest flow, becoming, process; they do not lend themselves to a logical structure in which 'to be is to be the value of a variable' as W.V.O. Quine once famously asserted (1961: 13). For Quine, and for other philosophers committed to binary logic, the purpose of that logic is to determine the truth (or 'truth-value') of statements, as we shall see; and it is for this reason that they emphasize the importance of the precision of concepts and their binary nature: not-A must be the opposite of A, so that we can determine that if A is true, not-A must be false. In order to think clearly and in order to communicate, it must be possible to establish the truth or falsity of our statements and claims. Therefore binary logic must always be assumed: indeed even an attempt at rejecting it would be self-refuting.

Now, as we shall discuss in the next section, there are plenty of other things for thought and communication to do than make statements and claims. But suppose that for the time being we restrict ourselves to that function of language. It is after all an important one, and is assumed by Irigaray (and by us) as surely as it is assumed by the most patriarchal logician. When Irigaray has I-woman say 'You have stopped my tongue' or 'You do not hear' (EP 7), these statements mean the opposite of 'It is not the case that you have stopped my tongue' or 'You do hear'. If the former pair of statements are true then the latter must be untrue. Although the images Irigaray uses are fluid, there is no possibility of dispensing with binary logic where untruth is the opposite of truth.

To bring this down to the most basic level, we can decide whether a statement is true or untrue only if we understand the meaning of its terms: for example we must know what a tongue is, and what hearing is, in order to know whether the claims made about them are true or false. The concept ('tongue' or 'hearing' or whatever is being spoken of) must be clear enough to rule out its opposite: A must rule out not-A if we are to be able to make any claims about A. And once we have seen that that is the case, then we have seen that binaries are indispensable.

Or have we? There are many concepts which seem not to lend themselves to such precision, and yet they communicate perfectly well. Suppose we say 'It is raining' (A): this is the opposite to 'It is not raining' (not-A). By the Law of Excluded Middle, it must be the case that 'Either it is raining or it is not raining' (either A or not-A). But what about drizzle? Does drizzle count as rain or as not-rain? And how hard does it have to drizzle before we say that the drizzle has turned into rain? There are of course plenty of other such examples, sometimes known as vague concepts (Coates 1996: 39f.) or loose concepts (Black 1970: 1–13). Is a man who has one hair on his head bald? How many stones are needed to make a heap? It seems that there is little to be gained by a rigid application of the

Law of Excluded Middle in cases like these. We could perhaps insist that 'either the man is bald or he is not bald'; but all we will have succeeded in is pedantry. Neither truth not communication would be served by such insistence. It was because of concepts such as 'bald' and 'heap' that Bertrand Russell conceded that 'the law of excluded middle is true when precise symbols are employed, but it is not true when symbols are vague' (Russell 1923: 85–6).

As Russell acknowledged, however, 'all symbols are vague' (86). To revert to the examples from Irigaray, is 'you have stopped my tongue' true if I can speak once in my entire life? Twice? Five times? Would 'you do not hear' become false if you were to hear for five minutes every twenty years? Every year? Every day? If these questions are worth engaging with (and in many contexts even that would be problematic) surely the only possible answer is 'that depends': depends on the quality of the speaking and hearing, depends on whether and how the subsequent silence has changed. Although it is of vital importance to partners in a relationship to decide whether it is true that they have been heard, and important not to be deceived or to deceive themselves, it is not obvious that an appeal to the binary logic of the Law of Excluded Middle is going to be of much use.

Now, the response of Russell to the acknowledged vagueness of ordinary language was to try to develop an ideal language, a 'logically perfect language' in which propositions were made up of 'logical atoms' each of which could be given precise truth values in a 'propositional calculus' (Russell in Wittgenstein 1961: x). Russell and the early Wittgenstein and others who held to this view which came to be known as logical atomism held that the world is ultimately built up from 'simples having a kind of reality not belonging to anything else' (Russell in Urmson 1956: 40), and that language should be made to reflect it. As Wittgenstein put it,

The idea is to express in an appropriate symbolism what in ordinary language leads to endless misunderstandings. That is to say, where ordinary language disguises logical structure, where it allows the formation of pseudopropositions, where it uses one term in an infinity of different meanings, we must replace it by a symbolism which gives a clear picture of the logical structure, excludes pseudopropositions, and uses its terms unambiguously. (Wittgenstein 1929: 163)

And so we are quickly back with the complex systems of symbolic logic and propositional calculus whose dubious merits we considered above. Rather than accept fluidity or vagueness as positive and creative, ordinary (fluid) language is forced into a strict system of symbols which retain a rigid binary structure.

However, another way is possible. We need not consider the vagueness of much of ordinary language and the fluidity of its concepts a defect, as the logical atomists did. Rather, it can be seen as a merit. If the reality about which we are trying to communicate is vague or ambiguous, then perhaps a vague or ambiguous concept will in fact be more accurate and convey our meaning better than would rigid concepts with precise boundaries. This was the view to which the later Wittgenstein came; it is well put by an apologist for 'common sense', John Coates:

> Russell pointed out the pervasive vagueness of words, but none the less combined this view with formal semantics by arguing that language only gets what meaning it does attain by approaching the ideal language of logical atomism. However, a more fruitful approach is to work in the opposite direction, by examining the ways in which vagueness may be a virtue in serving the purposes language must serve. It all depends on the function of the tool at hand: sometimes a blurred picture may communicate more meaning than a sharp one. (Coates 1996: 8)

There are times, of course, when precision is what is necessary. But there are also times when insistence on precision is inappropriate and leads to distortion: it can also be a technology of mastery.

With these considerations in mind we can return for example to Irigaray's meditation on the flower (EP chapter six). As I-woman sees it, you-man wants the flower to be open, opened by him, open for him. It is not to be closed: there is to be no ambiguity.

> The flower opened: the flower offered in its appearing. Without its dark becoming, without the pulse of its unfolding/folding. Without the movement of its opening/closing: the spreading apart of petals through another's affection and their touching each other again to safeguard the self-other. (EP 31)

> La fleur ouverte : la fleur offerte dans son apparaître. Sans son devenir obscur, ni le battement de son éclosion-déclosion. Sans le mouvement de son ouverture-fermeture : l'écartement de ses pétales par l'affection d'un autre et leur retouche pour la garde de soi-l'autre. (Pe 37)

If the flower is to be rigidly either open or not open, then it can only be artificial. A real flower, a living flower, opens and closes with the pulse of life, offers itself and withdraws in a rhythm which has everything to do with mutual affection and the flow between self and other and nothing to do with mastery. The fluidity, the rejection of the binary 'either it is open or it is not open', is required for life and love. If the function of language is to serve the purposes of mutuality, then here is an instance where insistence on precision would defeat its purpose. The refusal to allow his thinking to 'have a single crack in it', I-woman says to you-man, results in a world whose rigidity is the rigidity of death.

> You have built up an anaesthetic world. But when our greatest pains or greatest joys are abolished by calculation, is that not the worst destruction? A realm beyond pain, where suffering no longer exists. (EP 55)

> Tu as construit un monde anesthésique. Mais l'abolition de la plus grande douleur et de la plus grande joie dans le calcul, n'est-ce pas la pire destruction? Un au-delà de la douleur où rien ne souffre plus. (Pe 66–7)

For Irigaray, as we have seen, the most destructive aspect of binary thinking is that it does not allow for genuine sexual difference. Woman is not allowed to be defined (or to define herself) in her own terms, but is defined as what man is not, as not-A to man's A. The result of such binary opposition is clarity and control: Irigaray suggests that it is motivated by fear.

> What terrifies you? That lack of closure. From which springs your struggle against infinity. Origin and end, form, figure, meaning, name, the proper and the self: these are your weapons against that unbearable infinity. (EP 71)

> Ton angoisse? Ce sans arrêt. D'où ta lutte contre l'in-fini. L'origine et la fin, la forme, la figure, le sens et le nom, le propre et le soi ... sont tes instruments contre cet insupportable infini. (Pe 87)

If woman were to be allowed to become, not restricted to being the opposite of man, then who is to say how she would develop? How could she be defined? No longer would she be not-A; as herself, she might become anything: to infinity. There would be no closure, and there could be no control. Trust, respect and mutuality would have to replace mastery; and that is a threatening prospect for one who is already terrified.

Moreover, if binary logic is inadequate to define woman – if 'woman' is a concept which must be allowed to be fluid and expanding – then is not the same true of 'man'? As long as the universe is divided up into a neat system of Pythagorean opposites, man can see himself as normative over against his opposite. But if 'woman' is set free from this rigid conceptualization, then 'man' too floats free. He too will have to undertake the task of defining himself, reconceiving his identity; and for him, too, there is no fixed end point or closure. 'Man', like 'woman', becomes a vague – or, better, a fluid – term. And as we discussed in Chapter 6, what Irigaray develops in relation to sexual difference can be extended to multiple differences.

The result is that the universe, including the universe of logic and truth, becomes much less rigid, less structured by oppositional binaries and more open to continuous development towards a horizon of becoming. Although philosophers of logic might protest that we have here abandoned formal logic for psychology and sociology, we would reply that if clarity and truth (which logic claims as its province) has little to contribute to the understanding and development of difference and mutuality, then it is high time that logic should be reformed. Supplementing rigidity with fluidity, we suggest, would be an important step in the right direction.

Binary logic and creative thinking

This leads us directly to the second aspect of our challenge to binary logic. Philosophers of logic present their work, as we have seen, as involving itself with clarity and truth, as the paradigm of rationality. But even if binary logic were adequate to establish truth – and in the previous section we argued that it is not

– is that all that rationality is about? Surely much more is involved. If man and woman are each looking for new paths to enable their mutual becoming, and if the rejection of binary opposition which this involves is extended to many other forms of difference, then it will be necessary to engage in creative exploration, imaginative possibility, which cannot be restricted by binary oppositions.

Again, it is of course possible for philosophers of logic to say that their concern is only with establishing the truth-values of propositions, not with developing the resources for creative thinking. If that is the case, however, then logic should not present itself as a paradigm of rationality. Rationality has a far wider remit than assessing truth claims. Part of that remit is creative thinking, whether in relationships between people, in art and literature, or in science. Again, this does not mean that truth is unimportant or that binary logic has no place. But although it is indispensable, it is also insufficient. By focusing on formal logic the impression is given that, for clarity of thought, binary opposition is essential and adequate. Even more seriously, if little attention is paid to the dynamic of creative thinking, then it is effectively marginalized and we become less capable of it. We might be able to invent a computer program, based as it is on binaries, and with it put humans on Mars, but we will be less able to find creative solutions to human conflict over difference, and with it promote justice and peace on Earth. Which is more important? And how should our assessment of their relative importance affect what we consider to be the paradigm of rationality?

Creative thinking involves the imagination, and the flow of images mingling with one another, as we have found in *Elemental Passions*. Images cannot be kept in tidy boxes. They are excessive, expressive, and full of allusions and possibilities which may be contradictory. They carry echoes and resonances which indicate new images that may be in uneasy tension with one another. But it is out of these very tensions and echoes that new ways forward often can be found. Rigid literal thinking which insists on assigned truth values and precise meanings blocks the flow of imaginative thought and stifles creativity, whether in terms of the mutual relationship between different subjects or anything else.

In Chapter 1 we contrasted the insistence upon literal truth and binary truth functions (A or not-A) that has characterized early Greek and Christian thought with the patterns of Rabbinic interpretation in the Midrash. In these Rabbinic interpretations we can see an example of the uneasy tensions which occur when one Rabbi's thoughts seem different from – or downright opposite to – another's, yet are held together in a rich web of creativity. We suggested that the fluid patterns of Rabbinic thinking were an influence on Levinas and Derrida, and through them upon Irigaray, whether or not she was explicitly aware of the Jewish provenance of this style of thinking.

In addition to this, however, there is another major thinker whose work casts long shadows over all of twentieth-century French thinking, emphatically including Levinas and Derrida, and with whom Irigaray is always at some level engaging.

That thinker is of course Hegel. Hegel is sometimes considered the epitome of binary thinking, insisting as few others have done on the collision of opposites, A and not-A. Yet this is only one aspect of his thought. As we noted when we discussed Hegel's master–slave dialectic, it is only as the two work through their opposition to come to a place of mutuality that either of them can be satisfied and a creative break-through can occur. In Hegel's thinking, such opposition and break-through leads, stage by stage, to union with the Absolute; and in the French struggle with and against Hegel his ultimate totalizing conclusion is a major difficulty. In Irigaray's terms, little would be gained if the other is simply the other of the same, if woman is taken up into man's totalizing project.

But Hegel can be read in more than one way. If we read him as a flat-footed literalist in which binary oppositions clash, then we remain oblivious to the creative impulse of his logic. Judith Butler has argued that Hegel's sentences require an engagement of consciousness which enacts the movement he represents in his text: 'the rhetoric initiates us into a consciousness of irreducibly multiple meanings which continuously determine each other' (Butler 1999: 19) in a manner that reminds us of Rabbinic style.

In reading for multiple meanings, for plurivocity, ambiguity, and metaphor in the general sense, we experience concretely the inherent movement of dialectical thinking, the essential alteration of reality. And we also come to understand the role of our own consciousness in constituting this reality inasmuch as the text must be read to have its meaning enacted. (19)

Butler is talking about the text of Hegel's *Phenomenology*, but as we have seen, exactly the same could be said of Irigaray's *Elemental Passions*. It is as far from the rigid binary opposition of Anglo-American philosophical logic as could be imagined. The creativity necessary for mutual relationship requires plurivocity and movement, willingness to live with ambiguity and to find in it resources for the future.

Ultimately, binary logic is sufficient for death of the body but not for life or the living flow of ideas. The rigidity of a corpse can be described without allowing for growth and change, but a living body cannot. Conception, gestation and birth all depend on fluids; just as living creative thought and becoming require fluidity and movement, not binary principles. As Irigaray says, once again using sexual encounter as the model for creative encounters of many sorts,

In that living body, nothing and no one can be fitted exactly. Whole without parts. Indefinitely mobile. Impulse, change, the process of becoming, these cannot be imposed from the outside, from something considered as a law or principle. (EP 80)

En ce corps vivant, rien ni personne ne peut s'encastrer. Tout sans parties. Indéfiniment mobile. L'impulsion, le changement, le devenir, ne pouvant s'imposer d'un dehors qui ferait loi, ou principe. (Pe 96–7)

We have the choice, in our thought as in our relationships, to acquiesce in rigidity or to celebrate life. Life is forever fluid.

BIBLIOGRAPHY

Ainley, A. (1998) 'Luce Irigaray. Divine Spirit and Feminine Space' in P. Blond (ed.), *Post-Secular Philosophy. Between Philosophy and Theology*. London, Routledge: 334–45.

Anderson, P. S. (1997) *A Feminist Philosophy of Religion. The Rationality and Myths of Religious Belief*. Oxford, Basil Blackwell.

Angelou, Maya (1969) *I Know Why the Caged Bird Sings*. London: Virago.

Aristotle (1941) *The Basic Works of Aristotle*, ed. R. Mceown. New York, Random House.

Armour, E. (1997) 'Questions of Proximity. "Woman's Place" in Derrida and Irigaray' in *Hypatia* 12(1): 63–77.

Armour, E. (1999) *Deconstruction, Feminist Theology, and the Problem of Difference. Subverting the Race/Gender Divide*. Chicago and London, University of Chicago Press.

Bacon, F. (1964) 'The Refutation of Philosophies' in *The Philosophy of Francis Bacon. An Essay on its Development from 1603 to 1609 with New Translations of Fundamental Texts*, ed. B. Farrington. Liverpool, Liverpool University Press: 103–34.

Bannet, E. T. (1993) 'There Have To Be At Least Two' in *Diacritics* 23(1): 84–98.

Barnes, J. (1982) *The Presocratic Philosophers*. London, Routledge & Kegan Paul.

Barnes, J. (1987) *Early Greek Philosophy*. London, Penguin Books.

Bataille, G. (1962) *Death and Sensuality. A Study of Eroticism and the Taboo*. New York, Walker and Company.

Bataille, G. (1985) *Visions of Excess, Selected Writings, 1927–1939*. Minneapolis, University of Minnesota.

Battersby, C. (1998) *The Phenomenal Woman. Feminist Metaphysics and the Patterns of Identity*. Cambridge, Polity Press.

Beauvoir, Simone de (1954) *The Second Sex*, trans. H. M. Parshley. New York, Knopf.

Berg, E. (1982) 'The Third Woman' in *Diacritics* 12 (summer): 11–20.

Bergson, Henri (1910) *Time and Free Will*, trans. F. L. Pogson. London, Sonnenschein.

Berry, P. (1994) 'The Burning Glass. Paradoxes of Feminist Revelation in *Speculum*' in C. Burke, N. Schor and M. Whitford (eds), *Engaging with Irigaray. Feminist Philosophy and Modern European Thought*. New York, Columbia University Press: 229–46.

Black, Max (1970) *Margins of Precision. Essays in Logic and Language*, Ithaca and London, Cornell University Press.

Boothroyd, D. (1996) 'Labial Feminism. Body Against Body with Luce Irigaray' unpublished paper, University of Sunderland.

Boulous Walker, M. (1998) *Philosophy and the Maternal Body. Reading Silence*. London, Routledge.

Bowie, M. (1991) *Lacan*. London, Fontana Press.

Braidotti, R. (1986) 'The Ethics of Sexual Difference. The Case of Foucault and Irigaray' in *Australian Feminist Studies* 3: 1–13.

Braidotti, R. (1989) 'The Politics of Ontological Difference' in T. Brennan (ed.), *Between Feminism and Psychoanalysis*. London, Routledge: 89–106.

Braidotti, R. (1991) *Patterns of Dissonance. A Study of Women in Contemporary Philosophy*. Cambridge, Polity Press.

Braidotti, R. (1994a) *Nomadic Subjects. Embodiment and Sexual Difference in Contemporary Feminist Theory*. New York, Columbia University Press.

Braidotti, R. (1994b) 'Toward a New Nomadism. Feminist Deleuzian Tracks; or, Metaphysics and Metabolism' in C. V. Boundas and D. Olkowski (eds), *Deleuze and the Theatre of Philosophy*. London, Routledge: 157–87.

Braidotti, R. (1994c) 'Discontinuous Becomings. Deleuze on the Becoming-Woman of Philosophy' in *Nomadic Subjects*. New York, Columbia University Press: 111–24.

Bibliography

Brennan, Teresa (1989) 'Introduction' to T. Brennan (ed.), *Between Feminism and Psychoanalysis*. London and New York, Routledge.

Brennan, Teresa (1993) *History after Lacan*. London and New York, Routledge.

Brookes, E. H. (1968) *Apartheid. A Documentary Study of Modern South Africa*. London, Routledge & Kegan Paul.

Burke, C. (1980) 'Introduction to Luce Irigaray's "When Our Lips Speak Together"' in *Signs. Journal of Women in Culture and Society* 6(1): 66–79.

Burke, C. (1994a) 'Irigaray through the Looking Glass' in C. Burke, N. Schor and M. Whitford (eds), *Engaging with Irigaray. Feminist Philosophy and Modern European Thought*. New York, Columbia University Press: 37–57.

Burke, C. (1994b) 'Translation Modified. Irigaray in English' in C. Burke, N. Schor and M. Whitford (eds), *Engaging with Irigaray. Feminist Philosophy and Modern European Thought*. New York, Columbia University Press: 249–63.

Burke, C., et al. (eds) (1994) *Engaging with Irigaray. Feminist Philosophy and Modern European Thought*. New York, Columbia University Press.

Butler, J. (1990) *Gender Trouble. Feminism and the Subversion of Identity*. Routledge, London.

Butler, J. (1993) *Bodies That Matter. On the Discursive Limits of 'Sex'*. London, Routledge.

Butler, J. (1999) *Subjects of Desire. Hegelian Reflections in Twentieth Century France*. New York, Columbia University Press.

Canters, H. (1994) 'Towards a Feminist Philosophy of Religion', Gronigen, University of Groningen.

Canters, H. (1998a) 'Love I. Recognizing Differences between Bodies' unpublished paper presented to 'After the Body. An International Conference on Religion, Culture and Gender', University of Manchester.

Canters, H. (1998b) 'Vrouwen die Spreken en Gehoord Worden' in M. De Haardt, E. Maeckelberghe and Mathilde v. Dijk (eds), *Geroepen om te Spreken. Over Verbeelding en Creativiteit in Theologie en Pastoraat*. Kampen, Kok Pharos: 91–102.

Canters, H. (2000) 'Luce Irigaray. Beelden voor een Vrouwelijk Subject' in *Fier* 3(1): 1–7.

Cavarero, A. (1995) *In Spite of Plato. A Feminist Rewriting of Ancient Philosophy*. Cambridge, Polity Press.

Chanter, T. (1995) *Ethics of Eros. Irigaray's Rewriting of the Philosophers*. London, Routledge.

Cheah, P. and E. Grosz (1998a) 'Of Being-Two' in *Diacritics* 28(1): 3–18.

Cheah, P. and E. Grosz (1998b) 'The Future of Sexual Difference. An Interview with Judith Butler and Drucilla Cornell' in *Diacritics* 28(1): 19–42.

Clarke, B. (1999) *River, Cross my Heart*. New York, Little, Brown and Company.

Coates, John (1996) *The Claims of Common Sense. Moore, Wittgenstein, Keynes and the Social Sciences*. Cambridge: Cambridge University Press.

Code, L. (1991) *What Can She Know? Feminist Theory and the Construction of Knowledge*. New York, Cornell University Press.

Colebrook, C. (1997) 'Feminist Philosophy and the Philosophy of Feminism. Irigaray and the History of Metaphysics' in *Hypatia* 12(1): 79–98.

Collins, Patricia Hill (1991) *Black Feminist Thought. Knowledge, Consciousness, and the Politics of Empowerment*. London, Routledge.

Collins, Patricia Hill (1999) *Fighting Words. Black Women and the Search for Justice*. Minneapolis and London, University of Minnesota Press.

Cornell, D. (1991) *Beyond Accommodation. Ethical Feminism, Deconstruction and the Law*. London, Routledge.

Bibliography

Cornell, D. (1995) 'What Is Ethical Feminism?' in S. Benhabib, J. Butler, D. Cornell and N. Fraser (eds), *Feminist Contentions. A Philosophical Exchange*. London, Routledge: 75–107.
Cornell, D. (1998) *At the Heart of Freedom. Feminism, Sex and Equality*. Princeton, Princeton University Press.
Cornford, F. M. (1922) 'Mysticism and Science in the Pythagorean Tradition (I)' in *The Classical Quarterly* 16: 137–52.
Cornford, F. M. (1923) 'Mysticism and Science in the Pythagorean Tradition (II)' in *The Classical Quarterly* 17: 1–12.
Coxon, A. H. (1986) *The Fragments of Parmenides. A Critical Text with Introduction, Translation, the Ancient Testimonia and a Commentary*. Assen, The Netherlands, Van Gorcum.
Derrida, Jacques (1978) *Writing and Difference*, trans. Alan Bass. Chicago, University of Chicago Press.
Descartes, R. (1975) *The Philosophical Works of Descartes*, ed. Elizabeth Anscombe and Peter Geach. Cambridge, Cambridge University Press.
Descombes, Vincent (1980) *Modern French Philosophy*, trans. L. Scott-Fox and J. M. Harding. Cambridge: Cambridge University Press.
Deutscher, P. (1996) 'Irigaray Anxiety. Luce Irigaray and her Ethics for Improper Selves' in *Radical Philosophy. A Journal of Socialist and Feminist Philosophy* 80 (Nov/Dec): 6–17.
Deutscher, P. (1997) *Yielding Gender. Feminism, Deconstruction and the History of Philosophy*. London, Routledge.
Deutscher, P. (1998) 'Book review of I Love to You (1996)' in *Hypatia* 13(2): 170–4.
Drury, Shadia B. (1994) *Alexandrè Kojève. The Roots of Postmodern Politics*. London: Macmillan.
duBois, P. (1991) *Torture and Truth*. London, New York.
Duchen, C. (1988) *Feminism in France. From May '68 to Mitterand*. London and New York, Routledge & Kegan Paul.
Dyer, R. (1998) *White*. London, Routledge.
Fauré, C. and L. T. Robinson (1981) 'The Twilight of the Goddesses, or The Intellectual Crisis of French Feminism' in *Signs. Journal of Women in Culture and Society* 7(1): 81–6.
Felman, S. (1997) 'Women and Madness. The Critical Phallacy' in C. Belsey and J. Moore (eds), *The Feminist Reader. Essays in Gender and the Politics of Literary Criticism*. London, Macmillan: 117–33.
Ferry, Luc and Renaut, Alain (1990) *French Philosophy of the Sixties. An Essay on Antihumanism*, trans. Mary Schnackenberg Cattoni. Amherst: University of Massachusetts Press.
Flax, J. (1991) *Thinking Fragments. Psychoanalysis, Feminism, and Postmodernism in the Contemporary West*. Oxford, University of California Press.
Frege, Gottlob (1879/1970) *Begriffsschrift* in *Translations from the Philosophical Works of Gottlob Frege*, ed. Peter Geach and Max Black. Oxford, Basil Blackwell.
Frege, Gottlob (1967) 'The Thought. A Logical Inquiry', trans. A. M. and Marcelle Quinton, in *Philosophical Logic*, ed. P. F. Strawson, Oxford: Oxford University Press.
Freud, S. (1961) 'Female Sexuality' in *The Standard Edition of the Complete Psychological Works of Sigmund Freud*, ed. J. Strachey. London, The Hogarth Press. XXI: 223–43.
Freud, S. (1986a) 'Beyond the Pleasure Principle' in *The Essentials of Psychoanalysis. The Definitive Collection of Sigmund Freud's Writing*, ed. A. Freud. London, Penguin Books: 218–68.
Freud, S. (1986b) *The Essentials of Psychoanalysis. The Definitive Collection of Sigmund Freud's Writing*. London, Pelican Books.
Freud, S. (1986c) 'Femininity'. Lecture 33 of 'New Introductory Lectures on Psychoanalysis' in *The Essentials of Psychoanalysis. The Definitive Collection of Sigmund Freud's Writing*, ed. A.

Bibliography

Freud. London, Pelican Books: 412–32.
Freud, S. (1986d) 'Three Essays on the Theory of Femininity' in *The Essentials of Psychoanalysis. The Definitive Collection of Sigmund Freud's Writing*, ed. A. Freud. London, Pelican Books: 277–376.
Fuss, D. (1992) '"Essentially Speaking". Luce Irigaray's Language of Essence' in N. Fraser and S. Lee Bartky (eds), *Revaluing French Feminism. Critical Essays on Difference, Agency, and Culture*. Bloomington and Indianapolis, Indiana University Press: 94–113.
Gallop, J. (1982) *Feminism and Psychoanalysis. The Daughter's Seduction*. London, Macmillan.
Gallop, J. (1988) *Thinking through the Body*. New York and Oxford, Columbia University Press.
Garry, A. and M. Pearsall (eds) (1996) *Women, Knowledge and Reality. Explorations in Feminist Philosophy*. London and New York, Routledge.
Gatens, M. (1991) *Feminism and Philosophy. Perspectives on Difference and Equality*. Cambridge, Polity Press.
Gatens, M. (1996) *Imaginary Bodies. Ethics, Power and Corporeality*. London, Routledge.
Grayling, A. C. (1982) *An Introduction to Philosophical Logic*. Brighton, The Harvester Press, and New Jersey, Barnes and Noble Books.
Grosz, E. (1989) *Sexual Subversions. Three French Feminists*. Sydney, Allen & Unwin.
Grosz, E. (1990) *Jacques Lacan. A Feminist Introduction*. London, Routledge.
Grosz, E. (1993) 'Irigaray and the Divine' in C. W. Maggie Kim, Susan M. St Ville and S. M. Simonaitis (eds), *Transfigurations. Theology and the French Feminists*. Minneapolis, Fortress: 199–214.
Grosz, E. (1994a) 'A Thousand Tiny Sexes. Feminism and Rhizomatics' in C. V. Boundas and D. Olkowski (eds), *Deleuze and the Theatre of Philosophy*. London, Routledge: 187–210.
Grosz, E. (1994b) 'The Hetero and the Homo. The Sexual Ethics of Luce Irigaray' in C. Burke, N. Schor and M. Whitford (eds), *Engaging with Irigaray. Feminist Philosophy and Modern European Thought*. New York, Columbia University Press: 335–50.
Guthrie, W. K. C. (1956) *The Greek Philosophers. From Thales to Aristotle*. London, Methuen Press.
Gutting, Gary (2001) *French Philosophy in the Twentieth Century*. Cambridge: Cambridge University Press.
Haack, Susan (1974) *Deviant Logic. Some Philosophical Issues*. Cambridge, Cambridge University Press.
Haack, Susan (1978) *Philosophy of Logics*. Cambridge, Cambridge University Press.
Hall, C. (1995) *White, Male and Middle Class. Explorations in Feminism and History*. Cambridge, Polity Press.
Halsema, A. (1998) *Dialektiek van de Seksuele Differentie. De Filosofie van Luce Irigaray*. Amsterdam, Boom.
Handelman, Susan A. (1982) *The Slayers of Moses. The Emergence of Rabbinic Interpretation in Modern Literary Theory*. Albany, State University of New York Press.
Harding, S. (1986) *The Science Question in Feminism*. Milton Keynes, Open University Press.
Harding, S. (1991) *Whose Science? Whose Knowledge? Thinking from Women's Lives*. Milton Keynes, Open University Press.
Harding, S. (1993) 'Rethinking Standpoint Epistemology. "What Is Strong Objectivity"?' in L. Alcoff and E. Potter (eds), *Feminist Epistemologies*. London, Routledge: 49–82.
Hartsock, N. (1985) *Money, Sex and Power. Toward a Feminist Historical Materialism*. Boston, Northeastern University Press.
Hartsock, N. (1987) 'The Feminist Standpoint. Developing the Ground for a Specifically Feminist Historical Materialism' in S. Harding (ed.) *Feminism and Methodology*. Bloomington, Indiana University Press: 157–80.

Hegel, G. W. F. (1977) *Phenomenology of Spirit*, trans. A. V. Miller. Oxford, Clarendon Press.
Heidegger, Martin (1971) *Poetry, Language, Thought*, trans. Albert Hofstadter. New York, Harper and Row.
Heidegger, Martin (1978) *Being and Time*, trans. John Macquarrie and Edward Robinson. Oxford, Basil Blackwell.
Heidegger, Martin (1993) *Basic Writings*, revised and expanded edition, ed. David Farrell Krell. London, Routledge.
Hirsh, E. and G. Olson (1995) '"Je – Luce Irigaray" A meeting with Luce Irigaray' in *Hypatia* 10(2): 93–114.
Hodge, J. (1994) 'Irigaray Reading Heidegger' in C. Burke, N. Schor and M. Whitford (eds), *Engaging with Irigaray. Feminist Philosophy and Modern European Thought*. New York, Columbia University Press: 191–211.
hooks, b. (1982) *Ain't I a Woman. Black Women and Feminism*. London, Pluto Press.
hooks, b. (1984) *Feminist Theory. From Margin to Center*. Boston, South End Press.
hooks, b. (1991) *Yearning. Race, Gender, and Cultural Politics*. London, Turnaround Press.
hooks, b. (1994) *Teaching to Transgress. Education as the Practice of Freedom*. New York, Routledge.
Hussey, E. (1997) 'Pythagoreans and Eleatics' in C. C. W. Taylor (ed.), *From the Beginning to Plato. Routledge History of Philosophy*. London, Routledge: 128–74.
Irigaray, L. (1974) *Speculum. De l'autre femme*. Paris, Editions de Minuit.
Irigaray, L. (1977) *Ce sexe qui n'est pas un*. Paris, Editions de Minuit.
Irigaray, L. (1979) *Et l'une ne bouge pas sans l'autre*. Paris, Editions de Minuit.
Irigaray, L. (1980) *Amante Marine de Friedrich Nietzsche*. Paris, Editions de Minuit.
Irigaray, L. (1981) 'And the One Doesn't Stir without the Other' in *Signs. Journal of Women in Culture and Society* 7(1): 60–8.
Irigaray, L. (1982) *Passions élémentaires*. Paris, Editions de Minuit.
Irigaray, L. (1983) *L'Oubli de l'air. Chez Martin Heidegger*. Paris, Editions de Minuit.
Irigaray, L. (1984) *Ethique de la différence sexuelle*. Paris, Editions de Minuit.
Irigaray, L. (1985a) *Speculum of the Other Woman*. New York, Cornell University Press.
Irigaray, L. (1985b) *This Sex Which Is Not One*. New York, Cornell University Press.
Irigaray, L. (1987a) 'Egales à qui?' in *Critique* 43.480: 420–37.
Irigaray, L. (1987b) *Sexes et Parentés*. Paris, Editions de Minuit.
Irigaray, L. (1988) 'Equal to Whom?' in *Differences. A Journal of Feminist Cultural Studies* 1(2): 59–77.
Irigaray, L. (1989) 'The Gesture in Psychoanalysis' in T. Brennan (ed.), *Between Feminism and Psychoanalysis*. London, Routledge: 127–38.
Irigaray, L. (1990) *Je, tu, nous. Pour une culture de la différence*. Paris, Bernard Grasset.
Irigaray, L. (1991a) 'He Risks Who Risks Life Itself' in M. Whitford (ed.), *The Irigaray Reader*. Oxford, Basil Blackwell: 213–19.
Irigaray, L. (1991b) *Marine Lover of Friedrich Nietzsche*. New York, Columbia University Press.
Irigaray, L. (1991c) 'The Bodily Encounter with the Mother' in M. Whitford (ed.), *The Irigaray Reader*. Oxford, Blackwell Publishers: 34–46.
Irigaray, L. (1992a) *Elemental Passions*. London, Athlone Press.
Irigaray, L. (1992b) *J'aime à toi. Esquisse d'une félicité dans l'histoire*. Paris, Bernard Grasset.
Irigaray, L. (1993a) *An Ethics of Sexual Difference*. London, Routledge.
Irigaray, L. (1993b) *Je, tu, nous. Toward a Culture of Difference*. London, Routledge.
Irigaray, L. (1993c) *Sexes and Genealogies*. New York, Columbia University Press.
Irigaray, L. (1995) 'The Question of the Other' in *Yale French Studies* 87: 7–20.

Bibliography

Irigaray, L. (1996a) *I Love to You. Sketch of a Possible Felicity in History*. London, Routledge.
Irigaray, L. (ed.) (1996b) *Le Souffle des femmes : présente des credos au féminin*. Paris, ACGF.
Irigaray, L. (1999) *The Forgetting of Air in Martin Heidegger*. London, Athlone Press.
Jantzen, G. (1997a) 'Luce Irigaray. Introduction' in G. Ward (ed.), *The Postmodern God. A Theological Reader*. Oxford, Blackwell: 191–8.
Jantzen, G. (1997b) 'Power, Gender and Ecstasy. Mysticism in Post/Modernity' in *Literature and Theology* 11(4): 385–403.
Jantzen, G. (1998a) 'Necrophilia and Natality. What Does it Mean to Be Religious?' in *Scottish Journal of Religious Studies* 19(1): 101–21.
Jantzen, G. (1998b) *Becoming Divine. Towards a Feminist Philosophy of Religion*. London, Routledge.
Jardine, A. (1985) *Gynesis. Configurations of Woman and Modernity*. Ithaca and London, Cornell University Press.
Jardine, A. and Menke, A. M. (1991) *Shifting Scenes. Interviews On Women, Writing and Politics in Post 68 France*. New York, Columbia University Press.
Jay, M. (1993) *Downcast Eyes. The Denigration of Vision in Twentieth-century French Thought*. London, Routledge.
Jay, N. (1981) 'Gender and Dichotomy' in *Feminist Studies* 7(1): 38–56.
Kirk, G. S. and J. E. Raven (1969) *The Presocratic Philosophers. A Critical History with a Selection of Texts*. Cambridge, Cambridge University Press.
Kneale, W. and Kneale, M. (1962) *The Development of Logic*. Oxford, Clarendon Press.
Kojève, Alexandre (1969) *Introduction to the Reading of Hegel*, ed. Allan Bloom, trans. James H. Nichols Jr. New York, Basic Books.
Kozel, S. (1996) 'The Diabolical Strategy of Mimesis. Luce Irigaray's Reading of Maurice Merleau-Ponty' in *Hypatia* 11(3): 114–29.
Lacan, J. (1977) *Ecrits. A Selection*. London, Tavistock Publications.
Lacan, J. (1982a) *Feminine Sexuality. Jacques Lacan and the Ecole Freudienne*, ed. J. Mitchell and J. Rose. London and Basingstoke, Macmillan.
Lacan, J. (1982b) 'God and the Jouissance of the Woman' in *Feminine Sexuality. Jacques Lacan and The Ecole Freudienne* ed. J. Mitchell and J. Rose. London and Basingstoke, Macmillan: 137–49.
Larrington, C. (ed.) (1992) *The Feminist Companion to Mythology*. London, Pandora Publishers.
Le Doeuff, M. (1989) *The Philosophical Imaginary*. Stanford CA, Stanford University Press.
Levinas, E. (1979) *Totality and Infinity: An Essay on Exteriority*, trans. Alphonso Lingis. The Hague, Martinus Nijhoff.
Levinas, E. (1981) *Otherwise than Being or Beyond Essence*, trans. Alphonso Lingis. The Hague, Martinus Nijhoff.
Levinas, E. (1987) *Time and the Other*, trans. R. Cohen. Pittsburgh, Duquesne University Press.
Lévi-Strauss, C. (1949) *Les Structures élémentaires de la parenté*. Paris, Presses universitaires de France.
Lévi-Strauss, C. (1969) *The Elementary Structures of Kinship*. Boston, Beacon Press.
Lloyd, G. (1984) *The Man of Reason, 'Male' and 'Female' in Western Philosophy*. London, Methuen Press.
Lloyd, G. (1986) 'Selfhood, War and Masculinity' in C. Pateman and E. Grosz (eds), *Feminist Challenges. Social and Political Theory*. Sydney, Allen & Unwin: 63–77.
Macey, D. (1988) *Lacan in Contexts*. London and New York, Verso.
Merchant, Carolyn (1983) *The Death of Nature. Women, Ecology and the Scientific Revolution*. New York, Harper & Row.

Merleau-Ponty, Maurice (1962) *Phenomenology of Perception*, trans. Colin Smith. London and New York, Humanities Press.
Merleau-Ponty, Maurice (1964) *Signs*, trans. R. McCleary. Evanston IL, Northwestern University Press.
Mitchell, J. and J. Rose (eds) (1982) *Feminine Sexuality. Jacques Lacan and the Ecole Freudienne*. London, Macmillan.
Moi, T. (ed.) (1986) *The Kristeva Reader*. Oxford, Blackwell.
Moi, T. (ed.) (1987) *French Feminist Thought*. Oxford, Blackwell.
Moi, T. (1988) *Sexual/Textual Politics. Feminist Literary Theory*. London, Routledge.
Mortensen, E. (1994) 'Woman's Untruth and Le Féminin: Reading Luce Irigaray with Nietzsche and Heidegger' in C. Burke, N. Schor and M. Whitford (eds), *Engaging with Irigaray. Feminist Philosophy and Modern European Thought*. New York, Columbia University Press: 211–29.
Mortley, R. (1991) *French Philosophers in Conversation*. London and New York, Routledge.
Moulton, J. (1992a) 'A Paradigm of Philosophy. The Adversary Method' in A. Garry and M. Pearsall (eds), *Women, Knowledge and Reality. Explorations in Feminist Philosophy*. London and New York, Routledge: 5–20.
Moulton, J. (1992b) 'The Myth of the Neutral "Man"' in A. Garry and M. Pearsall (eds), *Women, Knowledge and Reality. Explorations in Feminist Philosophy*. London and New York, Routledge: 219–33.
Nye, A. (1990) *Words of Power. A Feminist Reading of the History of Logic*. New York and London, Routledge.
Nye, A. (1992) 'The Voice of the Serpent: French Feminism and Philosophy of Language' in A. Garry and M. Pearsall (eds), *Women, Knowledge and Reality. Explorations in Feminist Philosophy*. New York and London, Routledge: 233–49.
Plato (1994) *Republic*. Oxford, Oxford University Press.
Pluhacek, S. and H. Bostic (1996) 'Thinking Life as Relation. An Interview with Luce Irigaray' in *Man and World. An International Philosophical Review* 29(2): 343–60.
Plumwood, V. (1993) *Feminism and the Mastery of Nature*. London and New York, Routledge.
Quine, W. V. O. (1961) *From a Logical Point of View*, New York, Harper & Row.
Rosen, Stanley (2000) *G. W. F. Hegel: An Introduction to the Science of Wisdom*. South Bend IN, St Augustine's Press.
Russell, Bertrand (1923) 'Vagueness' in *Australasian Journal of Philosophy*, 1: 84–92.
Russell, Bertrand, and A. N. Whitehead (1910) *Principia Mathematica*. Cambridge, Cambridge University Press.
Sartre, Jean Paul (1969) *Being and Nothingness*, trans. Hazel Barnes. London, Methuen.
Saussure de, F. (1995) *Course in General Linguistics*. London, Duckworth.
Schor, N. (1994a) 'Previous Engagements. The Receptions of Irigaray' in C. Burke, N. Schor and M. Whitford (eds), *Engaging with Irigaray. Feminist Philosophy and Modern European Thought*. New York, Columbia University Press: 3–15.
Schor, N. (1994b) 'This Essentialism Which Is Not One. Coming to Grips with Irigaray' in C. Burke, N. Schor and M. Whitford (eds), *Engaging with Irigaray. Feminist Philosophy and Modern European Thought*. New York, Columbia University Press: 57–79.
Schutte, O. (1997) 'A Critique of Normative Heterosexuality. Identity, Embodiment, and Sexual Difference in Beauvoir and Irigaray' in *Hypatia* 12(1): 40–63.
Shildrick, M. (1997) *Leaky Bodies and Boundaries. Feminism, Postmodernism and (Bio)Ethics*. London and New York, Routledge.

Bibliography

Shurmer-Smith, P. and K. Hannam (eds) (1994) *Worlds of Desire, Realms of Power*. London, Edward Arnold.

Strawson, P. F. (1952) *Introduction to Logical Theory*. London, Methuen.

Urmson, J. O. (1956) *Philosophical Analysis. Its Development Between the Two World Wars*. Oxford, Clarendon.

Vasseleu, C. (1998) *Textures of Light. Vision and Touch in Irigaray, Levinas and Merleau-Ponty*. London, Routledge.

Venn, C. (1990) 'Women's Exile. Interview with Luce Irigaray' in D. Cameron (ed.), *The Feminist Critique of Language*. London, Routledge: 80–96.

Verhoef, P. (2001) *Nynke* (a film).

Wallace, J. (1998) 'The Feminine Mystique. An Interview with Luce Irigaray' in *The Times Higher Education Supplement*: 19.

Ward, G. (1996) *Theology and Contemporary Critical Theory*. London, Macmillan.

Ward, G. (ed.) (1997) *The Postmodern God. A Theological Reader*. Oxford, Blackwell.

Weed, E. (1994) 'The Question of Style' in C. Burke, N. Schor and M. Whitford (eds), *Engaging with Irigaray. Feminist Philosophy and Modern European Thought*. New York, Columbia University Press: 79–111.

Weekes, D. (1997) 'Shades of Blackness: Young Black Female Constructions of Beauty' in H. S. Mirza (ed.), *Black British Feminism*. London, Routledge: 113–27.

Weinbaum, A. (1994) 'Marx, Irigaray and the Politics of Reproduction' in *Differences* 6(1).

Weir, A. (1996) *Sacrificial Logic. Feminist Theory and the Critique of Identity*. London, Routledge.

Wenzel, H. V. (1981) 'Introduction to Luce Irigaray's "And the One Doesn't Stir without the Other"' in *Signs. Journal of Women in Culture and Society* 7(1): 56–60.

Whitbeck, C. (1992) 'A Different Reality. Feminist Ontology' in A. Garry and P. Marilyn (eds), *Women, Knowledge and Reality. Explorations in Feminist Philosophy*. London, Routledge: 51–76.

Whitford, M. (1989) 'Rereading Irigaray' in T. Brennan (ed.), *Feminism and Psychoanalysis*. London, Routledge: 106–27.

Whitford, M. (1991a) 'Introduction' in M. Whitford (ed.), *The Irigaray Reader*. Oxford, Blackwell: 1–15.

Whitford, M. (1991b) *Luce Irigaray. Philosophy in the Feminine*. London, Routledge.

Whitford, M. (1994) 'Reading Irigaray in the Nineties' in C. Burke, N. Schor and M. Whitford (eds), *Engaging with Irigaray. Feminist Philosophy and Modern European Thought*. New York, Columbia University Press: 15–33.

Wittgenstein, Ludwig (1929) 'Some Remarks on Logical Form' in *Proceedings of the Aristotelian Society*, supp. vol.9.

Wittgenstein, Ludwig (1961) *Tractatus Logico-Philosophicus*, trans. D. F. Pears and B. F. McGuinness. London: Routledge & Kegan Paul.

Wright, M. R. (1981) *Empedocles. The Extant Fragments*. London, Yale University Press.

Wright, M. R. (1997) 'Empedocles' in C. C. W. Taylor (ed.), *From the Beginning to Plato*. London, Routledge: 175–208.

INDEX

A and not-A 3, 4, 15, 18–19, 35, 45, 115, 131, 138, 144, 148, 151–3
abyss 117–18, 120
air 76, 85, 113, 120–1
Anaximander 29
Anderson, Pamela 10
Angelou, Maya 19
Aquinas 2
Aristotle 2, 9, 12, 18, 22, 78, 140, 142, 146
Augustine 27

Bacon, Francis 22–3
Barnes, Jonathan 10, 12
Bataille, Georges 25–6, 44
Battersby, Christine 24
Berg, Elizabeth 48, 56
Berry, Philippa 29
birth 14–16, 24, 54, 65, 73–4, 82, 89, 94, 102, 108, 137
Bowie, Malcolm 55
Braidotti, Rosi 5, 57, 106, 128
breath 62, 76
    see also air
Brennan, Teresa 17, 40
Burke, Carolyn 1, 38, 54, 57
Butler, Judith 128, 153

canon 2, 127–8, 138, 140
Cavarero, Adriana 10, 13–15, 25, 44
cave 81–3, 92, 96, 102, 109, 121
Chanter, Tina 141
Cicero 146
Cixous, Hélène 56
Clarke, Breena 20, 26
cloud 61–2, 103–4, 114
Coates, John 150
Code, Lorraine 24
copula 77–8, 94–5, 102, 109, 119–20
Cornell, Drucilla 40
Cornford, F. M. 9–10
Coxon, A. H. 11
creative, creativity 102, 108, 139, 152

death 25–6, 54, 61, 72–3, 75, 85, 153
de Beauvoir, Simone 17, 53, 127
Deleuze, Gilles 53

Derrida, Jacques 2, 14, 26, 28, 53, 56, 70, 78, 140–1, 152
Descartes, R. 2, 55, 69, 77–8, 115, 140
desire 33, 36, 70, 72, 83, 87, 108–9, 112, 133–4, 145
Deutscher, Penelope 127
divine 3, 58
    see also God
divinity 77
duBois, Page 12, 22
Durkheim, Emile 18
dwell 107, 113
dwelling 70, 84, 90, 95, 114
Dyer, Richard 20–1, 129

earth 75, 83, 96, 107, 119
elements 47, 83, 103, 114
    see also four elements
Empedocles 5, 23, 28–32, 47, 62, 64, 67, 73, 78, 92, 95–6, 103, 107, 136, 139–40, 142
essentialism 132

fear 70–1, 74, 78, 83, 91–2, 96–7, 99, 101–2, 118, 151
fecund, fecundity 78, 87, 95, 99
Felman, Soshana 125
fertilization 76
Fiorenza, Elisabeth Schüssler 127
fire 81, 83
flourishing 111, 134–5
flower 79–80, 88, 94, 103, 109–12, 114, 122, 148, 150
Fort! Da! 42–3, 45–6, 65–6, 70
Foucault, Michel 53
four elements 29, 31, 53, 80, 83, 96, 139
Frege, Gottlob 142–4, 146
Freud, Sigmund 2, 26, 28, 31, 33–4, 36–7, 41–2, 45, 48, 55, 70, 80, 106, 115, 127, 140

Gallop, Jane 48
Gatens, Moira 1, 13, 18–19
gaze 37, 54, 79–80, 82, 94, 99–100, 103, 110–12, 118–19
gift 61, 89, 94, 96–7, 138
Gill, Gillian 69

Index

God 14, 76, 85, 101, 115, 121, 143
see also divine
Grayling, A. C. 143
Grosz, Elizabeth 31, 39

Haack, Susan 143
Halsema, Annemie 54
Handelman, Susan 27
Harding, Sandra 24
Hartsock, Nancy 130
Hegel, G. W. F. 2, 16–17, 33, 41, 44, 69, 133, 140–1, 153
Heidegger, Martin 25, 53, 55–6, 64, 69, 70, 74, 81, 107, 113, 118, 127, 140–2
Heraclitus 29, 31, 142
Hill Collins, Patricia 20, 130
Homer 10–11, 29
Hussey, Edward 13

Icarus 81
image, images 5, 33, 39, 56, 58, 62, 68, 79, 91, 94, 103, 105, 124, 127, 131, 134, 148, 152
imagery 125, 139
imaginary 39, 139
imagination 152
infinity 91–2, 100

Jay, Nancy 1, 18–19, 22
jouissance 48, 68, 82–3, 96, 119

Kant, Immanuel 2, 72, 87, 91, 95, 107, 140
kiss 108–9
Kneale, William and Martha 142, 144–5
Kojève, Alexandrè 16–17, 41, 44
Kristeva, Julia 56

Lacan, Jacques 2, 5–6, 15, 17, 31, 33–4, 38, 42–5, 47–50, 53, 55–6, 64, 70, 80, 85, 87–8, 94, 97, 105–6, 110, 115, 117–18, 127, 133–5
lack 41, 44, 56, 80, 88
Law of the Excluded Middle 12
Law / Name of the Father 41, 44, 125, 130

Laws of Logic 77
Levinas, E. 28, 53, 140–2, 152
Lévi-Strauss, C. 61, 65, 89, 109
life 62, 74–5, 153
lips 46, 54, 63–4, 66, 72, 77, 88–9, 94, 103, 105–11, 114, 116, 120–1, 148
Lloyd, Genevieve 1, 14
Locke, John 2
logical atomism 149–50

Marx 70, 74, 87
Mary 121
mastery 108, 118, 120, 135, 150–1
maze 66, 114
Merleau-Ponty, Maurice 16, 53
metaphor 83, 89, 93, 105, 107
mirror, Mirror Stage 38, 40, 43, 56, 68, 73, 77, 85, 87–8, 94, 118–20, 135
mortal, mortality 72–4, 117
Moulton, Janice 24
mutual, mutuality 3, 5, 8, 74, 84, 86–7, 91, 93, 96, 108, 119, 122, 124, 131–2, 134–5, 147, 150–1, 153

Narcissus 81
narrative 58–9, 63, 65, 87, 135, 145–6
Nietzsche 55, 57, 140–1
Nye, Andrea 13, 16, 44, 144–6

Ockham 146
Oedipus complex 34–6, 40
one and not-one see A and not-A
origin 71, 73–5, 99
Ovid 140

Parmenides 2, 4, 10–16, 18, 25, 27–9, 31–2, 44, 73, 82, 117, 139–42, 144–5
passion 3, 145
Philo 2
Plato 2, 14–15, 22, 25, 44, 55, 81–2, 87, 92, 112, 140, 142, 145
Plotinus 140
Plumwood, Val 20–1, 24, 130
poetry, poetic style 13, 54, 94, 105, 125, 139–40

Index

power 21–2, 25, 32, 40, 69, 84, 101, 110, 132, 146–7
Pythagoras, Pythagorean table of opposites 9, 10–11, 15–16, 18, 20, 31, 33, 85, 139–40, 142, 151

Quine, W. V. O. 148

Rabbinic patterns of thought 26–8, 35, 43, 52, 152–3
race 128–31, 134
religion 90
Rosen, Stanley 17
Rousseau 2
Russell, Bertrand 149–50
Russell, B. and Whitehead, A.N. 143

Sartre, Jean Paul 16, 41, 53, 64, 69, 140
Saussure 43
Shildrick, Margrit 24
silence 67, 72, 97
Socrates 25, 115
song 60–2, 87, 91, 102–3, 111, 113–14, 116, 148
space 46, 54, 56, 71, 75, 84, 91–3, 100, 107, 146
Spinoza, B. 2
Strawson, P.F. 143

sun 81–3, 102, 120

tetralogy 53, 57
Thales 29
thread 65–7, 70, 72
time 54, 71, 84, 91–3, 107
tongue 63–4
touch, touching 54, 66–7, 70, 80, 91, 94, 103, 106, 108–9, 116, 118–20, 138
translating, translation 1, 53, 57

violence, violent 65, 68, 71–4, 78, 90, 100, 114, 117, 122, 132, 135
virginity 120–2
visual 37

Ward, Graham 41
web 85
Weed, E. 48
Weekes, Debbie 21
Wenzel, H. V. 57
Whitbeck, Caroline 24
Whitford, Margaret 1, 31, 56, 113
Wittgenstein, L. 2, 143, 149–50
womb 66, 68–9, 72–3, 80, 82, 85, 90, 95–6, 102, 114, 116, 135
Wright, M. R. 30

Lightning Source UK Ltd.
Milton Keynes UK
UKOW04f0424270614

234141UK00003B/32/P